"Small ac

Chicago-
intimate,
social an
from live

Carefully
Acts of Rep
the critic
performa
strategies

Small Acts
processes
the conti
collabora

Stephen
Universit
America

Matthew
group's works. He teaches at The School of the Art Institute of Chicago and is author of *39 Microlectures: In Proximity of Performance* (2000).

edited by
stephen bottoms and
matthew goulish

SMALL ACTS OF REPAIR

performance, ecology, and Goat Island

LONDON AND NEW YORK

First published 2007
by Routledge
2 Park Square, Milton Park, Abingdon, Oxon OX14 4RN

Simultaneously published in the USA and Canada
by Routledge
270 Madison Ave, New York, NY 10016

Routledge is an imprint of the Taylor & Francis Group, an informa business

Typeset in Joanna by
Florence Production Ltd, Stoodleigh, Devon
Printed and bound in Great Britain by
Cromwell Press, Trowbridge, Wiltshire

British Library Cataloguing in Publication Data
A catalogue record for this book is available from the British Library

Library of Congress Cataloging in Publication Data
Bottoms, Stephen J. (Stephen James), 1968–
Small acts of repair: performance, ecology, and Goat Island/
edited by Stephen Bottoms and Matthew Goulish.
p. cm.
Includes bibliographical references and index.
1. Goat Island (Performance group) I. Goulish, Matthew, 1960–
II. Title.
PN2297.G63B68 2007
792.0973–dc22 2007006605

ISBN10: 0–415–36514–7 (hbk)
ISBN10: 0–415–36515–5 (pbk)
ISBN10: 0–203–01656–4 (ebk)

ISBN13: 978–0–415–36514–7 (hbk)
ISBN13: 978–0–415–36515–4 (pbk)
ISBN13: 978–0–203–01656–5 (ebk)

To our children
Eleanor, Jake
and to our students

In the twenty-first century a return to basics, an ecologically sound art practice, will become essential—one that is respectful of the audience as well as the artist, the needs of the body, the mind, as well as the spirit, an art form with a goal and purpose, offering a recognition that there is little time to waste and small amounts of psychic energy to squander. Goat Island['s work represents] one innovation in form and approach that successfully "accommodates the mess." May it spawn others.

Carol Becker (1994: 64)

Ecology must stop being associated with the image of a small nature-loving minority or with qualified specialists. Ecology in my sense questions the whole of subjectivity and capitalistic power formations, whose sweeping progress cannot be guaranteed to continue . . .

Félix Guattari (2000: 52)

CONTENTS

List of illustrations viii

Notes on contributors ix

Notes on the contents and acknowledgments xi

Prologue xiii

A. Introduction(s) 1

B1. Performance 27

B1.1 Environment 29
B1.2 Response 50
B1.3 Body 69
B1.4 Time 90

B2. Process 111

B2.1 Environment 113
B2.2 Response 128
B2.3 Body 144
B2.4 Time 167

C. Teaching 185

Epilogue 222

Goat Island timeline 225

Bibliography 227

Index 237

ILLUSTRATIONS

1	Van Eyck playground: before and after	31
2	*We Got a Date*	33
3	*It's an Earthquake in My Heart*: floor plan	39
4	*It's an Earthquake in My Heart*	45
5	*How Dear to Me the Hour When Daylight Dies*	57
6	*The Sea & Poison*	68
7	*It's Shifting, Hank*	73
8	*The Sea & Poison*	76
9	*It's an Earthquake in My Heart*	79
10	*How Dear to Me the Hour When Daylight Dies*	82
11	*Can't Take Johnny to the Funeral*	92
12	*It's an Earthquake in My Heart*	98
13	*It's an Earthquake in My Heart*	103
14	*When will the September roses bloom? Last night was only a comedy*	108
15	*When will the September roses bloom? Last night was only a comedy*	110
16	Lin Hixson in conversation with the audience at a work-in-progress performance/discussion for *The Sea & Poison*	116
17	*The Sea & Poison*	125
18	*How Dear to Me the Hour When Daylight Dies*	137
19	*It's Shifting, Hank*	143
20	*Soldier, Child, Tortured Man*	148
21	Lin Hixson: body collages for *It's Shifting, Hank*	151
22	*When will the September roses bloom? Last night was only a comedy*	166
23	*When will the September roses bloom? Last night was only a comedy*	181
24	*When will the September roses bloom? Last night was only a comedy*	183

NOTES ON CONTRIBUTORS

Sara Jane Bailes is Senior Lecturer in Performance Studies at the University of Sussex. Her writing and teaching focus on comparative readings of a range of experimental theatre groups/artists. She is a contributing editor of *Women & Performance: a journal of feminist theory*, and is author of *Performance Theatre and the Poetics of Failure* (Routledge, 2007).

Carol Becker is Dean of Faculty and Senior Executive Vice President for Academic Affairs at The School of the Art Institute of Chicago. Her books include *The Invisible Drama: Women and The Anxiety of Change*; *The Subversive Imagination: Artists, Society, and Social Responsibility*; *Zones of Contention: Essays on Art, Institutions, Gender, and Anxiety*; and most recently, *Surpassing the Spectacle: Global Transformations and the Changing Politics of Art*.

Stephen Bottoms is a theatre researcher and practitioner, and is currently the Wole Soyinka Professor of Drama and Theatre Studies at the University of Leeds. He is the author of *Playing Underground: A Critical History of the 1960s Off-Off-Broadway Movement* (2004), *Albee: Who's Afraid of Virginia Woolf?* (2000), and *The Theatre of Sam Shepard* (1998).

Karen Christopher joined Goat Island in 1990 as a performer/collaborator. She received her BA in theatre arts from Pomona College, CA, and her MFA in film/video from Columbia College, Chicago. She has also worked with Chicago Actors Ensemble and the Neo-Futurists, and has recently collaborated with Chicago artists David Kodeski and Lucky Pierre.

Matthew Goulish co-founded Goat Island in 1987, and has performed in all the group's works. 39 *Microlectures*, a collection of his writings, was published by Routledge in 2000. He teaches in the Liberal Arts Dept and the MFA Writing Program of The School of the Art Institute of Chicago, and was awarded a Lannan Foundation writer's residency in 2004/5.

Adrian Heathfield is a writer, editor, and curator, and is Professor of Performance and Visual Culture at Roehampton University. Among his many publications, he has edited *Live: Art and Performance* (Tate/Routledge 2004), and *Shattered Anatomies: Traces of the Body in Performance* (1995).

Lin Hixson has mounted over thirty interdisciplinary performances since 1981. She co-founded Goat Island in 1987, and has directed all of the company's works. She is full Professor of Performance at The School of the Art Institute of Chicago. She has received three NEA fellowships in New Genres and one in Choreography, and three Illinois Arts Council fellowships.

Mark Jeffery joined Goat Island in 1996 as a performer/collaborator. He studied Visual Performance at Dartington College, UK, and is currently an adjunct Associate Professor at The School of the Art Institute of Chicago. He presented *Anteroom* at the Chicago Cultural Center's *Site Unseen Festival* in 2005.

CJ Mitchell joined Goat Island in 1998 as company manager, and now works with the company on development. He was General Manager of the Centre for Contemporary Arts, Glasgow, 1996–1998, and Programs Manager at Performing Arts Chicago, 2002–2004. He is Executive Director of Chicago's Link's Hall.

Peggy Phelan is the Ann O'Day Maples Chair in the Arts and Professor of Drama and English, Stanford University. She is the author of *Unmarked: the Politics of Performance* (1993) and *Mourning Sex: Performing Public Memories* (1997). She co-edited *Acting Out: Feminist Performances* (1993) with the late Lynda Hart, and *The Ends of Performance* (1997) with Jill Lane.

Bryan Saner joined Goat Island in 1995 as a performer/collaborator. He received his undergraduate degree in Sculpture and Religion from Bethel College, Kansas, studied at Chicago's MoMing Center, and was a collaborative performer with Sock Monkeys, 1989–1993. He runs his own carpentry business.

Philip Stanier is an artist and writer, and currently a senior lecturer and research fellow in Contemporary Theatre Practice at Manchester Metropolitan University. He founded the Strange Names Collective in 2001, and is on the board of directors of the New Work Network.

Litó Walkey joined Goat Island in 2002 as a performer/collaborator. She studied at the School for New Dance Development, Amsterdam, and has worked with Paz Rojo and Vera Mantero. In March 2005, as Artistic Associate at Chicago's Link's Hall, she curated *A Drop of Water: four contemporary duets from Europe.*

NOTES ON THE CONTENTS AND ACKNOWLEDGMENTS

Stephen Bottoms

This book represents an attempt to mirror, structurally, the workings of a Goat Island performance. As such, it has no single or dominant "author," but represents a creative collaboration between varying voices. The writing is mostly by the members of Goat Island, but their contributions here also sit alongside those of critics external to the company, creating—it is hoped—a sense of dialogue in keeping with the inclusive discursiveness that the company has always sought to foster, through talkbacks, work-in-progress showings, participatory workshops, and so forth. All contributions to the book have, however, undergone a process of editing and sequencing which itself mirrors the process of constructing a Goat Island performance, as diverse sources for movement and text are folded into the mix, setting up unexpected echoes and juxtapositions.

The overall structure of the book is also appropriated from Goat Island's work, just as they appropriate structures and sources from everywhere else. The company's 2004 performance *When will the September roses bloom? Last night was only a comedy* exists in two, alternate versions, because the long, central sections of the piece—known to the company as B1 and B2—were structured so as to mirror each other sequentially, and to be reversible in sequence. The shorter, introductory A section always begins the piece, and the shorter, concluding C section always ends it, but depending on which night one attends, one sees in between these bookends either B1 and then B2, or vice versa. So too, the reader of this book may choose, after reading the introduction(s), to read B1 or B2 first. The former considers Goat Island's work from the point of view of its reception in performance; the latter considers the company's creative process, leading up to the finished performance. Alternatively, you might choose to cross-reference the mirroring subdivisions of the B sections—looking, for example, at B1.3 and B2.3 on the subject of "Body." In fact, you can choose to do whatever you like.

In B1, my own voice and those of other critics external to the company are more apparent, and the ecological thematics of the book perhaps a little more explicit; in B2, the outside voices are appropriately less apparent, and the eco-considerations more implicit. Ultimately, though, the discrete concerns of B1 and B2 are inevitably less discrete than their separation here suggests: process and reception leak into each other; proving inseparable. Something similar applies to the closing C section, which seeks to address the company's approach to teaching performance, as opposed to creating it—an uneasy distinction at best.

The introductory A section provides readers with another choice; whether to read Matthew's contribution first, and then mine, or to seek somehow to read them simultaneously. The latter approach would, it should be noted, be more in keeping with the way they were written: these introductions developed—organically?—in response to each other's evolving drafts.

A note on responsibilities: Matthew edited the C section, working directly with the company. I edited both of the B sections, in consultation with Matthew and the company, and using a wide variety of previously existing writing as "found texts" to be folded together. Some of the found material was also adapted somewhat to suit the new context. In the B sections, where no attribution for previous presentation or publication is given, the writing is original to this volume—although my own contributions often build on my own previous writings about Goat Island.

Acknowledgments: We would like to thank Talia Rodgers and Minh-Ha Duong at Routledge, for their sterling support for this project. We are also deeply indebted to the various critics who have given permission for their work to be excerpted in this book, including Sara Jane Bailes, Carol Becker, David Hughes, Adrian Heathfield, Chris Mills, Peggy Phelan, Henry Sayre, and Philip Stanier. Special thanks also to Charles Garoian, whose work was an inspiration. Goat Island would also like to thank board members Lauren Martens and Smokey Hormel for years of generosity and encouragement.

PROLOGUE

An Application April 24, 2003

Dear Richard H. Driehaus Foundation,

In your guidelines, you invite us to write this narrative in letter form, to tell you what we think you should know about Goat Island. We accept the invitation. One thing you should know about us is this: how we communicate is as important as what we say. As a result, we often find ourselves speaking in modes considered nontraditional. Letter writing, however, constitutes a tradition. So while this application may appear nontraditional (as your guidelines state, "instead of a traditional proposal") it is in fact very traditional, although the tradition it adheres to is the wrong one. This resembles the way we make performances. Already, you know something about us. Because of this invitation, we feel we know something about you as well. We have taken your suggested points as section headings. Please read this not only as a proposal in the form of a letter, but also as an invitation accepted; that is, the kind of letter one might receive from an amateur who has just discovered the possibilities, and writes under their spell. You feel as if you know the writer, not only because of what is said, but also because of how.

A history of your organization / Why you began the company and what you hope to accomplish (i.e., your mission):

We began on Thanksgiving Day, 1986—Lin Hixson, the brothers Timothy McCain and Greg McCain, and Matthew Goulish. Eventually others joined—Karen Christopher, CJ Mitchell, Mark Jeffery, Margaret Nelson, Bryan Saner, Litó Walkey. But on that first day in 1986, when four people met in an apartment on West Caton Street, Wicker Park, Chicago, we did not know that we were beginning a performance group or even that we were beginning a performance. We only knew that we were beginning. We agreed that we would share a kind of "impossible problem" from which we would generate material individually, and then come together: a starting point.

Choose a specific incident from your past. Find a historical event that occurred at approximately the same time.

Create an environment and/or performance expressing the feeling of the memory in relation to the historical incident.

We had few skills and little understanding of performance. We unanimously elected Lin Hixson director. We needed confidence, and for that we turned to Lin. At the suggestion of a friend we eventually named our performance group Goat Island. We eventually created a performance and then another, and have so far made seven of them. They were theatrical, repeatable, carefully constructed. Eventually we were invited to perform in Britain, then invited to enough other places to tour for long periods: Belgium, Switzerland, Germany, Austria, Croatia, the Czech Republic. Lin received fellowship awards for her directing. The company became a non-profit, received funding for its activities, and commissions from the Vienna Festival, Arnolfini Live/Bristol, the BBC, and others. The McCain brothers departed. The work of making the performances became more in quantity and more difficult. We began teaching. We confused the tasks of teaching with the tasks of administration, documentation, fundraising, and making a performance. This confusion made things a bit easier. All of that happened eventually.

On Thanksgiving Day, 1986, we had no idea where our "impossible problem" would lead us, or when it would lead us there. Why did we start? Because of Tatsumi Hijikata, Ronald Reagan, Catholic school, Yvonne Rainer, Bela Bartok, the weather in Chicago. Because we were compelled to. Because we needed a container that could hold whatever we could imagine. Because it was what we did. Because Simone Weil said, "What is culture? The formation of attention" [Calasso 2001: 121].

A description of your organization currently:

We earned a reputation for working slowly. One critic described our process as "glacial." It was true. We took two years to develop a piece, and we still do. It takes us that long to get it how we want it. We perform work-in-progress events during those years, and have extensive audience dialogues. However, over the years, in addition to researching and rehearsing the new performance, more and more has begun to fill that two-year window: webpage activity, film-making, video documentation, Reading Companion artist books to accompany each performance, workshop teaching commitments, group talks and lectures, performing earlier-completed works, administration, fundraising.

Now we find ourselves working steadily on all the aspects of the company at all times, since those aspects have become so linked. We could all devote every waking hour to Goat Island if circumstances allowed, which of course, circumstances never do. Instead, we have committed ourselves to smallness. Rather than capitalizing on successful events for expansion, we prefer simply to continue to exist, and to produce more and varied events. If we can survive, hopefully our example will inspire others to pursue their own projects or organize their own companies.

How you market your company's work:

In some ways, the marketing presents an accurate window into the work. It gives people a point of entry, and a specific invitation. We must accomplish this instantly, using only a picture and words. In other ways, the marketing of the work becomes the work. The trace of the residue, years later, may work slowly but have a lasting effect, as in the following example.

A nineteen-year-old drama student finds a scrap in a box in the theatre section of the basement of a rural college library. The group Goat Island has long since vanished from the face of the earth. All that remains, at least for that student in that moment, is their marketing. She, the only one in her class fascinated by the dreary times before the hyperweb helmet and the hovercraft skateboard, reads the paragraph.

> *"We discover a performance by making it."*
>
> *Goat Island has begun creating their eighth performance work with the question: How do you repair? Drawing on diverse sources for dance/movement sequences, theatrical scenes, and spoken texts, the company has begun mining* The Wind *(a silent film from 1928), the history of the teaching of the alphabet in America, the time/space patterns of the Fibonacci sequence spiral, the poetry of Paul Celan, and household repair manuals and diagrams. The piece, scheduled for premiere in 2004, will question our place in a damaged world and our aptitude at repairing it.*

She receives the seed of an idea. For her it is a new idea. The search follows the discovery. She is less alone.

The challenges your company faces:

Today we face a challenge to our fiscal, aesthetic, and philosophical survival. The impossible has lost its rights. When we began it seemed that the possibilities of the impossible were endless. In our first rehearsals, we constructed our limits, set an impossible problem, and began our work. We felt as if we had discovered human-ness: speaking certain lines, enacting certain scenes, moving a certain way, with a certain intensity and concentration. We felt as if we were pressing against the outer walls of the world, and sometimes opening windows through them. We developed small habits: 1) trying to lodge ourselves in history; 2) pursuing the impossible.

We took as a kind of credo, especially for a performance called *The Sea & Poison*, something John Cage had written in 1983: "We're now surrounded by very serious problems in society. We tend to think that the situation is hopeless, that it's just impossible to do something that will make everything turn out properly. I think that this music, which is almost impossible, gives an instance of the practicality of the impossible" [Cage 1993: liner notes].

Today, what was once referred to as impossibility is being redefined as some kind of natural law, something that cannot be changed. "Neoconservative" forces have taken the ascendancy, and they celebrate themselves as the only way. They refuse to tolerate voices of dissent, and even reasonable voices who suggest this or that change, improvement, compassion, find themselves dismissed. Adhering to the Bill of Rights is a radical act. We have lived through history, we are told, history was a construction of the last century, and history is over. With Patriot Acts, rules of force, and an identify-pursue-destroy-celebrate videogame consciousness, America will now manage the world.

"The impossible has, so to speak, lost its rights," says philosopher Alenka Zupancic [2001: 75]. So, we must add, has history.

Our two foundations—history and the impossible—have become irrelevant. Now, in our new performance, as we investigate notions of repair or stage the visionary voices of the twentieth century (Paul Celan, Simone Weil) we find that previous strategies are no longer enough. Or are they too much? How do we speak from our irrelevance? How do we attempt less? How do we choreograph a dance to repair the world? How do we frame a performance in the eye of a needle? How do we stage a scene to bring the dead back to life?

Your vision for the company over the next 3–5 years:

For the next 3–5 years, we plan to survive. We are in this, as they say, for the "long haul." All invitations stand indefinitely.

How your company would spend the grant?

Our meeting has been so brief, we should call it a parting. We hope you have not grown tired of us already. Some people find us unrealistic, full of hyperbole. Actually, somebody recently accused us of being full of *parabole*. But we have tried to introduce ourselves responsibly. Virginia Woolf wrote this in a letter to a young poet: "I have had enough of the rules. How straight the path, and how strict. This you must do; this you must not. That explains why we repeat the same thing over and over again" [Woolf 1984: 262].

How would we spend the grant? We always find goodbye the most difficult. Thank you for the opportunity to write this letter. We will use the funds for general operating support, working toward the completion and Chicago premiere of our eighth performance: artist fees, material costs, rehearsal space, Reading Companion preparations. That is to say, we will try to live up to the words we have written to you today: to keep our promises, to be the people we said we were, to stage what we know in the stillest hour of the night to be true, to remind ourselves of the impossible, the historical, to choreograph a dance to repair the world, to say, "We have become human again."

Thank you,
Goat Island

A. INTRODUCTION(S)

A. INTRODUCTION(S)

Matthew Goulish

1 A history of ecology

Speaking to students in Houston, Texas in 1991, the architect Rem Koolhaas described his firm's attempt to design a ferry terminal on the North Sea. Managers of the lines between England and the Continent had decided to improve their facilities through the creation of palatial terminals, and one company asked for a colossal, two million square foot building, to accommodate simultaneous access to four boats as well as restaurant, casino, hotel, and convention space, built on a pier two miles into the sea at the Belgian coast town of Zeebrugge. "We found ourselves confronted," Koolhaas said, "with very artistic choices in that the only judgment we could make was no longer functionally based, because the problem was too complex to be analyzed in a rational manner. It was a myth that had to be assembled" (Koolhaas 1996: 20). At this mythic scale, the structure of the process takes on its own life. The finished building will remain as residue. Koolhaas framed the choice to his students:

> we proposed two different options to the client, each of which had structural and even philosophical implications. One option was to prefabricate the building and erect it quickly. By erecting a fireproof steel skeleton, we could cover the shape with chicken wire and spray concrete. We would then be able to assemble the building in record time—approximately 42 months—but the price would be a certain flimsiness to the building, and therefore a certain unreality. There was, however, another option in which the construction time could remain one of the attractions of the building. We proposed that a crew of just 24 Belgians begin the building in reinforced concrete and simply grow old with the construction. The minimal progress that the building would make, in the interval of different rides on the ships, would be a strong part of the building's appeal, while after 40 or 50 years, the Belgian construction workers, by then old men, would finally reach the top. The price of this option was that construction was very slow, but the end product would be a completely authentic and real building.
>
> (21–22)

continued on page 4

A. INTRODUCTION(S)

Stephen Bottoms

Perhaps only Matthew Goulish would open a book on performance practice with an anecdote about a ferry terminal. A performer with Goat Island since the company's inception, his writing nevertheless tends to operate "in proximity of performance" (as the subtitle of his book 39 *Microlectures* has it), rather than attempting to reflect directly on Goat Island's work onstage. "First of all, I don't believe in documentation," he explains:

> Whenever we try to make a piece of documentation, it becomes its own work of art, with little to do with the performance we had set out to document. But this is a good thing. Because there is no way to experience the performance other than to experience the performance. Its resistance to duplication in other media is in fact one of the reasons to do it in the first place.*

This book happily participates in the failure of documentation to capture or codify the eight Goat Island performances, premiered between 1987 and 2004, that it makes reference to. Indeed, reviewing videotapes of these pieces (an experience which is itself akin to watching them down a long tube), I am struck again by the *impossibility* of explaining or accounting for the beauty I find in this work on so many levels; and indeed by a palpable sense of loss felt in the reminder that I may never again get to see these now-disappeared events "live." Performance has no adequate surrogate.

Still, the critic in me will inevitably attempt to interpret the creative circuitousness of the artist. Looking across at Matthew's text, I might propose a link between the Koolhaas–Goulish equation of *slowness* = *authenticity* and the fact that Goat Island habitually spend a full two years developing each new performance piece from

* From unpublished introductory remarks to Matthew's paper "Memory is This" (see Goulish 2000b).

continued on page 5

Koolhaas's second option, *slowness*, proposes a process as the singular labor of a life. Zeebrugge/slow adopts the lifespan as durational measure. This measure, with its commitment implication—the investment not of 42 months of "man hours" but of 24 lifespans—accounts for the equation of *slowness* and *authenticity*. It also makes explicit the implicit economics of translation of human lifespan into commodity. It proposes the question, *What sort of North Sea boat terminal is my life?*

Any economics presumes an ecology—that is, the setting of a limit, which in turn presumes the existence of a unit. In Zeebrugge/slow, the unit is a life; the ecology one of duration, labor, and materials. Yet the *slowness* = *authenticity* equation perhaps takes for granted a nonexistent permanence. Might not the *slowness* option require a second crew, following the first after a 20-year delay, because in that time the finished part of the terminal, having suffered the effects of decay, would require repair? At the 50-year point of completion, would we not then see three crews on Zeebrugge/slow? Their schedules would stagger as follows: Crew #1 (construction) at completion point; Crew #2 (maintenance) 3/5 up the building, having followed Crew #1 at a 20-year delay for 30 years; Crew #3 (second maintenance) 1/5 up the building, having followed Crew #1 at a 40-year delay, and Crew #2 at a 20-year delay, for 10 years. Let us imagine that all these crews enter the building every day at sea level through the same door. When Crew #2 begins work after Crew #1 has been using the door for 20 years, they find they must replace the doorknob. Ten years later, they must replace it again, since its daily use, by two crews instead of one, has shortened its lifespan by half. When Crew #3 arrives 10 years after that, they replace the doorknob again, and, because all three crews use the door every day, they must replace it now at a rate of one doorknob per 6.6 years. At the point at which Crew #1 completes the building, the main entrance is on its fifth doorknob. Is it still accurate to consider Zeebrugge/slow a single building?

We may call this problem the Ship of Theseus.

What is the ship of Theseus? The question arises in a dialogue between two students of philosophy, Phaedo and Echecrates. Phaedo has witnessed the death of Socrates, while Echecrates has not. Phaedo re-enacts the death of the teacher for his colleague. For the duration of the performance, the re-enactment seems to bring the teacher back to life. Our teacher, says Phaedo, resembles the Ship of Theseus. What is the Ship of Theseus? asks Echecrates, and Phaedo tells him this story.

For many years Athenians had been forced to sacrifice seven youths and seven maidens to the Minotaur each year. Theseus claimed he could enter the labyrinth

continued on page 6

inception to premiere, making the rhythms of their everyday lives part of the making of each piece. A Goat Island show is one performed by visibly exhaustible bodies whose skin cells, hair and nails have—like organic Ships of Theseus—all grown out and been replaced many times over in the time since the process of building a performance began.

As Matthew implies, though, the equation of slowness and authenticity may itself be premature—a product of romantic thinking? Perhaps I need to slow down too—to resist the urge to summarise, and to ask myself, instead, "*what kind of ferry terminal is this introduction?*" Is it (and here I go interpreting) to be erected quickly, from chicken wire and sprayed concrete, to provide a flimsy superstructure on which to build the rest of this book? This is the habitual role of introductions—to provide a quickly accessible but necessarily sketchy outline of the ideas to be developed in detail later on. Yet I wonder if this introduction, like the prologue of many a Goat Island show, needs to ramble on a bit and create a bit of a muddle; to disorientate rather than reassure the reader. Let me try to develop this thought, circuitously, by introducing a transport analogy of my own.

In September 2000, nine months into the new millennium, a rag-tag alliance of British farmers and truck drivers decided to blockade Britain's oil refineries with roadblocks and pickets in protest at the high price of fuel—74 percent of which, at that date, was tax. We have the right, the protesters insisted, not to be forced out of our lawful businesses by exorbitant taxation of necessary resources. Apparently enjoying widespread popular support, the protesters succeeded in bringing the country to its knees within three days. With no fuel supplies getting out of the refineries by tanker truck, filling stations quickly ran dry, forcing motorists to abandon their cars. Many people could not get to work. Many schools closed. Meanwhile, thanks partly to the results of panic buying, shops and supermarkets began to run short of fresh food. Emergency services continued to receive fuel supplies, but since many individual health workers were unable to get to work, healthcare provision too began to be seriously affected. When this last factor became apparent, and when employers began announcing that the suspension of business would necessitate widespread redundancies within another two days, the protesters decided to call off their action before the disruption became too great, and while they still enjoyed public support. Even they, it seems, had no idea of the scale of the impact they would make in such a short time.

The fuel blockade was described by the press as "direct action," but it might as easily have been called "performance art," and certainly the vertiginous perspective shift on everyday reality that it precipitated would have made any artist proud. The action forced a remembering of facts conveniently forgotten; a making visible

continued on page 7

and slay the monster. The Athenians vowed that if Theseus succeeded, they would send his ship to Apollo's sacred island of Delos each year to give thanks. Theseus killed the Minotaur and escaped the labyrinth with the guidance of Ariadne's thread. Upon his safe return, the Athenians kept their vow and began sending the ship to Delos. Their gratitude moved them to continue this practice even after Theseus' death. After many such journeys, the ship needed repair. The Athenians resolved to make each replaced part indistinguishable from the original. Over the years, they replaced every component of the ship. Yet it showed no outward change in appearance.

Phaedo concludes his story to Echecrates: Socrates, our teacher, is like this ship —present and absent, reincarnated through an identical substitute.

The philosophy lesson ends there, but one question remains unasked. Phaedo originally came from Elis, where he was captured and brought as a slave to Athens. After his ransom, he became a student of philosophy. Phaedo the outsider knows the stories of Athens better than Echecrates, a native Athenian. Phaedo offers Echecrates' story back to him. Let us think of Phaedo as a sea terminal. The Ship of Theseus has sailed into his port in the form of the death of Socrates. This is the unasked question: is Phaedo the philosopher the same sea terminal as Phaedo the slave?

Consider a spider's web. The spider cannot measure the fly as a tailor measures a client before sewing a suit. Yet the spider determines the length of the web's stitches according to the fly's dimensions, adjusting the resistance to the force of impact of the fly's flight. The spider has constructed the threads of the web in exact proportion to the visual capacity of the fly's eye, so that the fly cannot see them, and flies toward death. The spider weaves the radial threads more solidly than the circular ones, coats the circular threads with a viscous liquid, and makes them elastic enough to imprison the fly. The spider travels along the smooth, dry radial threads, drops on its prey, and winds it finally in its invisible prison. The perceptual worlds of fly and spider remain uncommunicating, yet attune to one another in such a way that we may describe the spider's web as "fly-like." The spider's web is a performance of the intersection of two worlds.

So proposed Jacob von Uexküll, today considered one of the greatest zoologists of the twentieth century. Uexküll's early investigations into animal environments express the unreserved abandonment of every anthropocentric perspective in the life sciences, and radically dehumanize the image of nature. Where classical science imagined a single world containing all living species, hierarchically ordered from the most elementary forms to the higher organisms, Uexküll instead

continued on page 8

of the habitually overlooked. Suddenly it was apparent to all just how fragile a network of interconnections it is which holds contemporary life together. As a resident of Scotland, for example, I was unnerved to discover that the nation's five million inhabitants depend for their fuel supplies on just one refinery, at Grangemouth. Every last remote wee gas station in every last remote wee highland village has to be reached regularly by a tanker truck coming from that one location. Without that truck, nothing else would be on the roads. We have been "naturalised" into rarely thinking twice about how fuel reaches filling stations, or how food gets onto shelves in supermarkets. Yet deprived of these resources, millions of us are thrown into chaos. While we like to pretend that we are autonomous entities in control of our own destinies, the reality is that we are reliant on—indeed, subject to—supply systems over which we have little or no control. In a sense, we are all already cyborgs, physically dependent on the internal combustion engine.

Ecology, states the *Oxford Reference Dictionary*, is "the study of organisms in relation to one another and their surroundings." My Ecology 101 textbook puts it slightly more carefully: "Ecology is the scientific study of the distribution and abundance of organisms and the interactions that determine distribution and abundance" (Townsend *et al.* 2003: 4). There are finite resources in any ecosystem (man-made systems included), and the inhabitants of a given system are mutually dependent on each other's activities for the distribution of those resources. Ecologists often prefer to study islands (Great Britain, for example?), because clear geographical limits help to clarify the parameters of the systems they contain. What happens, though, if certain inhabitants of a system prioritise their own "rights" to resources over the needs of the whole system? The result, simply put, can be systemic imbalances with potentially catastrophic consequences.

Take, for example, the sugar beet crop in Norfolk, England. In order to maximise their yield, certain farmers colluded in genetic modifications of the sugar beet which would render it resistant to weed-killing herbicides. The crop did better, because the weeds it was competing with for resources were killed off. It turned out, however, that the local skylark population, which relied on "fat hen," a so-called weed, as its staple diet, was decimated (cf. Townsend *et al.* 2003: 32–33). Nationally, between 1972 and 1996, the skylark population fell by 60 percent (Guattari 2000: 7). In a world of finite resources, every economic decision has ecological implications. Some might say that a little less birdsong in Norfolk is a small price to pay to ensure we humans of our right to sugar. Yet "*the overall quality of every aspect of [a monocrop] system is in decline*," because (for example) while "pests" will eventually become resistant to pesticides, the incidental extermination of their more natural combatants (such as the skylarks) will eventually leave the crop undefended (McDonough and Braungart 2002: 34–35). In the long term, we lose both ways.

continued on page 9

described an infinite variety of equally perfect perceptual worlds, that, although uncommunicating and reciprocally exclusive, link together as if in a gigantic musical score. These distinct perceptual worlds, each with an animal at its center, he named *umwelt*: the environment-world constituted by a series of elements that he called "carriers of significance," or the only things of interest to the animal, in a closed unity with the receptive organs of the animal body (cf. Agamben 2004: 39–43).

In Uexküll's universe, there does not exist an objectively fixed wildflower stem, but only multiple wildflower stems as *umwelt*-specific carriers of significance. A child breaks one to weave a bouquet. An ant climbs on another to reach its nourishment at the flower's blossom. The cicada larva pierces a third and uses it as a pump to construct the fluid parts of its cocoon. The cow chews and swallows a fourth. Uexküll accords no particular privilege to any one among the infinity of wildflower stems, but only sees each as an element in a selectively sampled environment, one closed unity among the infinity of such unities.

Uexküll's studies on what we have come to call ecology situate themselves in German history in close proximity to the writings of Friedrich Ratzel on *Lebensraum*. Ratzel's theses, according to which all peoples are intimately linked to their vital space as their essential dimension, had a notable influence on Nazi geopolitics. In 1928, Uexküll wrote the preface to Houston Chamberlain's *Foundations of the Nineteenth Century*, a volume today considered one of the precursors of Nazism.

In Gregory Bateson's 1970 essay "Form, Substance, and Difference," we find a return to Uexküll's proposal of multiple closed worlds overlayed on the earth—and the link between ecology and closedness, or the limit. This limit concept has a double life: the limit of the world-environment (*umwelt*), and the limited units, or linked relations between carriers-of-significance and receivers-in-the-body, within the world-environment. Bateson's characterization of these two ecologies as subcategories, respectively, of (1) the world of the physical, mechanical, material, and (2) the world of mental processes, of mind, facilitates his redefinition of the animal at the web's center:

Ecology has currently two faces to it: the face which is called bioenergetics—the economics of energy and materials within a coral reef, a redwood forest, or a city—and, second, an economics of information, of entropy, negentropy, etc. These two do not fit together very well precisely because the units are differently bounded in the two sorts of ecology. In bioenergetics it is natural and appropriate to think of units as bounded at the cell membrane, or at the skin; or of units composed of sets of

continued on page 10

Similarly, on the macro-scale, our short-termist obsession with rapid returns is cultivating longer-term chaos in the earth's climate. Never mind the skylarks: how many humans will survive the rise in temperatures anticipated this century as a result of our profligate burning of carbon-emitting fossil fuels (by our cars, for example)? We are driving an atmospheric feedback loop that is heating up the global "greenhouse" we all occupy, turning fertile land to desert, and causing devastatingly destructive weather patterns as a side-effect. In this century, writes Mayer Hillman, "much of the earth's surface could become uninhabitable, and most species on the planet could be wiped out" (Hillman 2004: 9). Or, as Gregory Bateson wrote back in 1970: "It is in our power, with our technology, to create insanity in the wider system of which we are parts" (Bateson 2000: 473).

This heat is unbearable, but we all have to live with it.
Air conditioning—that's the best investment.
You certainly have achieved a good standard of living,
And you want to hold onto that for your family.

from *It's an Earthquake in My Heart**

Part of the problem here is that we in the West are so wedded to our speedy, convenience-culture lifestyles that we have been very *slow* to act decisively on the scientific evidence of impending eco-disaster, just in case that evidence turns out to be exaggerated. (What if, we might insist, Hillman's "could be" proves pessimistic?) And part of the problem *here* is that it takes a very long time for ecologists and climatologists to produce really overwhelming evidence of the need to act *right now*. In the introduction to their second edition of *Biogeochemistry of a Forested Ecosystem* (1995), a landmark study of the impacts of deforestation and acid rain in New Hampshire, the authors (Likens and Bormann) make pointed reference to three of their original collaborators who had died since they began collecting data in 1963. Rather like Koolhaas's ferry terminal, ecological research is literally a life's work. Yet the *economy* of knowledge acquisition is too often tied to short-termism: research results need to be produced on deadline to satisfy the bodies providing funding. We human beings love to believe we can cut corners.

In his carefully-titled book, *Steps to an Ecology of Mind* (first published 1972), Bateson cites another example of intellectual short-cutting, this time from the French neoclassical theatre:

Moliere, a long time ago, depicted an oral doctoral examination in which the learned doctors ask the candidate to "state the cause and reason" why opium puts people to

* Adapted from a passage in the film *How to Live in the German Federal Republic* (1990), directed by Harun Farocki.

continued on page 11

conspecific individuals. These boundaries are then the frontiers at which measurement can be made to determine the additive-subtractive budget of energy for the given unit. In contrast, informational or entropic ecology deals with the budgeting of pathways and of probability. The resulting budgets are fractionating (not subtractive). The boundaries must enclose, not cut, the relevant pathways.

In accordance with the general climate of thinking in mid-nineteenth-century England, Darwin proposed a theory of natural selection and evolution in which the unit of survival was either the family line or the species or subspecies or something of the sort. But today it is quite obvious that this is not the unit of survival in the real biological world. The unit of survival is *organism* plus *environment*. We are learning by bitter experience that the organism which destroys its environment destroys itself.

If, now, we correct the Darwinian unit of survival to include the environment and the interaction between organism and environment, a very strange and surprising identity emerges: *the unit of evolutionary survival turns out to be identical with the unit of mind.*

Formerly we thought of a hierarchy of taxa—individual, family line, subspecies, species, etc.—as units of survival. We now see a different hierarchy of units—gene-in-organism, organism-in-environment, ecosystem, etc. Ecology, in the widest sense, turns out to be the study of the interaction and survival of ideas and programs (*i.e.*, differences, complexes of differences, etc.) in circuits.

Moreover, the very meaning of "survival" becomes different when we stop talking about the survival of something bounded by the skin and start to think of the survival of the system of ideas in circuit. The contents of the skin are randomized at death and the pathways within the skin are randomized. But the ideas, under further transformation, may go on out into the world in books or works of art. Socrates as a bioenergetic individual is dead. But much of him still lives as a component in the contemporary ecology of ideas.

(Bateson 2000: 466–467; 491)

Bateson draws a loop from Uexküll around the monstrous misinterpretations of the middle part of the twentieth century, landing in 1970 to restore ecology to its central place in biological discourse. He revises ecology with a triple definition: as material economy, as economy of mental processes, and as economy of mind-in-environment:

It is the attempt to *separate* intellect from emotion that is monstrous, and I suggest that it is equally monstrous—and dangerous—to attempt to separate the external mind from the internal.

(470)

continued on page 12

sleep. The candidate triumphantly answers in dog Latin, "because there is in it a dormitive principle."

(Bateson 2000: xxvii)

The tendency to invent such tautological hypotheses is, Bateson suggests, characteristic of much scientific enquiry, and "all such hypotheses are 'dormitive' in that they put to sleep the critical faculty within the scientist himself" (xxvii). The whole process of intellectual specialization, argues Bateson (who was a notorious polymath, always muddling up discourses that didn't "belong" together), tends to involve the proliferation of artificial terminologies and self-enclosing logics, more often than it does the acquisition of worthwhile knowledge. Lost in their own spheres of specialization, researchers may find themselves unable to make necessary connections to other discourses, so that the doorways to pressing broader questions remain unopened. Meanwhile, the "lay reader" is forced outside, obliged to accept and submit to the supposed authority of impenetrable specialist thinking—which determines so many aspects of government, medical and corporate policy—rather than being allowed to engage with new ideas as an amateur. The spider spins a web of its own worldview; the flies are caught uncomprehendingly within it.

The US-based activist collective Critical Art Ensemble have argued for the necessity of "amateur" engagement in contemporary debates around issues such as the uses of new biotechnologies, precisely so that scientists and policy-makers are not left unaccountable: "until myths such as 'we must suffer long and hard to learn about a model' are done away with (which is not to say that specialization should be done away with) there will never be interdisciplinarity, nor productive public dialogue on various knowledge bases" (Schneider 2000: 122). Goat Island's work adopts a similar attitude, but whereas CAE always begin work on a project with a guiding political and pedagogic agenda, Goat Island really do attempt to start each new piece from a position of "not knowing." As performer Karen Christopher puts it:

One way to inspiration is to see as a new eye, as a novice, as someone who cannot possibly be jaded by fixed notions or blinded by familiarity to a subject. An amateur in a specialized environment will see all things differently than the specialist will see them. So to shake loose the restrictions of prior knowledge we take ourselves into areas in which we are not the experts. We have to go outside our scope of expertise, of knowledge, of comfort and familiarity. That doesn't have to mean a foreign country or even a new neighborhood. There are areas within our everyday life that we have not turned our attention to. The important thing is to find a new angle, a new point of view, a fresh perspective. The important thing is the information be unfamiliar.

(Christopher 1999a)

continued on page 13

Delicately, he concludes with a line from William Blake:

A tear is an intellectual thing.

2 Consistency

. . . enormous weight is attached to all the objects that Robinson Crusoe saves from the wrecked ship or makes with his own hands. I would say that the moment an object appears in a narrative, it is charged with a special force and becomes like the pole of a magnetic field, a knot in the network of invisible relationships. The symbolism of an object may be more or less explicit, but it is always there. We might even say that in a narrative any object is always magic.

(Calvino 1993: 33)

So writes Italo Calvino in his lecture on "Quickness"—one of his *Six Memos for the Next Millennium* from 1985, addressing the millennium in which we now find ourselves. In Calvino's formulation, a narrative is an island; an island, a narrative. We might say they share an ecology. Calvino suggests that while Crusoe chooses each rescued object out of necessity, in this ecology, salvaged things attain multiplicity: multiple uses, images, lives. The microcosm (*umwelt*) will intensify around each object (carrier of significance) as if around a magnetic pole. Perhaps the *magic* Calvino describes derives from this balance, between the necessary and the multiple, an overflow precipitated by the closed system of narrative and island:

. . . I found two saws, an axe, and a hammer, and with this cargo I put to sea . . .

(Defoe 2003: 42)

The island/narrative ecology delimits an implicit biopolitics—of survival, power, the administration of everyday life, of relations with animals and becoming-animals—extending to the encounter with the other, named for the day of the meeting: Friday, the famous island inhabitant who becomes Crusoe's slave of sorts:

But to return to my new companion. I was greatly delighted with him, and made it my business to teach him everything that was proper to make him useful, handy, and helpful; but especially to make him speak, and understand me when I spoke; and he was the aptest scholar there ever was.

(Coetzee 2004: 1)

This Crusoe passage begins the Nobel lecture of South African novelist J. M. Coetzee, a lecture titled *He and His Man*. Coetzee revisits Crusoe and Friday years after the shipwreck, when they have settled in England. Crusoe has become mute, can

continued on page 14

Goat Island's working process on a new performance habitually begins simply with a "seed," a deliberately open-ended question or enquiry, usually suggested by director Lin Hixson. Thus, for example, work on the piece that eventually became *It's an Earthquake in My Heart* (2001) began two years earlier "with nothing," Christopher stresses, other than:

> an idea to study cloud formations, which evolved into ideas about paths and chases, which evolved into research into cars and traffic patterns and then into hand gestures and the circulatory system. Like a system of roots underground the sources of material fan out in several directions with many forks and diversions along the way.
>
> (Christopher 2001)

This forking out is achieved by allowing each member of the group to respond individually to the initial investigation by bringing in materials which she or he sees as being laterally connected to it. Other members then respond to these responses —and so on and so on as the connections expand outwards in a multiplicity of directions, into the examination of architecture, poetry, musicology, pilgrimages, freakshows, or whatever else.

The translation of these diverse sources into performance sequences is also insistently "interdisciplinary": Goat Island's work collides normally separate performance registers, juxtaposing scripted, character-based scenes with extended, dance-like movement sequences and with the construction of kinetic-sculptural images combining bodies with inanimate objects. In each of these registers, the company adopts a pointedly non-expert, "amateur" approach: these are not "actors" or "dancers" but ordinary, untrained bodies carrying out ordinary tasks (though they are frequently sequenced into something extraordinary). Moreover, the careful balancing of image, movement and text means that the verbal is never allowed to dominate—to determine some neatly decodable "meaning" for the visual elements.

This resistance to reducing their work to unifying explanations is central to the company's philosophy. As the material for a performance accumulates, the various lines of enquiry being pursued gradually begin to suggest connections with each other. Over time—and time spent is *the* crucial factor here—the links proliferate organically, and are responded to in turn: the developing performance material is gradually sequenced into a densely constructed network of allusory cross-references. Eventually, it may become necessary to summarise a piece's predominant concerns, for publicity purposes as much as anything else. And yet, Christopher notes,

> I can say this piece [*It's an Earthquake in My Heart*] is about learning to live in the aftermath of disaster—but that puts much too fine a point on it. Disasters come in so

continued on page 15

only write by rewriting the letters sent to him by Friday, the educated slave who reports on his travels:

In Halifax, writes his man, there stood, until it was removed in the reign of King James the First, an engine of execution, which worked thus. The condemned man was laid with his head on the cross-base or cup of the scaffold; then the executioner knocked out a pin which held up the heavy blade. The blade descended down a frame as tall as a church door and beheaded the man as clean as a butcher's knife.

Custom had it in Halifax, though, that if between the knocking out of the pin and the descent of the blade the condemned man could leap to his feet, run down the hill, and swim across the river without being seized again by the executioner, he would be let free. But in all the years the engine stood in Halifax this never happened.

He (not *his man* now but *he*) sits in his room by the waterside in Bristol and reads this. He is getting on in years, almost it might be said he is an old man by now. The skin of his face, that had been almost blackened by the tropic sun before he made a parasol out of palm or palmetto leaves to shade himself, is paler now, but still leathery like parchment; on his nose is a sore from the sun that will not heal.

The parasol he has still with him in his room, standing in a corner, but the parrot that came back with him has passed away. *Poor Robin!* The parrot would squawk from its perch on his shoulder, *Poor Robin Crusoe! Who shall save poor Robin?* His wife could not abide the lamenting of the parrot, *Poor Robin* day in, day out. *I shall wring its neck*, she said, but had not the courage to do so.

(Coetzee 2004: 4–5)

Haunted, Coetzee's Crusoe has fallen silent. Echoes encircle him. His past extends beyond his foreseeable future, his life collapsed into itself. Of him, we may ask the question: one or many shipwrecks? As the poet Lyn Hejinian has written of "Devastation, or, the wreck":

One can't write the words "war," "atrocity," "horror," etc., and by using them as names communicate the effect of what's named. This is because of the relation of language (and, in particular, naming) to measurement. The problem (if it is one) is with measurement—with incommensurability and with scale. Either there is one continual horror or there are different, discrete horrors each of which is constituted by one or many horrible occurrences within it. In neither case can a horror be taken as representative—as a horror which has absorbed all others. Horror, war, and atrocity have to be kept in mind as wrecks. And the brutality they produce can only elicit an emotional response, not a written one.

(Hejinian 2000: 12)

continued on page 16

many forms large and small and of such varying qualities: the disaster of lost keys, the disaster of a traffic jam, the disaster of deforestation, the disaster of forgetting, the disaster of war . . . disaster of loss, disaster of fear, earthquake, flood, fire, tornado. Furthermore it tells you nothing about the experience of witnessing the piece in its own time and its own space, and nothing about the journey you would take through the contents of your own mind as you watched it.

(Christopher 2001)

Rather than offering a linear narrative or a ruling "theme" to which other elements of the performance remain subservient, a Goat Island piece is a complex information system which may be accessed and read in very different ways by different spectators, depending on the mental connections one makes with the material, in order to "complete the circuit."

I seem to have strayed into the cyborgian again—mixing the organic and the machinic in my metaphors. (Not inappropriate, perhaps, for a company which works its performers' bodies so hard, at times, that they read as automated flesh machines, pushed close to the point of breakdown.) Here too, though, Gregory Bateson provides precedent: one of the generation of scientists who laid the foundations for the modern computer era with their research on cybernetics in the post-World War II period, Bateson's thinking was fundamentally influenced by his wilful muddling of natural and artificial systems: "ecology, in the widest sense, turns out to be the study of the interaction and survival of ideas and programs in circuits" (2000: 491).

In the performative "metalogues" which open *Steps to an Ecology of Mind*, a father and daughter debate questions through dialogue, much as did Socrates and his interlocutors, but in the meandering, playful, miscommunicative manner so characteristic of parent–child conversations. Indeed, "muddle" is a recurrent theme in the metalogues, with a double edge. On the one hand, it is a child's way of describing the second law of thermodynamics, "the law of entropy," which applies equally to eco- and information systems. A bounded system, all other things being equal, will spontaneously run down. Things will fall apart; ordered patterns will get muddled. And yet, on the other hand, muddle may also be the very state of disorder through which new possibilities for progress or creativity become apparent. The more complex a system, the greater the possibility for its entropic disorganization, and the more energy we have to expend by way of "negative entropy" to keep it all in the established order. It is harder to keep orderly a Scrabble board full of letters than one with very few. Yet the more information (or letters) in the system, the greater the number of possible options for recombination and reconfiguration of that information. Sometimes, maybe, shaking things up and getting in a really big muddle can be the most constructive way forward. That may sound "unscientific,"

continued on page 17

Friday, on the other hand, writes with eloquence from his position of freedom, and from his mobility. In his voice we detect what Hélène Cixous has called a "frightful happiness" (1998: 47). Between Crusoe and Friday, the constraints have reversed, maintained a complementary balance, as if the two castaways somehow cohere as a single subjectivity, sharing a limited magnitude of freedom and captivity, paralysis and dianoia. What are the limits of a life? Do they share the limits of language, of writing? One places the pages in the suitcase. The suitcase closes. The words close with the suitcase; the life closes with the words. What has been written, what has been left silent, becomes defined and forever differentiated. The universe itself attains closure.

Italo Calvino died on the eve of his departure for the United States, where he was to deliver his lectures, *Six Memos for the Next Millennium*, at Harvard. In her introduction for the posthumous publication, Esther Calvino wrote:

About the title: Although I carefully considered the fact that the title chosen by Italo Calvino, "Six Memos for the Next Millennium," does not correspond to the manuscript as I found it, I have felt it necessary to keep it. Calvino was delighted by the word "memos" [. . .]

My husband had finished writing these five lectures by September 1985, at the moment of departure for the United States and Harvard University. [. . .] I found [them] all in perfect order, in the Italian original, on his writing desk ready to be put into his suitcase.

(Calvino 1993: np)

Calvino planned to write the sixth lecture in Cambridge. He had decided on its title: *Consistency*.

3 The death of Socrates

What was the reason for the long interval between the trial, in which Socrates received the death sentence, and the execution? A fortunate coincidence, Phaedo explains. It so happened that on the day before the trial they had just finished garlanding the ship in which Theseus sailed away to Crete. The story says that the Athenians made a vow to Apollo that they would send this ship on a solemn mission to Delos every year, and ever since then they have kept their vow to the god, right down to the present day. They have a law that as soon as this mission begins the city must be kept pure, and no public executions may take place until the ship has reached Delos and returned again, which sometimes takes a long time, if the winds happen to hold it back. The mission is considered to begin as soon as

continued on page 18

but it was in fact one of the foundational insights of cybernetics: "Identifying information with both pattern and randomness proved to be a powerful paradox," explains Katherine Hayles, "leading to the realization that in some instances, an infusion of noise into a system can cause it to reorganize at a higher level of complexity" (Hayles 1999: 25).

At one point in the metalogue, "About Games and Being Serious," Bateson's daughter protests at the conceptual tangle they have got into, over whether or not playfulness can also be in earnest:

D: But it doesn't make sense, Daddy. It's an awful muddle.
F: Yes—a muddle—but still a sort of sense.
D: How, Daddy?

The text is here interrupted by three asterisks—a visual representation, perhaps, of "noise" in the system; or a speech bubble with only a question mark in it. Then the father resumes:

F: Wait a minute. This is difficult to say. First of all—I think we get somewhere with these conversations. I enjoy them very much and I think you do. But also, apart from that, I think that we get some ideas straight and I think that the muddles help. I mean —that if we both spoke logically all the time, we would never get anywhere. We would only parrot all the old clichés that everybody has repeated for hundreds of years. . . . If we didn't get into muddles, our talks would be like playing rummy without first shuffling the cards. [In] order to think new thoughts or say new things, we need to break up all our ready-made ideas and shuffle the pieces.

(2000: 15–16)

New thoughts, Bateson suggests here, may be less the product of pioneering journeys into uncharted territory (since even pioneers take their personal baggage with them), than of looking afresh at the connections between knowledges we already possess. In 39 *Microlectures*, Matthew Goulish makes a similar point in explicitly ecological terms: "Maybe we need new thoughts less than we need to decelerate, to reduce our thoughts, to refold them into other thoughts, and to recycle them" (Goulish 2000a: 3). Hence Goat Island's insistent appropriation and recontextualization of texts, movements and images from pre-existent sources, and—perhaps more significantly—their use of repetition (at times machinically relentless, at others meditatively slow), as the same moves or words are restated again and again in different contexts, as if being turned over and over to see what new understanding they might render up if sufficient attention is paid.

It is, of course, up to the individual spectator to enter the world of a Goat Island performance, to acquaint herself with its vocabularies and resonances, and to

continued on page 19

the priest of Apollo has garlanded the stern of the ship. That is why Socrates spent such a long time in prison between his trial and execution.

The ship of Theseus extended the life of Socrates, while also producing the problem of the last dialogue. It gave rise to the metaphor of Phaedo becoming his teacher in the eyes of Echecrates. Before we ask *What is a metaphor?* let us ask *What dies with the death of Socrates?*

It has been said that ethics, more than a branch of philosophy, precedes philosophy. The study of responsibility frames the construction of the classroom, and the roles of student and teacher; both prerequisites for the study of philosophy. Philosophy, the "love of knowledge", is then practiced in an ethically determined forum, where knowledge never strays far from love, and where the question remains a question. The practice of philosophy then undoes ethics, reopens its closure, by keeping the experience uncategorized, by asking not *how should one live?* but *how might one think?* Where ethics fixes responsibility, philosophy leaves it unfixed; to keep open, to breach the narrative of ethics, to live in the moment that eludes narration. What transpires then when the student asks a question, and silence answers in the place of the teacher? What dies with the death of Socrates? The interruption that remains an interruption is the soul of philosophy. To experience the death and the dialogue preceding it, we rely on the re-enactment of Phaedo, slave turned philosophy student, now turned (temporarily) teacher. What dies is the fixed differentiation between ethics and philosophy, between student and teacher. The classroom becomes theater, the arena that contains identities in limited motion, as three particles occupying in turn three magnetic poles: teacher, student, slave. Here identity depends on metaphor, *to carry with change*, ferrying stability across the waters of difference.

Change, said Gregory Bateson, equals difference plus time. Metaphor produced his last question. In a lecture titled *Men Are Grass: Metaphor and the World of Mental Process*, he proposed that nature works to some degree according to metaphor. He attempted to detail the differences between the material world and the world of mental processes, which for him concerned metaphor, and the difference between quantity and pattern. The lecture was to be the opening address of the annual meeting of the Lindisfarne Fellows on June 9, 1980. A few weeks earlier, Bateson realized his health would not allow him to attend the gathering. He dictated the lecture, and a tape recording was played in his absence on June 9. Bateson died at noon on July 4. Mary Catherine Bateson, Dean of Faculty at Amherst College in Massachusetts, and Gregory's daughter, edited the lecture transcript, giving us the following extract (Bateson 1980: 8–11) by way of conclusion:

continued on page 20

"refold" again the assembled thoughts into something that connects personally. The results (for this observer, at least) can be utterly revelatory. And yet, in attempting to maintain such open-endedness, the company flirts forever with entropy, with the danger that their own creative process, or indeed the reception process of the spectator, may descend into confusion and frustration if wrong turns are made, or if delicate balances tip. To journey into Goat Island is to embrace an intricately structured poetics of muddle.

But hasn't my circuitous introduction itself become muddled? Haven't we slid sideways from "proper" ecological issues like climate change, into the use of ecology and recycling as mere metaphors for performance practice? Una Chaudhuri has argued the need for "a programmatic resistance to the use of nature as metaphor" in theatrical contexts (Chaudhuri 1994: 29): see Gertrude Stein's notion of "landscape drama," for instance, or the familiar use in modern drama of a character's desire to cultivate plants as a symbol for the need to bring renewed life to the soul. Such metaphors should be dispensed with, Chaudhuri suggests, in order that the urgency of the ecological situation may be addressed more "literally." Her concern is understandable, but we need to ask, also, whether nature and metaphoricity are in any way separable. Isn't the human relationship with nature always already performed and performative? Verbs such as "landscaping" and "cultivating," for example, imply a paternalistic role for humans, whereby unruly nature needs some tough love to become constructively cultured. (This despite the fact that nature ordered itself very nicely without our intervention for millions of years.) Meanwhile, the binary opposition of nature and culture—with its implicit privileging of the latter—persists in much of our most basic thinking, insistently setting masterful humanity apart from the rest of the earth's life forms. Indeed, if performance activity is a part of our "culture," then to speak of addressing nature "literally" within that context is already in danger of a kind of patronizing benevolence, like putting some "noble savage" on display in a museum and appealing for the preservation of the endangered tribe.

The point that such habituated thought processes tend to blind us to is that humans and their culture are already *a part* of nature, not apart from it, or superior to it. If our environment is endangered, then so are we. Yet, as Bateson argued, even our understanding of such fundamental processes as evolution has been skewed by an anthropocentrism which champions "the survival of the fittest" (and of the cleverest, most dexterous—i.e. us) rather than reminding us that we depend on air, water, sunlight, and the entire food chain for our survival:

In accordance with the general climate of thinking in mid-nineteenth century England, Darwin proposed a theory of natural selection and evolution in which the unit of survival was either the family line or the species or the subspecies or something

continued on page 21

What seems to be clear is that at least in smaller numbers the pattern differences, between say three and five, are drastic indeed, and form in fact major taxonomic criteria in biological fields. I am after all interested in this realm of pattern or number or mental process as a biological realm, and the biological creatures, plants and animals, certainly seem to think that their concern is much more with number than with quantity, though above a certain quantitative level, a certain size of number, as I pointed out in *Mind and Nature*, numbers become quantities, so that a rose has five sepals, five petals, many stamens, and then a gynoecium of a pistil system based on five. The contrast between four sides of a square and three sides of a triangle is not four minus three, being one, it is not even the ratio between four and three. It is very elaborate differences between the two numbers as patterns.

So it would seem that this pattern aspect of numbers at least belongs in the mental world of organisms. Now I want to introduce into that world another component, which I confess is rather surprising. It's been clear for a long time that logic was a most elegant tool for the description of lineal systems of causation —if A, then B, or if A and B, then C, and so on. That logic could be used for the description of biological pattern and biological event has never been at all clear. [. . .] On the other hand there is another solution which I would like to present to you. Would somebody please place on the blackboard these two syllogisms side by side.

1.
Men die.
Socrates is a man.
Socrates will die.

2.
Grass dies.
Men die.
Men are grass.

Thank you. Now, these two syllogisms coexist in an uncomfortable world, and a reviewer the other day in England pointed out to me that most of my thinking takes the form of the second kind of sequence and that this would be all very well if I were a poet, but it is inelegant in a biologist. Now, it is true that the schoolmen or somebody took a look at various sorts of syllogisms, whose names are now, thank God, forgotten, and they pointed to the "syllogism in grass," as I will call this mood, and said, "That's bad, that does not hold water, it's not sound for use in proofs.

continued on page 22

of the sort. But today it is quite obvious that . . . the unit of survival is *organism* plus *environment.* We are learning by bitter experience that the organism which destroys its environment destroys itself.

(Bateson 2000: 491)

To save ourselves and the planet, then, requires first for us to change our "general climate of thinking," because the survival-of-the-fittest approach propels us inexorably toward:

the species versus the other species around it or versus the environment in which it operates. Man against nature. You end up, in fact, with Kaneohe Bay polluted, Lake Erie a slimy green mess, and "Let's build bigger atom bombs to kill off the next-door neighbors."

(Bateson 2000: 491–492)*

There is, Bateson wrote, "an ecology of bad ideas, just as there is an ecology of weeds," and to point this out is not merely to invoke "metaphor," but to remind us that the *environmental* and the *mental* are inextricably interrelated: "if Lake Erie is driven insane, its insanity is incorporated in the larger system of *your* thought and experience" (492). Almost 30 years later—with the latest eco-research at his disposal—environmental scientist Peter Murchie made a very similar point in his personal response to Goat Island's *The Sea & Poison* (1998):

this is a really timely piece just now. . . . Some studies have come out recently showing that just slightly elevated levels of PCBs, polychlorinatedbiphenyls, in mothers' breast milk, have been causing subtle changes in their children's development. This is among mothers who eat Great Lakes fish. There are PCBs in the water, that get into the fish tissue, and then into the mothers' breast milk. And recently it's been shown that the children on average have fourteen IQ points lower on their intelligence test scores. . . . You have children who are behind, and can't understand things, and maybe react badly, or in a disjointed manner, or can't control their movements.

(Murchie 1999)

Prompted by the performance's thematics of poisoning (connecting everything from frog mutation to St Vitus's dance to the murder of Hamlet's father), Murchie read

* To be fair to Darwin, who is regarded by some as one of the first ecologists, it should be noted that he was not responsible for the term "survival of the fittest." Philosopher Herbert Spencer coined it in response to Darwin, and the fact that the phrase "stuck" says something about the climate of thought we still live with.

continued on page 23

It isn't sound logic." And my reviewer said that this is the way that Gregory Bateson likes to think and we are unconvinced. Well, I had to agree that this is the way I think, and I wasn't quite sure what he meant by the word "convinced." That, perhaps, is a characteristic of logic, but not of all forms of thought. So I took a very good look at this second type of syllogism, which is called, incidentally, "Affirming the Consequent." And it seemed to me that indeed this was the way I did much of my thinking, and it also seemed to me to be the way the poets did their thinking. It also seemed to me to have another name, and its name was metaphor. Meta-phor. And it seemed that perhaps, while not always logically sound, it might be a very useful contribution to the principles of life. Life, perhaps, doesn't always ask what is logically sound. I'd be very surprised if it did.

[A] man named E. von Domarus, a Dutch psychiatrist in the first half of [the twentieth] century pointed out that schizophrenics tend, indeed, to talk, perhaps also to think, in syllogisms having the general structure of the syllogism in grass. And he took a good look at the structure of this syllogism, and he found that it differs from the Socrates syllogism, in that the Socrates syllogism identifies Socrates as a member of a class, and neatly places him in the class of those who will die, whereas the grass syllogism is not really concerned with classification in the same way. The grass syllogism is concerned with the equation of predicates, not of classes and subjects of sentences, but with the identification of predicates. Dies—dies, that which dies is equal to that other thing which dies. And von Domarus said this is very bad, and it is the way poets think, it's the way schizophrenics think, and we should avoid it. Perhaps. You see, if it be so that the grass syllogism does not require subjects as the stuff of its building, and if it be so that the Socrates syllogism does require subjects, then it will also be so that the Socrates syllogism could never be much use in a biological world until the invention of language and the separation of subjects from predicates. In other words, it looks as though until 100,000 years ago, perhaps at most 1,000,000 years ago, there were no Socrates syllogisms in the world, there were only Bateson's kind, and still the organisms got along all right. They managed to organize themselves in their embryology to have two eyes, one on each side of a nose. They managed to organize themselves in their evolution. So there were shared predicates between the horse and the man, which zoologists today call homology. And it became evident that metaphor was not just pretty poetry, it was not either good or bad logic, but was in fact the logic upon which the biological world had been built, the main characteristic and organizing glue of this world of mental process which I have been trying to sketch for you in some way or other.

continued on page 24

the company's relentless movement sequences in light of this information: "I saw that disjointedness, and that jerkiness, that flailing. . . . Disconnectedness. And I think that's happening to our population as a whole. It's happening to our children." Everything, even disconnectedness, is connected.

In *The Three Ecologies*, Félix Guattari picks up on Bateson's emphasis on the interrelation of environmental and mental ecologies, and adds a *third* ecology to the mix—that of the social and economic; of the capitalist system which pumps out its pollutants into those other, notionally separate realms. There is an ecology of bad ideas, and for Guattari, this is where many of them proliferate. An example? An under-reported subtext to the story of the British fuel crisis in 2000 was that the oil companies tacitly co-operated with the protesters, failing to send trucks out even from those refineries where there were only pickets, not blockades. The logic of their position was obvious (if the tax on gas is cut as a result of the protest, the price comes down and we sell more gas); just one part of a system of thought, oriented towards short-term gains, which excludes any long-term perspective on carbon pollution. At no point during the crisis do I recall seeing anybody (politicians, protesters, newscasters) mention the environment, or suggest that the high price of fuel might be part of an attempt to limit road usage for sound ecological reasons. To be green was just not populist enough, and the news media, too, were far more preoccupied with the short term—with the headline value of a government in disarray—than with any longer term implications. In the society of the spectacle, it seems, it's the bad old binaries of us versus them, "the people" versus "the government," that hold sway. Confrontation is more fun to watch than co-operation; destruction more exciting than repair.

This is how it happened. I was in Aberystwyth, Wales, staying in a physicist's apartment in November, 2001, by the sea. There were nine books on the shelf in the living room. I read from two—a doctoral thesis on solar wind and a British repair manual from the 1970s called *Around the Home*. I particularly liked the instructions in the repair manual on how to grip a tennis-racket handle and how to re-face a table tennis bat. Small acts of repair. Calming the hands in a troubled world. Restoring damage to renewed use. Wiping a stain with a cloth. When I returned to Chicago, I went to the bookstore chains searching for repair manuals. I found few. Today we buy new and discard the old. But in the basement, in Michigan, at my in-laws, I found the 1957 *Better Homes and Gardens Handyman's Book*. A first directive to begin Goat Island's eighth performance work.

(Hixson 2002b: np)

This is Goat Island director Lin Hixson's account of the earliest stages of thinking for the piece eventually titled *When will the September roses bloom? Last night was only a*

continued on page 25

Well, I hope that may have given you some entertainment, something to think about, and I hope it may have done something to set you free from thinking in material and logical terms, in the syntax and terminology of mechanics, when you are in fact trying to think about living things.

That's all.

comedy. The seed question for that work—"How do you make a repair?"—was clearly one haunted by the distinctly un-comedic "last night" of September 11th, 2001. Yet rather than viewing the terrorist attacks on New York and Washington as some epoch-shifting singularity (a cause), requiring an equally decisive show of counter-attacking might (an effect), Hixson was among those who saw these events as symptomatic of an existing global ecology of bad ideas (not unconnected to the question of fuel distribution). Her looping of the crying need for "repair" back to everyday household objects might seem an odd connection to make, but in a climate of thought dominated by "us versus them" dichotomies, perhaps a little "noise" is needed in order that the debate reorganise itself on "a higher level of complexity." The 9/11 hijackings were themselves carried out with everyday household objects: if the terrorists could make an unlikely circuit out of kitchen knives, aeroplanes and tall buildings to effect their spectacle of destruction, isn't it the responsibility of artists to at least attempt to seed a more redemptive environ/mental system?

That sounds, of course, like an absurd objective for a small performance company making unapologetically complex work. And yet, as Jacques Derrida argued in *The Other Heading* (1992), any honest attempt at taking responsibility for one's place in the world (with all the contradictions and blind spots that implies), must bring us face to face with the impossible: "the condition of possibility of this thing called responsibility is a certain *experience and experiment of the possibility of the impossible*" (Derrida 1992: 41). Moreover, as Hixson notes, it was precisely "the smallness of [the minor repair instructions] that struck me, in comparison to this big event that had happened" (Hixson 2003). Perhaps we *need* to start small, given the scale of the problems confronting us. Perhaps Goat Island's performative thought experiments —their attempts to engage systematically with the possibility of the impossible— have an important role to play alongside the more overt activism of groups like Critical Art Ensemble.

"In order to comprehend the interactions between [the three ecologies], we must learn to think 'transversally,'" Guattari stresses. To do that requires what he calls "ethico-aesthetic" experimentation, muddled-up practices rooted in smallness: "It seems to me essential to organize new micropolitical and microsocial practices, new solidarities, a new gentleness" (Guattari 2000: 43, 41, 51). Perhaps, to return to Blake, a tear is indeed an intellectual thing. Perhaps collaborative process and lateral thinking matter after all. Perhaps these words of performer Bryan Saner (1998) make a kind of ridiculous sense: "I believe that the work Goat Island is doing right now is going to keep the world from destroying itself."

B1. PERFORMANCE

1.1 Environment

1.2 Response

1.3 Body

1.4 Time

B1.1 ENVIRONMENT

Minneapolis: February 27, 1992

KILLACKY: Hi, you're listening to *Artifacts* at KFAI Radio, and I'm John Killacky. Visiting with us today is Lin Hixson, the artistic director of Goat Island, who perform their show *Can't Take Johnny to the Funeral* tonight and tomorrow night at Hennepin Center for the Arts, Studio 6A. So welcome, Lin.

HIXSON: Thank you.

KILLACKY: I don't know if the listeners are aware, but Studio 6A at the Hennepin Center was a Masonic Temple. You said you seemed to be making the touring route of Masonic Temples these days.

HIXSON: Goat Island doesn't work in a proscenium situation. We're interested in dealing with space in different ways. So our pieces—Goat Island has done three pieces—in all of them, the audience plays an important part. Not directly, in that we do not drag you on the stage or anything, but we look at the audience as witnesses of the work. They're set up in this situation where they surround the work. In this particular piece, the audience is on all four sides. So what that means is when we tour, we end up in different spaces that can accommodate that, and the Masonic Temple has been one of those.

More Permanent Than Snow Lin Hixson (2004: 128–131)

Do you see the empty lot on the corner? The walked-over weeds on the ground. Imagine a playground filling it in. Remove the wall of the liquor store next door and sit down quietly in its place. Catch the ball thrown at you by the young boy and watch as the light fades. See five performers fall to the ground and hear the one reciting the alphabet. Don't forget to rebuild the liquor store wall when you leave. Hold the sum of all these places together. These are our lived-in conditions.

In the 1989 film *Batman*, a moon sits in the sky and a bat sits in the moon. When I sat in the theatre and watched the film, the audience applauded when seeing the bat in the moon. I did not understand the applause because I never saw the bat. I saw teeth. I foregrounded the background and backgrounded the foreground. Four golden teeth—two on the top, two on the bottom, on the edge of a pitch-black chasm—snarled out at me. I never caught the bat like the moon. Instead, a not-bat sat in my eye.

One of my tasks as the director of Goat Island when making a performance is to foreground the not seen and background the seen. To do this requires: (1) the formation of attention; (2) slowing the traffic of the mind; (3) an enclosed encounter area; (4) spaces between.

Throughout the 1950s, the Dutch architect Aldo Van Eyck foregrounded blind spots on the city map of Amsterdam. Neglected holes between buildings, formless stretches of land, abandoned urban lots were converted by his designs into playgrounds for children. When he embedded this neglected ground into a playground, formerly unseen spots came into view. Groups of citizens caught sight of them and said, "These are not playgrounds." As a result of popular demand, during a period of ten years, Amsterdam built the unprecedented number of 734 playgrounds.

These were all spaces that were dead; spaces between buildings: a vacant lot, a waste space that had been bombed or destroyed or was derelict. But Van Eyck would just claim it as if it was the right shape, and design a playground according to the dynamics of that left-over space. So these are playgrounds that are like irregular triangles, or parallelograms, or wedge shapes, and people could look at these vacant, in-between spaces transformed into a playground, and say, "Oh, look what that made." Retroactive retro-fit; function adapts to its form. A playground.

(Matthew Goulish 2003)

Goat Island rehearses and performs in a gym in a church on a basketball court. Red and black lines outline the game and the playing area on the floor. Each time we start a new performance, we mark our performing area on top of the game with taped lines. The lines foreground the performance site and background the basketball court. Eight performance works now sit in the basketball court. The floor holds the worn away remains of 15 years of work:

1987 *Soldier, Child, Tortured Man*. A large rectangle. Four lines.
1989 *We Got A Date*. An alleyway. Two long lines.
1991 *Can't Take Johnny to the Funeral*. A boxing ring. Four lines.
1993 *It's Shifting Hank*. A rowboat. Four lines.
1996 *How Dear to Me the Hour When Daylight Dies*. A small rectangle next to a large square. Seven lines.
1998 *The Sea & Poison*. Two sides and two walls. Two lines.

2001 *It's an Earthquake in My Heart*. A Chevron sign with one side tilted out. Eleven lines.

2002. We work on a new performance. Its lines on the floor stand out with fresh tape. Twenty to thirty schoolchildren from the childcare center three floors below run across the floor. The children pause within our taped lines and say "you lose." Catch the ball thrown at you and watch as the traffic slows. Focus on the free-throw line until a woman's foot replaces it. Listen as James Taylor sings "Fire and Rain" and "Sweet Baby James" as the woman stands on one foot for 377 seconds.

We began this latest work with the question of repair. We looked at repair manuals from the 1950s for we could not find any current repair manuals in Chicago bookstores. The United States no longer repairs. It "disposes of" instead.

Van Eyck's work seemed integrally related to this idea of repair, but how could we communicate that just with space? We thought, what if there are actually two grids at work, and the audience is seated on one, and the two house shapes marked at either end of the stage are skewed to a different one? You get the sense that the performance is happening in a kind of skewed thoroughfare. Like a performance that has resulted by accident, within these pre-existing, criss-crossing grids.

(Matthew Goulish 2003)

1 Van Eyck playground: before and after.
Photographs © courtesy of Amsterdam Municipal Archives

If you look at a map of Amsterdam with Van Eyck's playgrounds, you see that the city is not a collection of buildings but is defined by the spaces in between. The map recalls Piet Mondrian's "starry sky" paintings, in which the artist moved away from a monocentred composition toward a randomly distributed galaxy of points. Van Eyck, influenced by Mondrian, viewed the idea of the city as an open-ended pattern, a constellation of situationally arising units, bound to time, accident, and circumstance. He was also influenced by Camillo Sitte, the nineteenth-century Viennese urbanist who recommended city configurations that bring about protection, and the slowing down of fast traffic. Van Eyck's redesign of Amsterdam's open areas turned individual voids into connections between people and between cognitive frames. Protected encounter areas were foregrounded. Traffic slowed. The focus of attention shifted from remote vistas to localities of site. Classical geometric forms sat within anti-classical patterns. Children hung off rectangular steel bars, played in triangles of sand, climbed half circles, and ran in three dimensional "starry sky" patterns.

Place. Placeless. Other place. Two places in one. Two-ness with two ones, one shifting forward then back to be seen; one shifting back then forward to be not seen; there is no place not the reflection of others. It is the reflected others we must discover.

(Edmond Jabès qtd in Waldrop 2002: 154)

It's snowing. Van Eyck watches it fall. The snow covers sidewalks, streets, trash, weeds, and empty lots. The cars stop. There is silence. Children run by and throw snowballs. Catch one. A trick of the sky has made these children lords of the city for one afternoon. They move freely—thoughts gone away. Van Eyck stands and does not move. The snow melts. He waits. A playground emerges in need of repair and surrounds him. Then the lights fade. It is time to go. There are many things to be afraid of but don't be afraid of the dark. Re-build something before you go. Listen as you leave. Van Eyck's speaking. He says, "How do we give children something more permanent than snow?"

In the field of social ecology, men like Donald Trump are permitted to proliferate freely, like another species of algae, taking over entire districts of New York and Atlantic City; he "redevelops" by raising rents, thereby driving out tens of thousands of poor families, most of whom are condemned to homelessness, becoming the equivalent of the dead fish of environmental ecology.

(Félix Guattari 2000: 43)

I've never actually read that book *Towards a Poor Theatre*, but for us there was never any question of a set. We knew that the actual room itself was going to become our set—that it [the performance] was always going to be pretty much us, and what we were wearing, and what we were saying. And also I loved playing with lighting, and I knew how to do that pretty cheaply. So we've carried those things with us in terms of production values: that's really become our aesthetic. We've gotten a little bit more money, but we don't use it to buy set pieces very often, unless it's a really good investment, because if we do, people won't get paid.

(Matthew Goulish 1997)

Portable islands Steve Bottoms

Glasgow, May 1994. My first experience watching Goat Island. They perform their 1989 piece *We Got a Date*. The audience is separated into two long, parallel tramlines, facing each other as if across a parade route. The four performers, dressed in school gym shorts and white T-shirts, repeatedly make their way up the lane in between, as if competing in some defective "sports day"—running, sprinting, bunny-hopping; one of them sometimes dragging himself on his belly, using his shoulders for propulsion, like the "fat kid" left behind, or like some stranded whale frantically flopping its way ever higher up the beach. At the end of each passing, the performers turn and run back behind the audience lines, looping back to their starting point. As they brush past me, sweat drips onto my shirt. The low-slung lights opposite are glaring in my eyes. For a moment I catch the eye of another spectator; we both look away as if stung. The performers pass again. I feel myself falling in love.

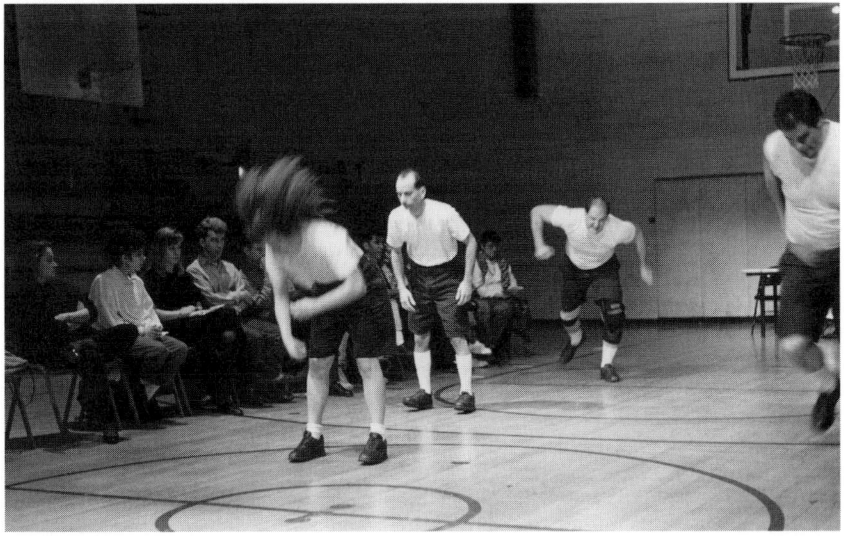

2 *We Got a Date*.

Photograph by Dona Ann McAdams. PS 122 at 14th Street Dance Center, New York City, 1990. Pictured left to right: Joan Dickinson, Matthew Goulish, Timothy McCain, Greg McCain

Within the existing literature on performance and ecology, there is general agreement that—as Bonnie Marranca has put it, "any elucidation of a theater ecology begins in the understanding of performance space" (1996: xvii). There is less agreement, however, about what such an understanding might entail. Marranca herself seems preoccupied with Gertrude Stein's notion of "landscape theatre," in which the traditional, anthropocentric emphasis on human characters caught up in linear narratives is replaced by an alternative emphasis on the simple, simultaneous occurrence of events or images spread across the proscenium stage. Marranca sees in the work of Robert Wilson one realization of Stein's ideal: his *Einstein on the Beach* for example (1976), ran on for many hours without linear progression, and spectators could come and go from the auditorium as they wished. The play was simply "there," like a landscape, to be viewed at leisure: "it is of no importance unless you look at it," wrote Stein (1985: 122).

This last phrase, however, surely signals the limitations of the landscape approach from an ecological perspective. Human agency may have been displaced from the stage action itself, but spectatorship is more anthropocentric than ever: the landscape is only of importance if we choose to look at it. As Baz Kershaw puts it: "Whether landscape is seen as a source of rejuvenating contemplation (a feast for the eyes of the Enlightenment) or a source of spiritual renewal (succour for the soul of romanticism), it is always so at the *service*, ultimately, of man (*sic*)" (2000: 128).

Rejecting the visual mechanics of the proscenium stage, Kershaw has instead made a case for what he calls "an aesthetics of *total immersion* in performance" (1999: 194). By placing audience members *within* a designated environment (artificial or "site-specific"), rather than having them look in on it from outside, and by inviting them individually to navigate its contours, he proposes that "the dualisms of modernism . . . particularly those between body and mind, analysis and creativity, thought and action" may be "transcended" (1999: 214). At the same time, though, Kershaw acknowledges that such "environmental" performances can sometimes be disorientating and disempowering for audiences made to feel vulnerable in such circumstances. One might add, moreover, that the dualisms he mentions may simply be reinforced if the novel sensory experiences (or indeed the feelings of vulnerability) arising from such "immersion" overwhelm any tendency toward critical reflection. Meanwhile, Una Chaudhuri is critical of the claims made for so-called "environmental theatre" on the grounds that it tends simply to reproduce "the logic of total visibility" already inherent in proscenium staging (Chaudhuri 1995: 26–27). In an environmental performance, audience members may not see everything laid out before them, but they are granted the mobility to go around corners to satisfy their curiosity. The anthropocentric right to omniscience thus tends to be reinforced rather than challenged; the "environment" is rendered *subject* to spectatorial penetration.

Goat Island's approach to staging suggests one possible solution to this eco-spatial conundrum. Neither proscenium-based nor conventionally "in-the-round" (another convention whose logics tend to assume "total visibility"), the company's work nonetheless locates spectators in fixed seating configurations around bare, floor-level performance spaces. The exact configuration is different for each new show, and is determined as part of the creative process, but in each case audiences find themselves located mere feet or inches away from the performers. (Director Lin Hixson maintains that, if there are more than three rows of risers around the stage, "a vital degree of intimacy" is lost.) Although this "poor theatre" staging approach was initially a reflection of Goat Island's economic limitations, the company's insistence, throughout its history, on maintaining this kind of audience–performer proximity has imposed "economies of scale" on their work that few would dare emulate. In the face of all the logics of touring—the obligation to tailor work to proscenium-based receiving houses—they have sought out ways to relocate their peculiarized performance spaces from site to site, with the result that they frequently find themselves playing in unorthodox spaces (Masonic lodges?), or treating conventional spaces in an unorthodox fashion: thus audiences at some locations find themselves seated literally "on stage" in a large theatre, perched on temporary risers around a demarcated performance area but with a dark, empty auditorium looming to one side. "Environmental theatre" this is not, but spectators nonetheless tend to find themselves sharply aware of the wider environment within which both they and the miniaturized world of the performance itself are located.

Similarly, spectators become aware of their own physical location in relation to the stage, not least because any given seat will tend to provide favourable views of certain actions (a body twitching on the floor right in front of your feet, for example), while setting others at more of a distance. The basic dynamic is sculptural. Bodies and objects are foregrounded or backgrounded, depending on one's particular vantage point, and still others may be partially or completely obscured from view (by the acute angle, by your neighbours' heads). Watching a Goat Island show is a process of learning to accept the loss of the spectator's habitual omniscience in performance situations, and an awareness of one's place in a larger system. As Gregory Bateson notes of ecological thinking, "a certain humility becomes appropriate" (2000: 467).

I have often felt that the ideal position from which to see [It's an Earthquake in My Heart] *would be from above. Here the full extent of its intricate patterns, its complex spatial and physical logics might be better mapped. But this is of course Goat Island's point: the ideal place is unavailable. There is no location from which to see the work in totality; there are only subjective and partial positions, fragments of a whole.*

(Adrian Heathfield 2001: 19)

Rather than a landscape (though it has something of the same simultaneity of event), a Goat Island performance can perhaps be thought of *as* an island (Robinson Crusoe's perhaps), surrounded by a "sea" of audience. Life on the island remains quite separate from the aquatic life: the performance is a closed eco-system, a rigorously rehearsed circuit sequence which coolly disregards the audience's immediate presence and seeks little participation from them. (Direct eye-contact between performers and spectators is studiously avoided for the most part, although when it comes, it tends to be warmly inclusive rather than confrontational.) Nonetheless, there is here a particularly intense occurrence of the "edge phenomena" that Baz Kershaw has cited as existing at the point of interaction between performers and audiences: "Edge phenomena are places, such as riverbanks and seashores, where two or more ecosystems rub up against each other to produce especially dynamic life-forms and processes" (Kershaw 2001: 136). On small islands, this rubbing-up-against is a constant and unavoidable aspect of life—a factor which, according to philosopher Gilles Deleuze, makes them particularly difficult places for human beings to come to terms with:

> *That an island is deserted must appear* philosophically *normal to us. Humans cannot live, nor live in security, unless they assume that the active struggle between earth and water is over, or at least contained. People like to call these two elements mother and father, assigning them gender roles according to the whims of their fancy. They must somehow persuade themselves that a struggle of this kind does not exist, or that it has somehow ended. In one way or another, the very existence of islands is the negation of this point of view, of this effort, this conviction.*
>
> (Deleuze 2004: 1)

So too, Goat Island's performances tend to challenge and to frustrate the assumption that spectatorship is an uncomplicated process. There is no relaxing into comfortable anonymity or "fly-on-the-wall" invisibility. Yet physical proximity goes hand-in-hand with the mental distance afforded by the avoidance of direct audience–performer contact. Critical awareness, and critical *self*-awareness, are practically unavoidable. (The frequent invitations to audiences at Goat Island work-in-progress showings to participate in post-show critical feedback discussions set up another "edge phenomenon" whose significance for both parties should not be overlooked.)

As Goat Island relocate their portable islands from city to city, they take their "lived-in conditions" with them, looking always to approximate the functional basics of the run-down church gymnasium that is sweet home, Chicago. Bare wooden floorboards are usually a requirement, so that the pounding beat of feet and limbs—running, jumping, falling—can be heard hammering out their insistent pulse. Exposed windows, too, add another dimension, locating this tiny, enclosed world in relation to a much bigger universe of lingering daylight, visible architecture, and muffled traffic sounds.

Goat Island takes up fleeting possession of their usual Chicago space, the third-floor gymnasium of an old (by Chicago standards, a century or so) church. The fading afternoon light, as the "daylight dies" into evening blue, grey and black, replaced only gradually by overhead track lighting, accents without overly accentuating both the transience and intensity of their visitation.

(Loren Kruger 1999: 87)

Alternative Spaces and Vision Bryan Saner (2001)

In order for humans to believe or say anything with certainty we tend to select what we view. This selection is sometimes related to the characteristics of our physical body. We don't have eyes in the back of our head so we tend to ignore half of the 360 degree panorama we are standing in. The best we can see with our full vision is 180 degrees. Most comfortably however, we focus on an even smaller picture plane, a sheet of paper, an electronic image monitor, a film screen or a stage. We close one eye and look through a telescope to see the universe.

Yet sometimes what we see through these lenses shakes our world and challenges our previous identities or philosophical and spiritual ideologies. We thought that the world was flat, now we think it is round. That realization was a catastrophic shift for us. Scientific and philosophical upheavals throughout history that have totally changed our view of life and the universe are based on these glimpses of the part, without totally understanding the whole. Any philosophical or theological construct we have to live by, any ethical standard or concept of reality, is based on us looking at the world through a keyhole.

Maybe we don't need to see the whole truth of the universe. We may not be ready for it. Maybe it's best that we get bits and pieces slowly, as in a process of becoming. Perhaps what we should concentrate on is becoming comfortable with not understanding everything that is going on. Perhaps we should be comfortable with not seeing everything. After all, the beginning of knowledge is not knowing.

This is all by way of thinking about how Goat Island uses performance space. We like to play our performances in nontraditional spaces, and create problems for ourselves to solve. By nontraditional, I mean not the usual proscenium venue where the raised stage is at one end of a room and the seating for the audience is at the other end. Proscenium stages arrange the audience and the players in a fixed position with fixed rules:

- Performers should not turn their backs to the audience.
- The audience sees one side of a performer, three at most, but not all four.
- Performers play to the audience in one direction.
- Spoken text goes in one direction.
- Exits lead performers off to unknown, unseen areas.
- Performers and audience are often separated by a minimum of 15 feet to the front row and up to 300 feet to the back rows or balconies.
- Performers must "act" in a stylized form to communicate across this gap of space. They must speak loudly, and exaggerate movement in a manner that we would not encounter in an everyday living situation.

What happens to the human body when it has to act this way? We feel that it flattens into a two-dimensional cut-out designed to be seen only from the front, destined to conform to the acting precepts of the current method, worried that it isn't being heard by the audience in the balcony. We are trying to set up another kind of relationship with audiences. Take the floorplan for our staging of *It's an Earthquake in My Heart*. This began as a miniature, tennis-court-shaped space approximately 10 feet wide by 20 feet long, with the audience placed on all four sides. We experimented with performing traffic patterns, and so added "pits" on the two longer sides to create places for us to park. The new shape reminded us of the Chevrolet logo. Later, it was afflicted with oblique angles after being struck by the lightning-bolt design of Daniel Liebeskind's Jewish Memorial Museum in Berlin, which we visited while on tour. Splitting the space diagonally, we created exits in opposing corners. These also function as additional performance areas at each end of the main performance space. They remind me of Renzo Piano's design for the Beyeler Foundation Gallery in Basel: in addition to rooms for showing specific works of art, that space invites you to look outside the gallery onto a cornfield and vineyard in the far distance.

In our new space we realize quickly why the fixations and rules of the proscenium were established in the first place. The proscenium stage makes things simpler and we recognize the elegance of that simplicity. Our new space has its own set of problems to solve—including variations on the ones listed above:

- It's difficult to understand a performer if her/his back is turned to the audience.
- Movement that looked good from the front now looks flat when viewed from the back.
- Setting up risers in this configuration is more difficult because it's not commonly done and so a new dialogue with venues happens. These alterations cost more for the venue or ourselves, or require that we find alternative venues to perform in.

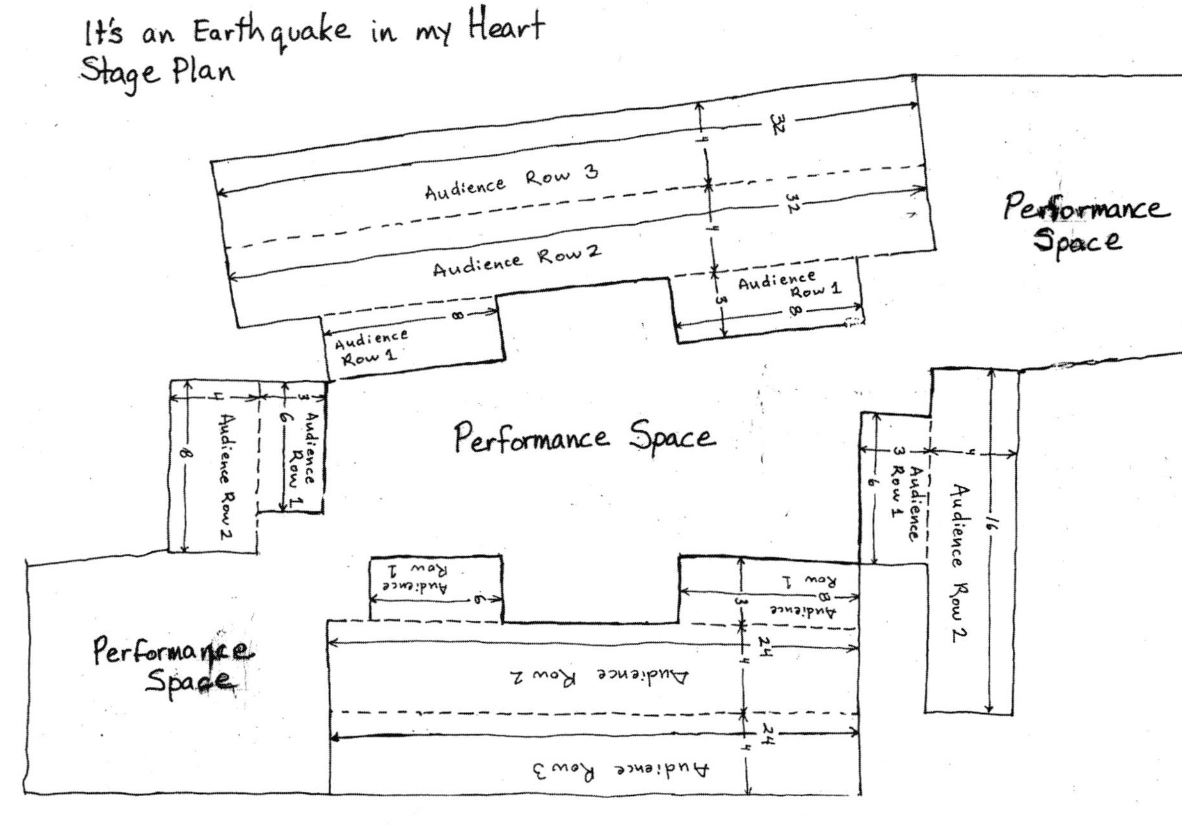

3 *It's an Earthquake in My Heart*: floor plan.

- Activity that happens in the exit spaces is missed by people who can't see or don't look into these corners, or is seen as a sketchy, diminished event through a small aperture between other audience members' heads.

We've never intended to condemn the proscenium stage. We are interested in making a contribution to an alternative. And we are interested in complexity—both as an aesthetic and as a working process. We find that dealing creatively with the problems of physical space adds something to the form and content of the work:

- We repeat events in different directions so the audience can hear the texts.
- The repetition contributes to a new rhythmical order in the work. The repetition allows for a contemplative delivery or transfer of the texts. It promotes the development of a history in the work, as we see the same text recurring alongside different visual images on stage at different times.
- The search for alternative spaces connects us with architecture as opposed to theater. Here we begin to function on a slightly different human scale.
- In addition to it feeling like a living space instead of an acting space, the distance between the audience and the stage has been reduced to a minimum of 3 feet and a maximum of 15 feet.
- The exit spaces at each end allow us to extend performed movement into the periphery of vision, and perhaps to advance the contextual components of the work.

The performer now becomes a whole person conscious of the back of the body and of being at least partially visible in all parts of the space. This expanded consciousness has implications for how we perform. We begin to see the performance material itself in more multi-dimensional terms. We think that audiences too find something new in the experience of dealing with these difficulties and differences.

In the early stages of work on a performance, when we are deciding on the shape of the playing space, we consider how the audience will see things and make changes accordingly: this is from the very beginning a collaboration with the future audience. Yet despite this, no one person sees everything and so audience members also find themselves having to collaborate with each other. As spectators, we compare notes during and after the performance. We watch other observers across the way as they respond to the performer who has her/his back to us: are they smiling or concentrating or bored? Their response tells us what is happening. We also project responses to what the backside of the performer is doing. After the performance we talk to each other over coffee or beer and tell each other what we saw. We recommend developing a comfort with not knowing everything in order to know something.

One of the ways we proved that the world was round was to place two equal-length sticks upright in the ground about five hundred miles apart; then at an exact moment a person at each location measured the length of the shadow. If the world was flat, the shadows would be the same length but the shadows were not the same length so we began to think that the earth is round. This experiment was conducted by Aristosthenes around 250 BCE. Over a thousand years later, when we finally agreed that the earth is round, we catapulted ourselves out of the middle ages into the Renaissance.

A triangulation must occur in order for us to make sense of these performances. Like two scientists measuring the shadows to prove that the earth is round, we must collaborate. It took two points of view to visualize the earth as a round surface. It also took time (roughly a millennium) to come to this understanding. Perhaps it is through a collaboration of these elements (multiple points of view and time) that we are able get a more accurate view of our selves. Perhaps we should only trust our own perceptions when measured against the perspectives of others.

The Materiality of Lightness Mark Jeffery (2004a)

A Goat Island performance space will generally begin empty. The space will be delineated with tape on the floor and an audience will sit around it. For the duration of the performance bodies will come and go, objects will come and go, echoes and structures will sequence the material, histories will appear and disappear. In this time, the audience's engagement with the material will focus and refocus on different aspects: configuration of people, arrangement of objects, arrangements in subtimes and subspaces. Environments and worlds will arrive, accumulate, be constructed, taken apart, introduced, destroyed, revealed.

In all of our pieces materiality has its own language, its own parameters, and its own development in the trajectory of the performance. Materiality becomes another inquiry, another investigation, an extension to the space, body and time. The materials we use are generally connected to the everyday, to the banal, to the ordinary. Their mundane status reflects our concerns towards finding a vocabulary of ecology, a response towards recycling. The cardboard that we began working with for *When will the September roses bloom? Last night was only a comedy* came from publicity packages that the group was working with 12 years earlier.

The question: "How do you repair?"

One of the ideas introduced in response to this question was for us to consider working with lightness. It was a response to the question, and also to previous pieces and their engagement with materials that had not necessarily been light

—and thus not necessarily easy to transport. A plough from a family farm, artificial trees, metal tables, rolls of Astroturf, insecticide sprayer. One example of lightness that we came up with was the material of cardboard, which not only flat-packs nicely in a case, but which suggests an aesthetic aiming towards the non-flashy, the pre-technological, the almost redundant, the throwaway.

As the new piece developed, other materials connected to lightness also began to be introduced. As these materials engaged and absorbed themselves into the piece, ideas of collapse, fragility, falling, uncertainty, failed magic shows and tricks, comedy juxtaposed with darkness, and perverse interrogations all emerged from our working with these lightweight materials. In engaging with fragility and repair, we have constructed: tables of cardboard; chairs missing legs and forever unbalanced; crutches of wood and cardboard to hold people up as if trees; stabilizers to connect lightness with growth and stability. In states of repair tables teeter, topple, collapse. Chairs with one leg can never stay upright. Repairs are made with parcel tape and cardboard. Lightness creates its own weight. As more weight and pressure is applied, rigid temporary states become states of fragility. Objects are always in a state of imbalance, instability.

Working with these reconfigured, everyday materials makes us reconsider our responses to the world, to the familiar. Whether in its collapse or in its interaction with itself, with other materials, or with our bodies, the newly transformed material or object helps us to look at possibilities for change, for renewal, for sustainability.

Our approach to material strives not to make a set, but to embody and absorb objects as part of the language of performance, as elements of a process which demand to connect with us conceptually, spatially and physically.

Material makes a demand. Material has the need to illuminate, propagate, shift and polarize our concerns, consciously and unconsciously. Material becomes flexible, rigid and fragile, brittle and light. In combination with objects, the human body has the potential to become a fountain, a forest, a dancing bear, a lighthouse, a car, a fog horn, a receptor, a tree, a disaster, an error, a machine.

Fake plastic trees Steve Bottoms

When a Zen priest ceaselessly clips, prunes, weeds, and trains his garden, wrote Alan Watts, "he is not interfering with Nature because he is Nature" (Watts 1957: 187). A similar point is made more prosaically by David Crouch in his discussion of British allotment owners, individuals working their small patches of land less for the sake of crop "productivity" than for the sake of the ongoing interaction with nature itself: "The air is always different and alerts the skin," notes one such smallholder, "unexpected scents are brought by breezes. Only when on your hands and knees do you notice insects and other small wonders" (Crouch 2003: 22). Goat Island's assembly of "found objects" within their allotted performance spaces suggests something similar—a working with and for these materials, rather than a use of them as mere "props" for predetermined ends.

The crucial distinction, of course, is that the materials used are patently man-made rather than "natural." But then, any natural object placed onstage would immediately become acculturated, subject to cultural assumptions: "Any attempt to comprehend 'nature' from within 'culture'"—Kershaw notes—"is similar to thinking you can turn on a light quickly enough to see what the dark looks like" (2002: 119). Kershaw, in fact, makes a connection here with Plato, for whom the arts can only ever provide copies of copies of the ideal forms suggested by nature: thus a table in a painting is a mere shadow of an actual table, which is only one manifestation of an ideal tableness that stands in natural relation to the scale of human bodies (Plato 1987: 336–339). What, then, of the moment in *When will the September roses bloom?*, when the stage becomes populated with a forest of child-sized cardboard tables, all wobbling precariously on hastily assembled cardboard-tube legs? Does the image perhaps foreground, through a kind of awkward comedy, the eternal failure of culture that Plato identifies?

By making space on its stage for ongoing acknowledgements of the rupture it participates in —the rupture between nature and culture, forests and books, sincere acting and real fish—the theater can become the site of a much-needed ecological consciousness.

(Una Chaudhuri 1994: 28)

In *The Sea & Poison* (1998), a performance which alludes repeatedly to human pollution of the natural world, Goat Island nonetheless avoid, systematically, any use of "real" or "natural" materials onstage. We are presented instead with a synthesized world of plastic grass, plastic fish, a plastic songbird, and a rainstorm of plastic frogs bouncing off a thundersheet (creating fake theatrical thunder). Even the dirt which the performers trample underfoot is from plastic sacks—a processed compost rather than "the real thing." Far from appealing to some myth of naturalness or authenticity (a myth which, it must be said, has long appealed to certain practitioners and critics of performance art), *The Sea & Poison* acknowledges and plays with the inescapable reality of the artificially synthesized world in which we now live.

This is not to say that ghost traces of the authentic do not persist in Goat Island's world: we see the actual exhaustion of performers' bodies (visible in sweat; audible in laboured breathing); the thud and creak of floorboards; the dying of the daylight. Yet the use of rough, bare floors itself requires a use of sturdy footwear which—as dancer Litó Walkey observed after joining the company in 2002—already imposes a basic separation between feet and "earth," very different from the "naturalness" of barefoot movement. In *It's an Earthquake in My Heart* (2001), that separation is enacted strikingly by one of the company's rare uses of "natural" materials: near-cubic blocks of rough-hewn wood are periodically used as perilously awkward platform shoes, elevating performers still further from the ground, as they clatter clumsily about the stage.

Perhaps these blocks are the dismembered corpses of some of the trees whose names Bryan Saner slowly, tenderly pronounces as a kind of litany later in the same piece—as if in remembrance of the cut-down dead:

Oak . . . Cedar . . . Tulip—the lumbermen call it yellow poplar . . . Sycamore . . . Gum —both sweet and sour . . . Beech . . . Black walnut . . . Sassafras . . . Willow . . . Butternut . . . Cypress . . . Larch . . . Box elder . . . Yew . . . Catalpa . . . Cherry . . . Pear . . . Hemlock . . . Hazel . . . Persimmon . . . Mountain-ash . . . Hickory . . . [etc.]

(list appropriated from Walt Whitman's *Specimen Days*)

The litany is complemented by the creation of a dreamy, miniaturized Christmas landscape, as the stage becomes populated with a forest of tiny, artificial fir trees, and a light carpet of snow is created by a showering of paper circles ("holes" cut out by a hole-punch). Again, though, the artifice is inescapable: one thinks less of "real" woodland than of *It's a Wonderful Life*. Our acculturated perspectives prevent us from seeing the wood for the trees.

Perhaps, moreover, the shrunken scale of the trees, of the cardboard tables, and of so many other Goat Island objects points to the shrinking *scale* of our perceptions of our environment. As Paul Virilio has argued, "the world of tangible experience . . . its 'life-size quality'" has become eroded and retarded by "the *microphysical* proximity" of the computer and television screens that now drip-feed so much of our reality (1997: 62). We confuse the "apparent horizon" of that which technology permits us to see ghosted in front of us with the disconcertingly "deep horizon" of terra firma:

the geophysical environment is undergoing an alarming diminishing of its "depth of field" and this is degrading man's relationship with his environment. *The optical density of the landscape* is rapidly evaporating. [Soon] there will not be much left of the expanse of a planet that is not only polluted but also shrunk, reduced to nothing, by the teletechnologies of generalized interactivity.

(Virilio 1997: 21–22)

And thus—like Goat Island's performers—we stride as life-size giants among miniature, virtual forests. "Americans today recognize fewer than 10 trees," Matthew Goulish notes, "but over 1,000 corporate logos" (Goat Island 2001a: 4).

4 *It's an Earthquake in My Heart.*
Photograph by Rebecca Groves. Mousonturm, Frankfurt, Germany, 2001. Pictured left to right: Mark Jeffery, Matthew Goulish, Bryan Saner, Karen Christopher

The wind flung the door open. It knocked over my water cup.
I went outside. I looked up at the sky.
This event appeared to confuse the birds, but I was not afraid.
I saw a cloud in the shape of a country church—the country church
from my home town—two smaller clouds in the shape of my parents,
a car-shaped cloud with a "Just Married" sign hanging on it.
The clouds were showing me my parents' wedding day.
It was nice of nature to imitate reality in this way.

(from *It's an Earthquake in My Heart,*
writing by Goat Island)

Artificial Ice Mark Jeffery (1999a)

During the making of Goat Island's *The Sea & Poison*, I brought in some incomplete material. The image was of a wake-up call/statue of liberty/lighthouse reading an anti-war letter. I stood in bare feet in a pail of water and poured a 99-cent pack of ice over my head. Ice fell in and around the bucket. A sea-flare was then lit with the assistance of Karen Christopher, and I held the burning firework/torch high above my head. This lasted until the flame extinguished: ice melted on the wooden floor, tiny sparks began to burrow and burn into the ground, smoke filled the air. As the flame burned, I read out an anti-war letter, written by a father to his son, who is asked to read it on his sixteenth birthday. The text of the letter was taken from the 1948 film *The Boy with Green Hair*.

Artificial objects had begun to present themselves during this time in the rehearsal process, and Matthew Goulish suggested we work with fake ice and discover another possibility to a burning flame. Plastic ice was bought at the camera store: this ice is normally used for photographic work, and for take after take the ice in your cocktail glass never melts. The sea-flare turned into a battery-operated light, bought at a boating store, normally used in distress, when lost at sea among the waves.

This point of departure and difference allowed me to discover a new approach to the making and performing of live work.* For me, the approach to performance had always been toward presenting the authentic; to be true to time and space, to the real body, to this which is happening *now* and only now. Yet the acceptance of different approaches and possibilities has led me to think that we might see the artificial in performance as being more "real" than the authentic in performance. Artifice gives us another way of looking, another way of connecting to and working with both the fake and the real.

No smoke. No flames. No coldness. No melting. A dry world where the moisture and emotion come through from the accent of the edit and the sequencing of bodies moving and talking within the parameters of structural form.

An Artificial List for *The Sea & Poison*:
3 Lines of white paint; 3 pieces of Astroturf; 1 drawing table; 1 metal garden stool; 1 wooden chair; 1 yellow backpack (full of plastic green frogs); 1 plastic clear bowl; 2 plastic goldfish; 1 plastic drink bottle; 11 plastic ice-cubes; 2 plastic frogs; 2 yellow bags; 1 flashing light; 1 torn, handwritten letter; 48 plastic leaves; 1 plastic bird; 1 elastic strap; 1 Dictaphone; 1 microphone; 1 microphone stand; 2 wooden pegs; 1 child-size wooden piano; 1 audiotape; a certain amount of water.

At 9.30 p.m. on the first Thursday of every month, BBC television broadcasts a programme titled *Crimewatch UK*. Each month, *Crimewatch* asks its viewers to become part of, and interact with, the programme—as three reconstructed crimes are transmitted into our homes; crimes ranging from murder to arson to bank raids. Each month we are invited to become witness to each crime, possibly for a second time, in order to help to solve it and convict the offenders. As each reconstruction

* *The Sea & Poison* was the first Goat Island performance that Mark Jeffery was involved in creating from the outset.

is presented, a high-ranking police officer provides a voice-over to the ten-minute crime. As the teleplay of actual crime unfolds, actors recreate and play out the past, the present and the possible future, in the hope that a specific viewer at home will recall the actual event that we are reliving, and phone in with new information. The videotape of the crime is generally overdramatic, insincere and unreal, as the witnesses and characters somehow cross over into theatre. Here we watch bad actors with bad props; bad wigs, bad clothes and bad dialogue, re-enacting these vital definitive moments, allowing the non-authentic to aid our memories. The gigantic scale of the artificiality somehow pulls at us in desperation to remember, to aid and assist.

In April 1999, the presenter of *Crimewatch*, Jill Dando, was murdered outside her London home, a gunshot to the head. The following month the show still aired, but this time it showed Jill's crime story. TV real + her real became a reel.
An out-of-work actress became Jill Dando.

Towards the latter part of *The Sea & Poison*, four performers situate themselves within a box frame painted onto the floor with white lines. The lines demarcate the length and width of an incomplete rectangle within the frame of the stage—a rectangle previously marked out by approximately 3360 jumps on and around its four corners. Three smaller rectangles of Astroturf are laid onto three quarters of the demarcated floor space, and it becomes the little stage at the back of the garden we all once played on. An end-of-term school play we never got to perform, rehearsing in the school holidays.

In her book *On Longing*, Susan Stewart describes an experiment with time and space that took place at the University of Tennessee's School of Architecture. Here, researchers had adults observe scaled-down environments at 1:6, 1:12, and 1:24 of their full size. The environments were living rooms, with scale figures and chipboard furniture. The adults were asked to respond by imagining themselves in these living spaces and re-enacting activities with the scale figures. The researchers asked the adults to state when they felt they had been engaged in such activities for 30 minutes. What occurred was that the temporary time compressed itself within the scale of the environment: 30 minutes was experienced in 5 minutes at 1:12 scale, and in 2.5 minutes in 1:24 scale. "In other words, miniature time transcends the duration of everyday life in such a way as to create an interior temporality of the subject," Stewart concludes (1993: 66).

Within our miniature stage-within-a-stage, four performers give testimonies and stories from past, present and future—a concertina of images and texts from fact and fiction, from newsclippings and films, an experiment in reconstruction. Here the artificial spinning-top knocks and reframes the lens/eye of our moving film camera. Time and space become abstracted for the audience, through the material and the miniature. Connections are made to what we may or may not have seen, past present future.

Earlier in *The Sea & Poison*, Karen has come into contact with a cloud of white mist, pumped from a chemical spray can. The mist has turned her hair white, ageing her. Here in our school-play world, whilst Karen sits on a metal stool, a soft, pink, plastic bald-cap is taken from a sidepocket of the backpack she is wearing. Matthew applies the bald-cap to her head by use of double-sided sticky tape. Karen's ponytail is hidden underneath the collar and shoulders of her clothing. She is transformed; her hair disappeared. Out of another sidepocket of the backpack, Matthew pulls a brown, synthetic, ponytail—an artificial stand-in for Karen's hair. Bryan walks over to Mark, pulls off a dollar bill attached to his shirt, and places it on the table Mark is resting on. Matthew walks over, places the hair on the table, picks up the dollar bill, and holds it in his hand. Karen stands and walks to the microphone. She speaks of being a Gulf War veteran, of deformities to babies, and eventually of being an incredible shrinking man, affected by pollution from a mist cloud, diminishing to microscopic scale. Within this short scene we have referenced several different social, historical, cultural and political contexts.

Through this merging of factual and imaginary narratives, we question the double-edged neatness with which our culture separates "truth" from "fiction"—actuality from artifice—and ask audiences to think again about the stories we are part of, about the crimes we are committing against our bodies and environment. To identify and reveal the secrets that we hide from ourselves.

In a world which really is topsy-turvy, *the true is a moment of the false.*

(Guy Debord, *The Society of the Spectacle*, statement 9)

Puppet show # 1 Lin Hixson (Goat Island 1996b: 6)

When I was nine, I received a puppet theatre for Christmas. It was too big for my bedroom so it ended up in my brother's room. Consequently, he began to perform puppet shows for me by hiding behind the yellow castle with its red and blue Bavarian patterns.

Three hinged panels formed the castle theatre. The main stage was an open-air rectangle cut into the centre panel and framed by scarlet curtains. In height it was just the size of my brother's head if you included his neck. In width, he could fit two hands with his fingers spread. The two side panels adjusted to provide his secret chamber. Of course the task was never to see the hand or head of my brother, but only the adventures of the king and queen or the lion and the mouse. The beginning of his plays usually went well; the king and queen danced; the lion bit the mouse's head. But soon my brother's foot would creep out off to the side, looming larger than the full figure of the queen. The top of his head would appear bobbing visibly with the king as he waltzed. Sometimes the sleeve of his shirt became the bottom of the mouse's body. And then, finally, when tired, he'd sit up, his big head taking up the whole rectangle and becoming the Godzilla backdrop to the lives of these smaller beings.

I grew to love these breakdowns; these scenes filled with the tension of his imminent arrival. How long would the fantastic world of the miniature people and animals last before they were disrupted by my brother's head? When would the lion become the lion-sleeve, or the queen become the queen-ear?

> I am continuing to shrink.
> To become—what? The infinitesimal?
> What will I be? Still a human being?
> Or am I the man of the future?
> If there were other bursts of radiation—other clouds drifting across seas and continents—will other beings follow me into this vast new world?
>
> So close—the infinitesimal and the infinite . . .
> But suddenly I know that they are really two ends of the same concept.
> The unbelievably small and the unbelievably vast eventually meet like the closing of a gigantic circle.
>
> I feel my body dwindling, melting, becoming nothing.
> My fears melt away, and in their place comes acceptance.
> All this vast majesty of creation—it has to mean something.
> And then I mean something too.
>
> (from *The Sea & Poison*; adapted from Richard Matheson's screenplay for *The Incredible Shrinking Man*, 1957)

B1.2 RESPONSE

Where to begin when speaking of the work of Goat Island? A company whose art practice is bent against the very idea of beginnings and endings, whose spare performance aesthetic seems at times so dense and complex that it trips up your tongue and ties it in knots. But I must say something, so why not start in the experience itself: extreme self-consciousness, physical discomfort, confusion, frustration, near boredom, vague recognition, déjà vu, fleeting identification, sudden epiphanies of meaning, an entranced or mesmerized state, a creeping accumulation of emotions, subterranean alteration. Perhaps you have felt one, or some, or all of these things while watching the work of Goat Island. You might have found these things "difficult," against some other desired effect. Traditions of watching within live arenas may lead us to expect that such experiences should and will have been cut down or out. And when we find ourselves inside them, that voice in our heads—at once natural and deeply conditioned—tends to ask, "I have paid for this. Where is the pleasure? Where is its meaning, its utility?" Goat Island's work holds you inside the duration of these experiences, then asks you to return to them again and again. It asks you to suspend your viewing habits and stall that inner voice, to linger openly in its moments, which are difficult to evaluate, identify and know. . . . Each performance quietly requires you to phase-shift your perceptions, and move into a state of *being with* the work that is sensory, associative, contemplative and unresolved. This work is not without its pleasures.

(Adrian Heathfield 2001: 16–17)

How can the audience be caught up when there is no character development, no plot, and the most minimal of props? It would seem that the goal could be achieved by creating various points of entry and enough silence so that the viewer can bring a series of personal/cultural associations. There is also the implicit emotional plea of the work which circumvents the intellect and aims for a response that is more direct. We become invested in the investment of the players—their commitment to their actions sparks our own.

(Carol Becker 1994: 60)

Beginnings Karen Christopher (1998, 1999b)

The audience: what do you want the audience to be, to think, to do? Do you want to alter the audience? Persuade, tease, stimulate, gratify? Do you want to tell them? Do you want them to tell you? Do you ignore them, do you perform for someone else while they are there? Do you take them for who they are? Do you look at them? How do you approach them?

We make words for what is important to us and the words we choose to talk about audience tell what our relationship is to the audience and to the idea of performance. We like to talk about audience as witness. A witness watches and makes judgements and is an active participant in the outcome of the event. The event is changed because of the presence of the witness. The performance remains unfinished until it is witnessed by an audience, and then it's finished again the next night, and the next night, and the next. When the show is over, another process begins—the shifting and the changing of emotion and memory, of experience and thought. This process is individual to each person.

What we try to do is create a history within a span of time and among a group of people sharing an experience. Though our style has changed over the years in some ways, one thing that has remained constant is the need to facilitate a breakdown at the beginning of the performance—to pull spectators away from wherever they have been, mentally, during the day, and to bring them into this space, now. Our attempts to do this often involve the manipulation of time through the extension or duration of a similar gesture, or a series of images repeated for a longer-than-expected length of time. These periods of activity test the stamina of both the performers and the spectators: we are asking the audience to go somewhere they don't know and to follow without understanding.

In Hollywood film-making the craftsmen involved are instructed, even forced, to make sure the audience knows what is happening within the first five minutes. The first ten will explain the entire story. This is done so as not to lose people: this is the hook, the set-up. We have our own set-up but it works differently because we are working with a completely different set of rules. During this early part of a performance we are stretching the limits of expectation. We are teaching the language of the piece and we are laying the groundwork for a history of movement and understanding. Language learning is a slow process that requires repetition and cross-referencing and identification and memory. And you have to see it used, this language you are learning. If not, then you don't see its dynamic qualities.

In the performance *Can't Take Johnny to the Funeral* (1991), the first 15 minutes contains a series of moves and jumps and falls to the floor and a lot of huffing and puffing and all this for no apparent reason. There were two large fellows, Tim and Greg

McCain, as well as Matthew Goulish and myself in that piece, and the McCains picked me and Matthew up and twirled us over their shoulders, and then did the same to each other. There was a lot of effort being expended, but no explanation as to what was going on. Some people found this puzzling, some found it troubling, and even the most patient observers found it a bit of a strain toward the end of the sequence. There was no music mediating the experience, no sound except the huffing and puffing of people trying to do something the worth of which had not at all been established. Even those who loved this sequence, as pure, gymnastic movement, would probably agree that it was an ordeal—something appreciated in hindsight but tortuous, to some extent, at the time it was taking place. As a performer, I could feel a seal being stretched. Then, when the music began at the end of this sequence, when all four performers—now flat on the floor heaving for breath and drenched in sweat—got up and moved about the space in a more relaxed and familiar way, the relief in the audience was visible and audible. They moved, they sighed, they spoke to one another. Some sat very still but began to relax, perceptibly. We had all survived the storm, but also, something chemical had happened. We had come through a threshold, through a liminal phase where change is made possible.

I think of storms because, here in Chicago, whenever we have big storms—especially snowstorms—something happens on the street once the worst is over. Everyone becomes very cheerful and talkative, chatting with strangers as if they feel very alive—and glad to be so. The ordeal in some way reminds us that we feel, that we care about life, that we are here and nowhere else. To experience ordeal in this way is to be actually here and thinking about here as well—not thinking about yesterday or tomorrow.

To me, though, the most important function of this ordeal process within a Goat Island piece is the extent to which expectations or preconceived notions are broken down, disappointed, frustrated. And that is a preparation for what comes after. To use another analogy, the process is a little like sitting in a darkened room. At first there appears to be no light at all, but as you sit there, if you keep your eyes open and you keep looking, you slowly begin to see more and more. Eventually you begin to see not only objects in the room but whole streams of light, formerly invisible, that now appear to shine through gaps in walls and above doors.

A young Canadian audience member in Lethbridge, Alberta, told me of his response to our 1996 piece *How Dear to Me the Hour When Daylight Dies*. By contrast with the extreme physicality of *Johnny*, this performance begins (after an opening monologue) with a fairly long period of near-stillness, during which Matthew slowly rubs the top of one hand with the fingers of the other, repeating the same gesture over and over with only slight variations. This occurs firstly in silence, continues for the full duration of Joe Heaney's Irish folk song, "The Rocks of Bawn," and persists into the silence that follows it. Then all four of us begin the "puppet jump," a series of movements involving jumping, reaching, falling and spinning, which continues for several more minutes, before we kneel down in a line to begin the "shivering homage" sequence: we shake, tremble, and then rub our hands (as if washing them) to the accompaniment of Doris Day's "Que Sera?" Many audience members found all this a trying experience, but this young man's comment was roughly as follows:

at first I was very frustrated, and then I thought these people are crazy and I didn't get it, and then I felt bored into anger. But then I felt a decision coming. I realized I could just check out and reject this performance or I could relax and not worry about understanding it and just accept it. I don't want to call it a religious experience [those were his exact words], but I chose to relax and suddenly I started getting all these ideas and began to have all sorts of associations with the movements and gestures I was seeing. It was because I was able to make this decision to accept the performance without understanding it. I was able to make that choice.

A misunderstanding Matthew Goulish (2000a: 31–32)

A few years ago, a producer whose name was Rollo made a special trip to see a performance of Goat Island's piece *It's Shifting, Hank*. Afterwards he wanted to give us his reaction, and I was elected to talk to him. I can summarize the conversation now as follows:

Rollo said: What is the reason for all this repetition?
And I said: What repetition?

Although at that moment I had no idea what he meant, I did sense that a significant insight lay somewhere at the heart of our misunderstanding.

Take for example the process of memorizing an alphabet. Is the act of recitation repetitious? One says one letter, and then another, and then another. But if all the letters are different, one could say there is no repetition. It is only at the point where a letter returns, and we recognize its return, that familiarity has occurred. But is even that a repetition? Perhaps the letter returns changed by time and events, altered by the nature of the intervening letters. At this point, can we say that there has been an occurrence of music?

To state the problem: what some see as a single moment repeating, others see as a nonrepeating series of similar moments. The difference in perception indicates not only how closely one is prepared to examine any given moment, but also a basic difference in philosophy. As John Cage said in his "Lecture on Nothing,"

"Repetition is only repetition if we feel that we own it" (Cage 1961: 110). To restate the problem: does one see the repeating / nonrepeating moment as occurring *inside of* or *outside of* a language? Because with his invocation of *ownership*, Cage perhaps refers not only to possession, but also to understanding, recognition, and especially familiarity. An authority on dance, whom we may refer to as an informed viewer, upon seeing a dancer perform two similar moves, may conclude, "The dancer repeated the step." One who is ignorant of dance and claims no ownership of its language, whom we may refer to as an ecstatic viewer, at this same moment might say, "The dancer performed two similar movements—the first in one place in the room, the second a little later in a different place in the room." The differences observed by the second viewer might seem so insignificant to the first viewer that he chose to ignore them altogether, concentrating instead on the larger patterns that conform to the language of dance which he feels he owns.

At this point we must question the dancer's intention. A creative artist, just like a creative audience member, may function as informed or ecstatic, or may switch back and forth at varying moments of the performance. But if the artist's intention is to step outside of the language (to the extent that such an action is possible), and function creatively as an ecstatic over a sustained period of time, then no difference between two moments is insignificant. Stepping outside of familiar languages requires an attempt not only to generate a new language, but also to reinvent the very notion of familiarity. . . . Processes of repetition and differentiation, of microelements combining and recombining to generate familiarities, lead us into a ritual of the possible occurrence of learning.

❖❖❖

MARK: The Breeze or Waspflie saith *ds ds* Z z
The Ass brayeth *y y y* Y y
The Frog croaketh *coax* X x
The Jay cryeth *tac tac* T t
The Dog grinneth R r
The Cuckow singeth cuckow *kuk ku* Q q
The Chicken peepeth *pi pi* P p
The Dog cryeth O o
The Bear Grumbleth *mum mum* M m
The Woolf howleth *lu ulu* L l
The Duck

BRYAN: Unfortunate . . . I have the unfortunate task of informing you that we are missing the "n", the "s", the "u", and the "w" . . . And we are missing . . . and we would like to apologize for the obvious favorites . . . the "f", the "v", the "h" and the "j."

Alphabet Matthew Goulish (2004a: np)

We return, repeatedly in our work, to originating structures (the alphabet) and pedagogical modes (teaching and learning). People have told us that our work starts with nothing and builds something. But I have never been convinced about the "starts with nothing" part. Maybe the alphabet explains why. A gesture, a dance move, a dog grinning—these small performative units are not without meaning. They are articulations of infinite meaning; infinite but limited, like allegory. When the grin of the dog becomes the sound of the letter R (Rrrr), a threshold has been crossed. "The image" has confronted "its meaning." Allegory (dog grinning) has encountered utility (R). There is brutality in this, as there is change, and learning. Cross that threshold in reverse, and one defines a zone of indiscernibility. Can we, by means of performance, remain in that zone? In the proximity of both learning and unlearning? Both the R and the dog grinning?

Becoming informed Steve Bottoms

Images of schooling and teaching recur persistently through Goat Island's performances—from Matthew-as-Ezra Pound teaching grammar in *It's Shifting, Hank*, through an insurance sales seminar conducted on tiny schoolroom chairs in *It's an Earthquake in My Heart*, to Mark's comic-grotesque recitation of alphabetic animal noises in *When will the September roses bloom? Last night was only a comedy*. This work, however, is anything but didactic. Rather, it compels an *unlearning* on the part of audiences, by challenging or frustrating habituated modes of response—such as the search for a linear narrative, or for a central, organizing "theme": learned behaviours both. We might speak, in Guattari's terms, of Goat Island's work inviting a certain *deterritorialization* of the mind—opening out time and headspace to facilitate a more personal, intuitive *process* of response than is normally experienced. "Process . . . strives to capture existence in the very act of its constitution, definition and detteritorialization" (Guattari 2000: 4).

As Matthew's discussion of "ecstatic" and "informed" audience members implies, it may indeed be harder for the ostensibly knowledgeable to cope with such a challenge. During my years of watching Goat Island, in confidently applying what I think I already know about the company, their working methods and objectives, to what I'm seeing in front of me, I have periodically found my "ownership" of this knowledge frustrated: "now, *why* are they doing that?"; "oh dear, this isn't as good as the last show." And then, witnessing the engaged responses of those around me, I've had to kick myself for missing the point; the point being that this work is not some fixed, predetermined *object* to be scrutinized for the meanings enclosed within, but an ongoing *experience*—"finished again the next night, and the next, and the next"—which asks only that I participate in being present rather than remaining pointlessly removed on some superior plane of "understanding."

A nod is required here in the direction of "process philosophy"—as developed by early twentieth-century thinkers like Henri Bergson and Alfred North Whitehead. Their approach to mental ecology rejected the rationalistic assumption that human consciousness is a fixed (disembodied?) entity that remains separate from the objective world of "things" that it observes and uses. Instead, they proposed, we are submerged (mind and body) within a world of flow and perpetual becoming. Hence Matthew's notion of the "ecstatic" spectator, which perhaps references Bergson's use of the term: to be *ec-static* is to be out of stasis, in motion (*or*: to be standing outside oneself, "beside oneself," rather than claiming self-unity). Conversely, if one assumes oneself already "informed," one is in danger of simply subjecting new experiences to the same old assumptions, the same old analytic habits, enclosing them within a static processing loop.

To break this vicious circle, Bergson called—as I think do Goat Island's performances—for a systematic nurturing of *intuition* in our response to what we experience; intuition being, in Bergsonian terms, "neither a feeling, an inspiration, nor a disorderly sympathy, but a fully developed method" (Deleuze 1991: 13). This "method" generates a kind of creative feedback loop between two forms of habituated mental process—the rational intelligence so celebrated by humans, and the hardwired instinct more usually associated with animals and insects: the instinct that allows a spider so perfectly to trap a fly in its fly-sized web, for example (note: Bergson is regarded by some less as philosopher than as sociobiologist; a critic of Darwin whose 1907 study *Creative Evolution* examined human behaviour in animal/biological terms). Intuitive process enables intelligence and instinct to inform each other creatively, just as Goat Island's work encourages responses at both the mental and emotional level by carefully blending referential texts, characters and ideas with compelling images and movement sequences that defy easy, rational assimilation.

Moreover, as Gilles Deleuze notes in his study *Bergsonism*, "intuition presupposes duration, it consists in thinking in terms of duration" (1991: 31). The period permitted between stimulus and response determines the degree of reflection and recollection that can be interpolated into the process. Hence the need for all that (non-)repetition in Goat Island's work; the insistence on providing *time* in which to process the mental connections being thrown up—a quantity of time that simply exceeds our ability to "know" rationally what to do with it. One example that immediately springs to mind for me is the "puppet jump" sequence early in *How Dear to Me the Hour When Daylight Dies*. All four performers execute variations on the same movement sequence:

The body bends forward at the waist, both arms swinging down, before one swings up, reaching high aloft, as the other stabs a fist into the small of the back. The body is driven into a vertical leap upward, before coming down to land in a kind of spasmodic whirling motion, arms and legs flying. The body comes to rest, repositions itself elsewhere in the space, and then begins the movement again. This continues for several minutes, with the group working through seemingly endless variations in the positioning and sequencing of the jumpers.

(Bottoms 1998: 421)

The sheer, repetitive insistence of the movement seems to demand an appreciation on the spectator's part which goes beyond the formalistic, and for me, various possible "readings" began to suggest themselves. Perhaps this was an image of a human yearning for transcendence, always followed by a spiralling fall to earth. Perhaps the precise regimentation of the performers pointed to a kind of

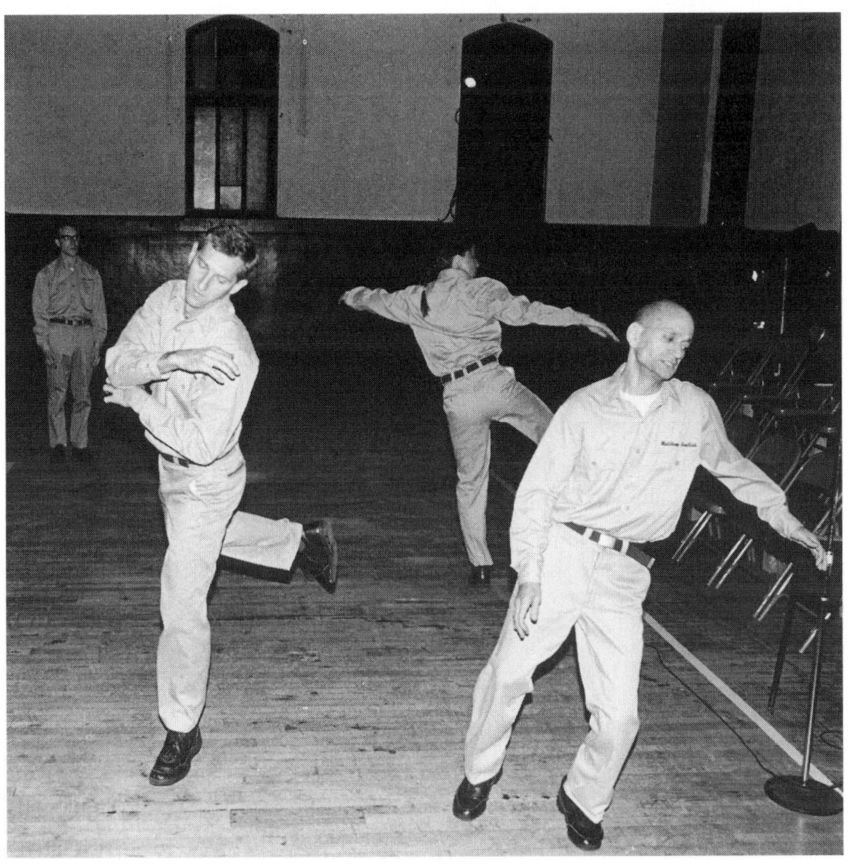

5 *How Dear to Me the Hour When Daylight Dies.*

Photograph by Nathan Mandell, Wellington Avenue Church, Chicago, 1996. Pictured left to right: Mark Jeffery, Bryan Saner, Karen Christopher, Matthew Goulish

manufacturing of identically frustrated dreams. The longer the sequence continued, however, the less adequate such rationalizing interpretations seemed, even as the sequence came to seem increasingly unsettling. It was as if my initial interpretation of what the movement might represent gradually gave way to an intuited, gut recognition of what it might therefore "mean" on a more personal level (an encounter with my own experiences of failure?). The effect was somewhat akin to that which Hal Foster describes in discussing Andy Warhol's 1963 car crash paintings—in which the actual content of the silk-screened photographic image seems oddly cold and distanced, and yet is given a disturbing resonance by Warhol's insistence on reproducing the same image in multiplicity. This strategy produces for the viewer:

> a second order of trauma, here at the level of technique, where the *punctum* breaks through the screen and allows the real to poke through. . . . Through these pokes or pops we seem almost to touch the real, which the repetition of images at once distances and rushes toward us.
>
> (Foster 1996: 136)

The term "punctum" derives, of course, from Roland Barthes' discussion of photography in *Camera Lucida*, in which he consciously avoids "following the path of a formal ontology (of a Logic)," and instead attempts to examine his own intuited responses: "a photograph's accident is that which pricks me (but also bruises me, is poignant to me)" (Barthes 2000: 21, 27). In Goat Island's case, I would note only that this accident is probably no accident: though the particular point of "wounding" may be different for each spectator, the experience occurs within a temporal landscape that has been carefully structured to facilitate such responses —through its deftly paced juxtaposition of speeds and slownesses, repetition and difference, and its gradual building up of a performative vocabulary which seems both emptied of and pregnant with meaning.

> *In the sixth grade, by the time I heard what Mrs Ferguson was explaining about long division on the chalkboard, she was asking me to come forward and repeat what she had just done. I had missed the entire lesson because I was focused on her bright red lips, which caused me to change those numbers of long division coming from her red mouth to Italian opera notes from Carmen. This was fueled by Clifford Kiracofe telling me at recess that Mrs Ferguson was forced to abandon her opera career. I think my initial impulse to slow things down stemmed from my wish to understand long division and have my experience of opera at the same time.*
>
> (Lin Hixson 2000)

What we see Matthew Goulish (Goat Island 1996b: 8)

In 1929, the philosopher Alfred North Whitehead attempted to make adjustments to the world of Isaac Newton. Where Newton's world of 1687 was one of actions and reactions, Whitehead's world of 1929 was one of organism and process. In his book *Process and Reality*, in Part I, "The Speculative Scheme," in Chapter 1, "Speculative Philosophy," in Section II under the heading "Defects of Insight and Language," Whitehead states that: (1) The sole justification for any thought—any thought at all—is the elucidation of experience; and (2) the starting-point of any thought—any thought at all—is the analytic observation of components of experience. Since this starting point cannot arrive without sense perception, Whitehead continues by examining what it is that we see.

In *Process and Reality*, in Part II, "Discussions and Applications," in Chapter II, "The Extensive Continuum," in Section IV on the world of 1929 as distinct from the world of 1867, Whitehead defines an event—any event at all—as follows: the actual world is built up of actual occasions. Whatever things there are, in any sense of "existence," are derived by abstraction from actual occasions interrelated in some determinate fashion I shall call an "event." This brings us to what we see.

What we see is never more than the evidence of an event—an event which, along with its myriad composition of occasions, we can never entirely know, but only begin to guess at. For example: when we see five neat rows of casserole dishes lying on the ocean floor, we can only guess that we see them because they are the result of an event which includes the occasion of the *Titanic* striking the iceberg. And: when we see Mike Walker, America's fattest man, lying immobilized at 1,187 pounds in the middle of Kansas, which is in the middle of the United States, we can only guess that we see him as a result of an event which included the occasions of the US war in Korea, which lasted from 1948 to 1953, left 54,000 Americans, 200,000 Chinese and 2 million Koreans dead, and left Mike Walker with an insatiable appetite.

Whitehead went on to explain that this piece of [grey stone] he had hold of contains everything you can find in it; and that, try as you will, you will never exhaust what it contains. You may find in it a fossil, and that is an item in which the whole pageant of organic life on earth is focussed; you may find in it calcium carbonate, and in that resides the whole history of chemistry; you will find a colour, shape and texture, and you have the whole of painting and sculpture in your hands; it might be a slingshot, and David and Goliath are beside you . . .

(C. H. Waddington 1969: 113)

Finger Karen Christopher (Goat Island 1996b: 8)

In Goat Island's *Can't Take Johnny to the Funeral*, when I hold my first finger pointing straight up and it describes a circle in the air, my hand swiveling at the wrist, I am thinking of a woman I once knew who had to leave her children in the custody of the state. I am not doing an imitation of her or of anything. The gesture comes from a gesture I made spontaneously once while describing the way my own mother listened to a particular 45 record over and over again. One woman told me that when she saw this gesture in the performance, she saw a woman waiting for her husband to come home from war. Another saw her two-year-old winding up to wreak havoc. These things were really seen by these women, and other people saw their own images too. Because of what led to this moment, what came after, each person's reference points, and my own intentions and those of Goat Island, the moment does not look the same to everyone. The moment occurs with the involvement of all parties.

The possibility of a moment opens a hole in time. A chasm between the sensation of the moment, which can occur in the moment, and the rational effort to recognize, classify, or respond to that sensation, which can arise only after the moment and while other moments are still occurring behind it.

(Leo Charney 1998: 30)

Stealing Bryan Saner (1996: 71–74)

The first time I saw a Goat Island performance, I thought I had never seen anything like it before. Now, occasionally, after a show people will tell us that they have never seen anything like it before. The truth is, we've seen it all before. Just about everything you see in a Goat Island performance has been taken from somewhere else. We've stolen it; except in a few cases where we've asked for permission, but generally we operate on the principle that it's easier to ask for forgiveness than to ask for permission.

Actually, we do credit the sources of our material. We pay for the use of our sources when required. To say that we steal things is a bit dramatic, and it's typically American to just take anything we want. The notion of stealing is inspired by my son Jake's love of the Robin Hood legend. Taking from the rich and giving back to the rest of the world. The library is free. We take stories from there and re-tell them. The point is that we don't do much creative writing; it's more accurate to say that we practice creative research and assembly.

The sources we are presently using, in *How Dear to Me the Hour When Daylight Dies* are: *The Harp of Burma* (film by Kon Ichikawa); *The 39 Steps* (film by Alfred Hitchcock); *Dreams* (film by Akira Kurosawa); *Grand Illusion* (film by Jean Renoir); the videos of Leslie Thornton; the writings of Herman Melville; the paintings of Sue Coe; the photographs of Jacques Sert; the life of Amelia Earhart; the life of Bob Fitzsimmons; the life of J. M. Bottle (known as Mr Memory); the life of Mike Walker.

The elements we steal from these sources are never meant to be seen alone or on their own merit. Each is like a layer in a collage: something happens over it, something happens under it. The physicalization that we layer over a spoken text often reveals new insights, or changes the meaning completely. Taking a text completely out of context is permitted. If we steal a movement from another dance company, we proceed under the principle that if we can perform it exactly the way they do it, we can't use it. Hopefully, it loses something and gains something else in the act of being stolen and transported to our work.

I think that the use of pre-existing texts and movements and characters offers the work a familiarity that allows people a way to get into the performance. Ballet has a set of pre-existing movements that people are familiar with. The movements have names and we endow them with content which gives us a common foundation with which to view and understand the dance. New performance works often do not have this common foundation, so using familiar characters and sources sometimes gives people a handle with which to view the work.

A side effect of this is the phenomenal synaptic impulses that happen in the brain when you see these familiar fragments on the stage. For example, you see Amelia Earhart, or someone pretending to be Amelia Earhart. You begin thinking of your connections with this character and your mind begins to lay a foundation. We think about her, we think about the things we've read about her, the newsreels we've seen about her, where she lived, where she flew, where we were when we first heard about her. We think about the story our grade school teacher told us about her. We think back to grade school. This reminds us of our first kiss on the playground, and our minds are able to take all these layers in. I think one of the most interesting things about using familiar historical characters and sources is that it allows our minds to go into the regions where our first kiss is, and lets that layer affect the experience of seeing something on stage. Our performances are crafted to allow meditative, mind-wandering space for this phenomenon to happen. The person sitting next to you might have a completely different understanding of the performance because of what Amelia Earhart means to her.

One product of this process of taking pre-existing texts and movement is that it makes a global collage. I like the idea of collage because it illuminates the individual pieces that go into the final picture. Each piece or layer of our performance—each gem that we've stolen—should be allowed to be seen on its own, as well as being part of the larger treasure. If our performances do reflect the world we live in, it's important for me to distinguish them as a collage, which is different from the "melting pot" image which is sometimes used to describe America or the world today, because the individuals tend to lose their identity in the melting. So I like to encourage people to view our performances as a collage; as if they were looking at a Rauschenberg or Hans Hoffmann painting. I like how Hans Hoffmann mixes yellow and blue. The two colors put together don't make green. The yellow is laid down and dries and the blue is painted over it, but between the brush strokes the yellow shows up in its pure form and becomes the initial foundation, a layer of the collage.

The theatrical effect we're trying for is to make the whole greater than the sum of its parts. Each individual piece of text or movement has a set value when viewed on its own, but when it's shared, when it's put together in one large chest, the whole treasure seems to have unlimited value. One solution for progress or the advancement of thought and art is to beg, borrow and steal from each other.
In the true spirit of Robin Hood.

Rhizome Steve Bottoms

The idea of stealing is, of course, stolen: collage is one of the defining art-forms of the twentieth century (ever since Duchamp, Picasso, Dada). But Goat Island's use of this method in performance is nonetheless distinctive. One could contrast it, for example, with the approach of the Wooster Group—the New York theatre collective that exerted a significant influence on Goat Island and many other performance practitioners through its pioneering approach, in the 1970s and 1980s, to the collaging of "found" texts as part of the devising process. Thus they took Spalding Gray's autobiographical narratives, or classic plays by Thornton Wilder, Arthur Miller and others, and spliced them together with forgotten or despised "low" culture sources, with documentary reconstruction, and architectural forms. Yet where Wooster Group performances typically reference a handful of sources in some depth, and appear—in their collaging—to pass comment on, or even "deconstruct" those texts (see Savran 1988), Goat Island's work tends to draw from a much wider range of sources: so many, in fact, that an audience will be unaware of most of the references. The program for *How Dear to Me the Hour When Daylight Dies* lists 17 separate sources of spoken text, and this is not to mention the even greater variety of materials drawn on to construct the movement sequences.

This Wooster/Goat distinction is not—to borrow a phrase of Bergson's—simply one of *degree*, but a difference *in kind*. Perhaps we should steal David Graver's distinction, in his book *The Aesthetics of Disturbance*, between collage and montage. As in the Wooster Group's work, *collage* tends to point "persistently back to the world from which [the appropriated fragments] came" (Graver 1995: 31). Some familiarity with the sources is thus required, or at least desirable: clearly, for example, knowledge of avant-garde theatre history is of benefit to anyone witnessing the 2004 Wooster Group piece *Poor Theater (A Series of Simulacra)*, which is explicitly based around the recreation and juxtaposition of performance work by Polish director Jerzy Grotowski and German-based choreographer William Forsythe (cf. Bottoms 2004; Savran 2005). Conversely, watching Goat Island, one would not need to know that substantial sections of the choreography for *It's An Earthquake in My Heart* have been plagiarized from assorted works by Pina Bausch. Nor, indeed, would one need to know anything about the British magician/comedian Tommy Cooper, some of whose jokes are reproduced in *When will the September roses bloom?*

> *I said to this waiter I says this chicken 'ere I've got is cold.*
> *He says well it should be, it's been dead two weeks.*

Remembering Cooper as part of my own childhood landscape, I might be moved to reflect—via Mark's snarling delivery of the lines—that yes, there was something curiously dog-like about Tommy (who died on stage, in the literal rather than metaphorical sense): didn't he often growl rather curiously—"Rrrr"—before delivering his catchphrase, "Just like that!" This association could trigger further reflections or memories, just as one might have personal associations with, say, Amelia Earhart. Yet even without such background knowledge, another (non-British?) spectator might be equally struck by the disturbing way in which the Cooper jokes are intercut with the memories of a torture survivor (performed by Matthew; text by W. G. Sebald). Joke-telling and torture turn out to be strangely connected; both crafted to elicit involuntary responses from the victim. Moreover, in laughing at the jokes, and at the same time feeling acute discomfort at doing so, in this context, the viewer of *September roses* might experience this connection viscerally.

For Goat Island, the objective in assembling appropriated fragments is to treat them less *as* fragments (deconstructed originals) than as constituent components in a new structure, a new ecology of interconnected points. In montage, Graver notes, "the disparate fragments of reality are held together and made part of the work of art by the work's constructive principle"; they "participate in a project that is greater than themselves," even as unproblematic unity remains inaccessible: "montage flaunts the cohesive power of its constructive procedures through its intentional incompleteness" (1995: 33). Compare that description with Henry Sayre's description of the "absolutely unpredictable and original structure" of *How Dear to Me the Hour When Daylight Dies*:

> [It] starts like high modern theater of the Beckett variety, changes to dance in a sort of post-Judson mode, heads off into stand-up, mutates into what David Antin has called "exercise time in a prisonyard," transforms itself back into dance, veers off again toward something resembling the activity room in a mental institution, comes back again to theater, recreates a tortuous pilgrimage march, and then fades to black as

what can only be described as a ballet gone awkward continues on in the growing darkness. Somehow it manages to give the impression of a single work.

(Sayre 1996: np)

A single work, perhaps, but not a unified one: the sheer diversity of the sources used, and the multiplicitous connections they throw up, defy any attempt on the part of the spectator to interpret a piece like *Daylight Dies* according to a singular frame of reference: "the piece frustrates when a founding concept or a resolution or a straightforward meaning is sought" (Hughes 1996: 32). Instead, the performance can be read as a dense, associative network of inter-related images, allusions and oblique narratives, but a network whose lines criss-cross ceaselessly rather than pointing inward—like some conceptual spider's web—toward a central point.

Goat Island's work might usefully be thought of in terms of an eco-analogy suggested by Deleuze and Guattari's *A Thousand Plateaus*—that of the *rhizome*. A rhizome is a form of "undisciplined" organic growth (such as crabgrass) which is inherently decentred, spreading out in all directions on a horizontal plane (ground level), with "lines of flight" shooting off in all directions, tangling, overlapping, cutting back. Similarly, a rhizomic text is constantly looping, rather than linear, and cuts indiscriminately across generic and disciplinary boundaries: "The rhizome connects any point to any other point, and its traits are not necessarily linked to traits of the same nature" (Deleuze and Guattari 1987: 21). The reader is freed to wander amidst the undergrowth, following his or her nose.

To facilitate this movement, Deleuze and Guattari insist, "a rhizome or multiplicity never allows itself to be overcoded, never has available a supplementary dimension over and above its number of lines" (9). This they contrast with those forms of collage text which, in assembling cut-up fragments, nonetheless seem to point toward a centralizing interpretation—such as the suggestion that this fragmentation reflects our experience of contemporary life in postmodern times: "The world has become chaos, but the book remains an image of the world. . . . A strange mystification: a book all the more total for being fragmented" (6). Similarly, one could point to any number of performance ensembles whose publicity literature speaks of finding a stage language to reflect contemporary experience. Goat Island, however, carefully avoid "overcoding" the sources they appropriate with any implied commentary on them, or with ironic or camp inflections of the sort now so familiar in postmodern theatre practice. Rather, the same attitude of even-handed enquiry is applied to whatever materials their working process leads them to—from Tommy Cooper's jokes to Simone Weil's meditations to James Taylor's songs. Though Goat Island performances are at times very funny, the humour comes *through* the material rather than *at its expense*, and even those sources which many might regard as tacky or laughable are treated with unexpected dignity. The corniest of songs, after all, might evoke very particular emotional memories for certain audience members. The group's performances thus operate on what Deleuze and Guattari would call a *plane of consistency*, "a plan(e) that . . . can only be inferred from the forms it develops and the subjects it forms, since it is for these forms and these subjects. . . . The plane is not a principle of organization but a means of transportation" (1987: 266–268).

She's leaving now 'cause I just heard the slamming of the door
The way I know I've heard it slam a hundred times before
If I could move I'd get my gun and put her in the ground
Oh Ruby, don't take your love to town

Kenny Rogers, "Ruby" (sung a cappella by Bryan in *Daylight Dies*)

A means of transportation. Goat Island frequently speak of wishing to facilitate individual spectatorial "journeys" into unexpected territory, and this is achieved, in effect, by what Maureen Turim refers to as "the spatialisaton of time" (qtd in Sayre 2004: 42). While a performance event necessarily begins and ends at certain points in linear time, it may also gradually create a mapping-out of interconnected points: when this begins to be apprehended by the spectator, his or her mind may be as likely to wander back to the past—to cross-reference the immediate moment with a previous one—as to look toward a future fulfilment. "Perhaps one of the most important characteristics of the rhizome," Deleuze and Guattari stress, "is that it always has multiple entryways" (1987: 12). Like grass, "it has neither beginning nor end, but always a middle (milieu) from which it grows and overspills" (21). Or, as David Hughes remarks in his *Dance Theatre Journal* review of *How Dear to Me the Hour When Daylight Dies*:

in some sense the piece is running backwards, meaning is flowing back towards ts source. . . . Perhaps for me, what gave the piece this centre, this omphalus, this navel from which all meaning flows (but in a great tangle and knot of meanings) was a sequence with an anchor which literalized a half-forgotten anecdote in the opening.

(Hughes 1996: 33)

This refers to Bryan Saner's construction of a head-high "anchor" from the pieces of an old plough and a microphone stand, a task he enacts in the piece's closing stages, but which resonates with a line from his opening speech (from Kon Ichikawa's 1956 film *The Harp of Burma*). For Hughes, this connection focused his attention on the question of how to "anchor" ourselves to the memory of the evils of war, so that they not be repeated in future. Conversely, my own "entry-point" for this performance came much earlier in the piece—something to do with my response to the puppet jump, which then connected with later images suggesting a carnival freakshow of dysfunctional figures forgotten or rejected by society. For other audience members I spoke to, the impressions were different again. For someone who had spent time in jail, the piece evoked the waking nightmare of imprisonment; to a friend who used to work in construction, the exhausting movement sequences, combined with the earthiness of imagery such as the plough, suggested an honouring of manual labour. For Henry Sayre, working on developing a theory of authenticity in performance, "it is death, and the ultimate authenticity of dying, that drives this performance" (1996: np). All of this is there to be found in the piece, in its dense network of associated points, but ultimately these varying interpretations say as much, if not more, about the processual journeys gone on by the individual spectators. The performance becomes a kind of psychic funhouse mirror in which the participant spectator is enabled to meditate creatively on deeply felt concerns, experiences, and memories.

There's a story.

The ghost of a dead sailor tied himself to an anchor, wrapping the rope around his body nine times, and threw himself backwards from a rock into the sea . . . I don't recall the rest of the story, and I don't know why this part of it came back to me this morning . . .

But now I can't forget it . . .

Re-authorship Matthew Goulish

Our performances, I believe, are relentlessly and formally structured to such a degree that the act of structuring the material—the evidence of arching structural composition—is legible and evident to any audience member who pays attention. The structure appears as a second intelligence at work, shaping and forming and modulating the performance experience. The organization of time communicates to the audience to some extent what they are *not* experiencing: chance or improvisation. Instead, the performance is a series of parts that have been measured, metered, sequenced, balanced, and unbalanced, patterned and ruptured—according to an intelligence distinct from the intelligence of the parts themselves, and located in relation to the parts both internally and externally. The fact that the performance is a loosely closed system, inscribed and encircled with limits, however porous, and that this closure's visibility signifies the presence of an author, carries its own associative meanings, while also facilitating the free roam within the piece. It is as if we are saying one may wander within the performance as if in a sort of neighborhood, through which we suggest a particular route, although you are free to stray from that route if you choose. The limits grant permission to stray. The straying is the act of creative response.

Stopping Time Karen Christopher (2002); CJ Mitchell (1999)

KAREN: There is a moment in *The Sea & Poison* when Matthew Goulish stands still for a long time. He has just poured a bucket of dirt on his head, set a seed down in it, and sprinkled it with water. Now he plays some music to it while shining a light on it to help it grow. As he stands there, Mark Jeffery sits down in front of him and writes a letter. In the preceding moments of the performance, the events have cascaded with an increasing intensity, each action gathering up all the other actions and a weight of meaning threatens to become meaningless until this moment is opened up as a rip in time: all the focus comes together in one point on top of one person's head; and then on top of another person's desk. The train stops. And in this moment, which rapidly becomes several moments, the audience spontaneously takes over authorship of the events. Everything has ceased to change. In this lapse, a shift in control occurs. Associations and realizations begin popping up everywhere.

CJ: Mark stops writing, pauses, considering his words, then continues. One sheet of paper is eventually covered with writing. He finishes, pulls the sheet of paper out of the metal-covered notebook and leaves the page of writing on the table. Karen walks over to the table, rips the page of writing cleanly into two pieces, folds the paper up tightly and puts it in Mark's breast pocket. . . . It is a subdued sequence within a performance which at other times is energetic to the point of the performers' exhaustion. The act we have watched—the act of writing—has been quiet, private. What is being written? Is this a diary, a story, a letter? A plea, an apology, a request?

It has been happening for some time, and I know it will continue for some time into the future. When will it end? There is too much to see all at once. The audience is included in this action. Are they getting it? What will the others have to say about this? I need to find out before I say what I think. "Why were the audience laughing? Don't they know the character is dying?" There is an echo elsewhere within the work—will I know this? There seemed to be very little happening; and then I realized there was actually a lot happening. *With my two arms I don't think I could reach the sky.*

The everyday action of writing: bringing a private action into a public space.

Watching someone thinking about the next words they will write down.

This takes time. This process takes time.

The audience begins to hear itself in the silence.

6 *The Sea & Poison*.

Photograph by Claude Giger. Theater Festival Basel, Switzerland, 1999. Pictured left to right: Mark Jeffery, Matthew Goulish

B1.3 BODY

Minneapolis: February 27, 1992

KILLACKY: We're talking to Lin Hixson from Goat Island, who are appearing tonight and tomorrow night at Studio 6A at Hennepin Center. It's part of a Chicago exchange weekend that the Walker Art Center and the Minnesota Dance Alliance are sponsoring together. Lin, you may not consider your work radical, but your work is in fact radical. If it's seen in a dance context, it's often called anti-dance. It is in many ways a return to the stripping of all virtuosity in movement. Tell us a little bit about your choices in that way.

HIXSON: There's nothing illusionary about the work. What you see in front of you, that's what you're getting. The people in the group are not trained dancers. Some of them are overweight. They would not like me saying that. But the body is not this taught body. For me, being the person who is outside looking at it, I love that. I love that I can identify with them, because they—also being a woman in this society, having grown up with fashion photography telling me how I am supposed to look—I like that these people that I'm watching are the people that I feel you would see on the street. So they're people you can identify with. . . . But we've learned a lot from dance. I think we're influenced particularly by the work done at the Judson Church in the 1960s, where there was a certain respect for pedestrian movement—like Yvonne Rainer pushing a vacuum cleaner as dance.

(Hixson 1992)

Part of the dynamism of the body as medium in work like Rainer's and Goat Island's [lies in] these performers' employment of everyday or "do-able" acts, [which] rupture a long history of a particular kind of form that was unavailable to most people. . . . Rainer's process—especially her task dances that are free of gender specificity or necessity—remain central to any history of feminist performance practice. Goat Island's case is less direct, yet in its evocations and careful elisions, the group attempts an ethical encounter with a world (our world) in which the attempts to name and categorize ourselves and, especially, each other, often generate brutality, violence and loss. In their actions, the group sets up a space of contemplation, albeit one full of activity and movement, for the audience to consider how these brutal actions could be, or could have been, *altered. They manufacture a space of engagement between subject and object. It is in this labor that the heart of the feminism lives, for the drive to confront our actions with their results, to see the icon in the context of its history or the monument surrounded by what it memorializes, exists as a prototypically feminist impulse.*

(Chris Mills 2000: 2–3)

Feminisms Lin Hixson (1995: 22)

Yvonne Rainer's writings and interviews about her dance works in the 1960s examined a terrain of performance that, in retrospect, laid a foundation for many of the issues that inform my ideas about performance. Some elements that Rainer elucidated and that I still find relevant today are:

1 The non-hierarchical relationships of performers in space. Hierarchies arise the moment performers begin to relate to one another. These relationships shift depending on the interactions between performers; depending on who does what to whom. I find the relationships between the performers to be non-hierarchical when all the performers are equally required to complete a task.
2 The use of found movement and task-like activity: "removing the body from the gaze by returning it to an activity, to the condition of *always doing something*" (Sayre 1989: 118–119). I always wanted to work with movement in performance, but I did not have the training of a dancer. Task and found movement provided an entrance into this territory for the non-dancer. While exploring task-like activity with non-dancers, I discovered what happens when movements are difficult to perform. Self-consciousness and pretension fall away, leaving an immediacy to the activity. Furthermore, when the body is always moving and not creating a two-dimensional, pictorial image, it is harder to objectify.
3 The reduction of dance to its essentials. "NO to spectacle no to virtuosity no to transformations and magic and make-believe no to glamour and transcendency of the star image no to the heroic no to the anti-heroic no to trash imagery no to involvement of performer or spectator no to style no to camp no to seduction of spectator by the wiles of the performer no to eccentricity no to moving or being moved" (Rainer 1965: 166). I do not say "NO" to all of the above, but this statement reminds me to question constantly why a movement or scene or text is in the work. Is it necessary for the integrity of this specific piece or am I attached to it for the wrong reasons?

All these things inform the work, but we also are interested in urgency. The group is very committed to pushing themselves in terms of endurance:

Matthew Goulish: *There's a practical reason why we work so physically. We have our bodies as performers and we don't have a lot of money. So we try to create from the beginning a heightened state of physical urgency. A lot of what we do is organized around a task or a series of tasks, and the way to deal with those tasks—I'm talking as a performer now—is with a feeling of urgency. It's very real when it comes over me. There are all these people watching and I don't have anything to give them except, like, moving this chair. So we have to drill it for precision of timing, for speed or slowness, grace or lack of grace, lightness, weight: if you fly through the air, how you land on the ground. All those things become so rehearsed and so precise even though they don't seem precise. In performance we become possessed by the spirit of the action, by the impossibility of doing it correctly. Sometimes we try to dance and we can't dance. And the pieces become about watching these people trying to dance when they can't, but we're really trying.*

(Goulish and Hixson 1990: 13)

Commitment Carol Becker (1996: 137–138)

Because [Goat Island] are willing to work themselves to exhaustion to alleviate the anxious urgency that appears to motivate the work, we become committed to their excessive action . . . willing to suspend analysis of its symbolic meaning while we give ourselves over to its unravelling. [For *Can't Take Johnny to the Funeral* (1991)] the inspiration for the movement was derived in part from sports photos—rugby, lacrosse, water polo—frozen moments reactivated, translated into dance/gymnastics. [Yet] here, as in other Goat Island works, we cannot resist wondering what has set these performers in motion and what hidden necessity motivates their action.

When the performers do slow down enough for us to study them, they appear as lost souls wandering inside their own intent, a bit like the inhabitants of Dante's hell. . . . They appear as part of some social interaction, yet inevitably apart. At times they become ontologically regressed, adults reduced to infancy writhing in convulsions. They also appear phylogenically regressed, wild dogs gnawing on each other's legs, humans reduced to a lesser species. Or they simply appear helpless, deranged inmates of a sanatorium, caught in the privacy and isolation of their illness. They re-enact obsessive patterns and appear to obey silent directives whose meaning they alone can understand.

Karen rotates her finger in the air and swivels her body while looking sidelong off into space. Matthew spins and collapses as if shot; with a circular movement of his hand he appears to torque down his mouth. There are times when they do interact. Karen crawls into a fetal position on top of Greg's prone body. Tim rubs his head against Matthew's leg like a cat. They cover their mouths with their hands, politely, almost with a slight gasp, as if they are remembering some unspeakable event, as if they must restrain the words they might otherwise utter. All motion is laboriously synchronized, separate scenarios woven into one complex, perfectly choreographed nightmare.

Pressure Karen Christopher (1999b)

In Goat Island's piece *It's Shifting, Hank* (1993), four performers would come on stage and, taking big, visible breaths, they would exhaust these breaths over and over in front of the audience by the repetition of a single spoken line. *Tom bring the boat nearer.* A plea not completely clear or understood, a prayer perhaps, a last hope. These people are gasping for air but they are not under water. The breathing of the audience is altered. Their own lungs are aching for a bit more air.

Later in the performance, a large man, former Goat Island member Greg McCain, thrust his head into a bowl of water, and held his breath. Matthew Goulish would perform a few tasks and then come over and touch Greg's shoulders, and Greg's head would come out of the water while Matthew stood next to him. Matthew would then go about performing his other tasks, returning at intervals to pull Greg's head out of the water again.

This was a simple event, not in and of itself particularly dangerous or daring. And yet an audience member once asked what would happen if Matthew came back late to pull Greg's head out of the water. Such was the stress in the audience during that sequence that she unconsciously felt that Greg was in reality incapable of lifting his head out of the water without Matthew's help. Greg, a big, grown-up man, was simply placing his head in a bowl of water. She said you expect a lot from the audience, you expect the audience to trust you, you expect that the audience will trust that you know what you are doing. She was upset. She had been upset for Greg, the man with his head in the water. The man dependent on another man to help him, over and over again. To understand this reaction, we had to look further back in the piece, to what happened before this moment, the moment when Greg's head was landing in the water. What set this up, this tension?

In the preceding sequence, all four performers crawled backwards on their forearms and toes, and they did this until they collapsed in puddles of sweat on the floor. One by one they failed to continue and ended up being dragged out of the way by the survivors who then carried on crawling. The crawling went on for a long period of time and the strain it caused on the performers' bodies was both visible and audible. The rubbing of the bony part of the forearm on the floor caused the skin to peel back and the elbows were bloody by the end of this sequence. Partially because

7 *It's Shifting, Hank.*
Photograph courtesy Belluard Bollwerk International Festival, Fribourg, Switzerland, 1994. Pictured left to right: Matthew Goulish, Timothy McCain, Karen Christopher, Greg McCain

of the obvious physical exhaustion brought on by these strenuous movements and partially because of their inexplicability, the audience altered during this phase. The audience began to lose a sense of the force that was in play. What was making these people on stage do what they are doing? Why do they continue even though it hurts them? What compels them? What does it mean? And more of these questions were unanswered than were answered. This put a great pressure on the scene that followed in which Greg McCain put his head in the bowl of water. What would this performer do? Would he sacrifice himself in one foot of water for the sake of the performance?

Biochemically stressed Steve Bottoms

The meditative dimensions of Goat Island's work begin and end not with concepts or mental abstractions but with the bodies of the performers, under pressure. Yet if there are parallels here with Jerzy Grotowski's notion of a "poor theatre" in which the actor performs a kind of physical sacrifice for the audience's benefit, there is no appeal in this work—as there was in Grotowski's—to the flaying and exposure onstage of the performer's inner self or soul. Instead, Goat Island's performers more often than not resemble automata, carrying out their mysterious and often tortuous physical tasks with a deliberately blank, unemotional facial glazing that betrays no outward expression of inner self. We cannot presume to "know" these people: they are like palimpsests, figures to be *read onto* by their observers.

Like so much else in the company's aesthetic, a link can perhaps be traced back to the Judson Dance Theater (based at Greenwich Village's Judson Memorial Church from 1962–1964): Steve Paxton's choreography was emphasizing facial blankness as early as 1963 (cf. Banes 1993: 167). Goat Island's work, however, retrieves and redevelops the often-neglected Judson experiments in rigorously awkward new directions. If the performers often seem devoid of individual agency and even personality—somewhat "beside themselves"—it is in part because of the impossible tasks they are charged with, but also in part because of the way their movements are so often plagiarized from other sources, models that they cannot quite live up to. Thus, they are not quite "in possession" of themselves or their activities. As Adrian Heathfield notes of the extensive copying of Pina Bausch's choreography in *It's an Earthquake in My Heart*:

It's no accident that the performers occasionally seem to be moving like puppets, or rehearsing a set of moves that they do not yet know. The movement is exposed as a repetition. We are watching them learn how to move. That the performers only "half-inhabit" the movement is crucial to the work since it creates a question over the source of the movement and the performer's volition. Their physicality seems to originate simultaneously from outside and inside the performer: from some notional instruction, pattern or plan, but also from a psychic force, which grips the performer within a repetition of a gestural form.

(Heathfield 2001: 18)

TSATSOS: [Goat Island's work has] been defined as a "dark vision of human relations and the power systems that control them" and as being "less overtly political than radically humanistic."
GREG MCCAIN: I agree. We're less overtly political.
DICKINSON*: Yeah, but radical humanism?
GOULISH: Because there are some problems with humanism.
DICKINSON: Yeah, I have some problems with humanism.
GOULISH: Maybe radical humanism is OK.

(Goat Island 1991a: 72)

We live, we are sometimes told, in a posthumanist age. Man is not the independent, self-realising entity that liberal humanism imagined him to be (and one of the problems with humanism was that it was usually a "him"; rarely a her: *she* remained peripheral to *his* self-centrality). Instead, the individual is conceived as a component

* Joan Dickinson was a member of Goat Island between 1988 and 1990. One of the creators of *We Got a Date*, she preceded Karen Christopher as the company's lone female performer.

part in a networked system—a fact hard to avoid when confronted with the daily spectacle of laptop users and cellphone wielders. The next stage of "cyborgization," claim the techno-prophets, will be to *upgrade ourselves* by implanting such devices within our bodies. "The body is obsolete," insists the Australian performance artist Stelarc, whose work insistently attempts to imagine future reconstruction of the human body, by violating its traditional epidermal limits through the use of implants and prostheses. Thus, for Stelarc, one goal would be to ascertain ways to boost brain and memory function with computerized assistance: "a 1400cc brain is an [in]adequate biological form. It cannot cope with the quantity, complexity and quality of information it has accumulated" (Stelarc nd.).

Contrasting strikingly with Matthew Goulish's suggestion that "we need to decelerate . . . our thoughts, to refold them into other thoughts and to recycle them" (2000a: 3), Stelarc's is the techno-capitalist logic of perpetual expansion and "progress"—a progress which, according to his own rhetoric, pushes toward "exit velocity" from the earth itself; the discovery of new, "extraterrestrial" possibilities. Yet such fantasies represent a convenient avoidance of facts which a 1400cc brain can readily comprehend: if we continue to insist on current rates of economic and developmental "growth," our planet's ecosystems simply will not be able to sustain us:

The present Ecological Footprint of a typical North American represents three times his or her fair share of the Earth's bounty. Indeed, if everyone on Earth lived like the average Canadian or American, we would need at least three such planets to live sustainably.

(Wackernagel and Rees 1996: 13)

Stelarc's, in short, is a posthumanism which perpetuates the worst aspects of traditional humanism—its "cultured" disregard for humanity's systemic dependence on nature; its assumption that the march of "progress" (bigger, better) will be good for all. Tellingly, though, not all futurians share his assumptions. In William Gibson's cyberpunk novel *All Tomorrow's Parties* (1999), for example, an artificial intelligence expresses the wish to "download" herself into a flesh-and-blood human body. This knowing reversal of the familiar sci-fi trope of seeking to "upload" human consciousness into the immortality of cyberspace is explained to the A.I.'s bewildered fleshly admirers as follows: "This is human . . . what you are, biochemically, being stressed in a particular way. This is wonderful. This is closed to me" (Gibson 1999: 165).

Similarly, the exhaustive celebration of bodily pressure and stress in Goat Island's work can be read as suggesting a different kind of posthumanism; one informed not by macho expansionism but by the feminist- and eco-inflected thinking that also drives Donna Haraway's influential "Cyborg Manifesto" (see Haraway 1991) and Katherine Hayles's *How We Became Posthuman*:

I see the deconstruction of the liberal humanist subject as an opportunity to put back into the picture the flesh that continues to be erased. . . . If my nightmare is a culture inhabited by posthumans who regard their bodies as fashion accessories rather than the ground of being, my dream is a version of the posthuman that . . . recognizes and celebrates finitude as a condition of human being, and that understands human life is embedded in a material world of great complexity, one on which we depend for our continued survival.

(Hayles 1999: 5)

The automaton-like bodies of Goat Island's performers, far from being merely the incidental vessels of subjectivity, are foregrounded in performance as flexible but depletable material, viewed always in relation to each other and their spatial contexts, as constituent parts of micro-social systems.

That concern has been apparent in the company's work from the outset: the earliest, most thematically explicit works like *Soldier, Child, Tortured Man* (1987) and *We Got A Date* (1989) used extensive sequences of drilling and regimentation to allude to the Foucauldian technologies of "bio-power" which operate to create "normalized," "docile bodies" in contexts as diverse as the military and the school gym class (cf. Bottoms 1996; Foucault 1979). By the time Goat Island made *The Sea & Poison* (1998), however, such regimentation had become abstracted to the point where the performers' bodies are presented simply as flawed cogs in a precision-timed

8 *The Sea & Poison.*

Photograph by Claude Giger. Theater Festival Basel, Switzerland, 1999. Pictured left to right: Bryan Saner, Mark Jeffery, Karen Christopher, Matthew Goulish

machine. The opening, exhaustingly long "dance" sequence places the four performers at four corners of an invisible rectangle, on which they begin to pound out a machinic beat by jumping up and down on the spot with jackhammer regularity. (You can almost feel their "ecological footprints" ramming into the earth.) With the beat firmly established, individuals then begin to break out into complex physical sub-routines (on the spot, or in small circlings, or in diagrammatic crossings of the stage space), thereby setting up a mesmeric polyrhythm of counterbeats. Periodically, in a great whirl of flailing bodies, all four collapse horizontally to the floor before forcing themselves up again (and again, and again) to restart the base-line jumping rhythm.

This "impossible dance," as the company calls it, which forces them through hundreds of jumps in a matter of minutes, was devised with the aid of a computer program in order to subject the performers to unrealizable requirements. What we see here is bodies perpetually and inevitably *failing* in their attempts to execute the prescribed movements. One instruction, for example, demands that they be flat on the floor on one beat, and fully upright on the next: since this cannot be done, the performers are perpetually having to play catch-up to a punishing rhythm escaping ahead of them. Where conventional choreography asks the body to soar, to express its capabilities as beautifully and seamlessly as possible, Goat Island's performers are subjected to a kind of strategic humiliation, exposing their awkwardness, their vulnerability, their limits. At times, though, there is real poignancy in this: as the impossible dance goes on and on—as breathing becomes laboured and the execution of moves more erratic—the performers also, necessarily, become more autonomous in their strategies for coping, in improvising un-prescribed physical adjustments in order to catch up to speed as they fall behind.

It's a vivid demonstration of Goat Island's long-standing emphasis on interrogating the particularities of individual physicalities—the involuntary tics and idiosyncratic variations which begin to distinguish different bodies when asked to perform similar tasks, repeatedly. Moreover, if a sense of individual humanity emerges from this uniform subjection to physical stress, this too can be read as a feminist concern. As Jane Blocker argues persuasively in *What the Body Cost* (2004), male body artists have historically tended to assume a kind of universal authority by casting their own bodies as generally representative of "the body" (Stelarc is a primary case in point here, insistently using that designation to reference his experiments on himself). Conversely, Blocker suggests, feminist artists have more humbly and strategically assumed a plurality of bodies placed within an establishing context, each of interest and value.

In *The Sea & Poison*, the establishing context suggests associations with workforces engaged as flesh machines in hazardous, toxic environments—a new literalization, perhaps, of the company's characteristic presentation of performance as labour;

as the necessary completion of complex, awkward physical tasks. Here, their uniform costuming—another habitual Goat Island strategy for de-gendering and de-hierarchizing the performers' bodies—resembles workers' fatigues in earthy greens and browns. (At a certain point, their reversible jackets are turned inside-out, switching from brown to radioactive yellow.) Over time, their overalls become visibly drenched in sweat, smeared with dirt, and in one case, plastered with dollar bills. They become caught in germ sprays, are subjected to sirens, and end up dragging each other's broken bodies around like sacks on their backs. *The Sea & Poison*, I would suggest, asks us to meditate not on the shiny, exciting, virtual world of information superhighways, but on the dirty, sweaty, poisoned, exhausted physical world of expanding global capitalism. "No, human beings are not machines," Deleuze and Guattari note, mock-humanistically: "we don't treat them like machines, we certainly don't confuse variable capital with constant capital" (1987: 457).

Body / machine #1 Bryan Saner (1999b)

The beginning of the new work is the epilogue of the old work. The old work *The Sea & Poison* contained a dance section we entitled the impossible dance, which was scored with the help of a computer and was impossible to perform. In beginning the new work, which became *It's an Earthquake in My Heart*, we became fascinated by recent advances in biotechnology and nanotechnology. We began thinking about pacemakers and internal body hardware. Earlier, Mark had constructed a large fan in a suitcase, which he performed with, strapped to his back. This made him look like a future man from a 1950s sci-fi film. The fan eventually shrank into hand-held, heart-sized models which fix themselves to our clothing in *Earthquake*, like chest implants.

We were directed: create a circulatory chase or a circulatory lullaby with your body. The direction included a diagram of veins in the human head. We developed a movement sequence in which fingers carefully trace the lines of veins in the head and neck. We developed another in which we are cars chasing and almost colliding while weaving through traffic. In the performance, the two sequences combine: nanotechnological widgets cruise the highways of our vascular systems. We discussed the very prevalent use, today, of psychiatric drugs like Prozac, Paxil and Zoloft—names with x's and z's. These pills that we swallow resemble the rounded capsule shapes of the Airstream mobile homes that take us away from our routine repetitions and compulsions and give us the freedom to let ourselves go on down the road. Airstreams polluting the airstream. Prozacs pumping our minds. It's an earthquake, an earthquake in my heart.

Everybody knows in a second life we all come back sooner or later
As anything from a pussycat to a man-eating alligator

Now you may think my story is more fiction than it's fact
But believe it or not my mother dear decided she'd come back
As a car
She's my very own, guiding star
A 1928 Porter, that's my mother dear,
She helps me through everything I do and I'm so glad she's here.

"My Mother the Car" (1965 television theme song);
from *It's an Earthquake in my Heart*

Body / machine #2 Adrian Heathfield (2001: 20)

Perhaps this is the dominant logic of *Earthquake*'s strange transformations from the animate into the inanimate: the human becoming automata (the engine in the heart, the body as car) . . . How to live when the late-capitalist complex has buried its mechanisms deep inside our flesh? What to trust in if we cannot trust ourselves? How to judge, if our judgement is always emoted? How to feel, in the knowledge that our emotions are both genuine and synthetically produced? Towards the end of *Earthquake* Goat Island adjust their image of the engine inside the heart, placing a burning flame at its centre [a fragment of red cloth,

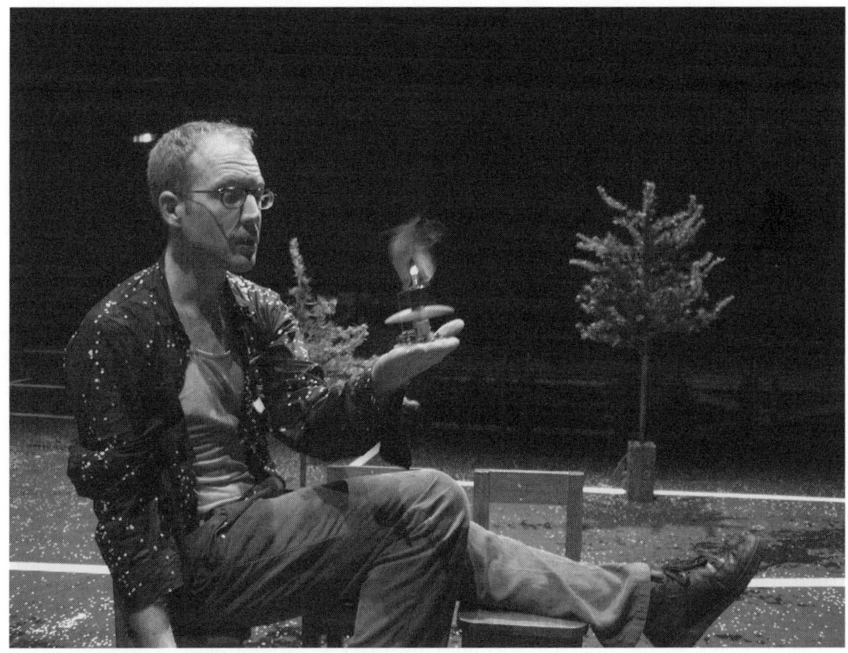

9 *It's an Earthquake in My Heart.*
Photograph by Rebecca Groves. Mousonturm, Frankfurt, Germany, 2001. Pictured: Mark Jeffery

fluttering in the fan's airstream]. A small thing, but also something fundamental. For me this is the most shattering and haunting image of the piece: the heart both fabricated and real; the flame, a flame of passion but also of destruction. Could it be that the catastrophe of which the piece speaks, the catastrophe in whose shadow we must ask again and again "how to live?", is not simply happening to our hearts but coming from them? How to live, then, with the knowledge that personal and social destruction emanates from the same place as love? It's an earthquake, an earthquake in my heart.

Assemblages Steve Bottoms

Heathfield's exposition of what he calls "the problem of the machine inside our hearts" eloquently expresses one dimension of *It's an Earthquake in My Heart*'s human-machinic implications. To get to another, we can turn the problem inside-out, by reminding ourselves that the heart is not in fact a mythic repository of emotion but *literally* a machine, a pump, which may stop pumping at any moment when a particular valve gives out or seizes up. In this respect too, *Earthquake*'s layering of pacemaker fans and traffic patterns seems deeply poignant: walking steadily in patterned lines, bends and roundabouts, the performers' traffic movements are not fast and frantic (not an impossible dance) but gradual, calm, almost serene; the studious carrying out of daily routines. When a bump or near-collision occurs, and the meditative quiet is suddenly shattered by the blare of Matthew's hand-held electric car horn, Mark falters, loses balance slightly, pauses with a hand to his chest, then continues. A heart flutter. A warning presaging the crash itself. We witness here again an intimation of vulnerability, mortality, within the heart of the machine.

This too is posthumanism. The body not a sovereign body, a wholeness unto itself, but partial, conditional, penetrated by pace-making medical technologies to help it operate more reliably. The "cyborg" not merely as a sci-fi nightmare of human-turned-machine, but as a mundane reality. Indeed, as Gregory Bateson observed in one of his classic examples, the blind man with his cane is a cyborg too, a cybernetic organism reliant on a tap-tapping prosthesis for the gathering of information that will make his environment navigable (cf. Bateson 2000: 465). Prostheses are a recurrent trope in Goat Island's work—the performers becoming constituent parts of strange assemblages that fuse their bodies with man-made objects. Like the machinic regimentation of the dance sequences, these too function to expose the performing body as awkward, vulnerable. (This as opposed to the god-like power that Stelarc apparently believes will be his, through body enhancement.) One thinks, for example, of the wobbling cardboard crutches on which Karen must rest her arm and leg in *When will the September roses bloom? Last night was only a comedy*, or the strange, too-high chin-brace on which Mark is propped in the same piece, as a grim-looking feeding funnel is inserted into his mouth. In *Earthquake*, performers carry miniature speakers about to amplify their voices, as though afraid they will not be heard. Bryan hunches awkwardly for what seems like hours over a microphone set up too low for him, but which he doesn't seem to think he has the authority to adjust.

Fast rewind to *The Sea & Poison*, to a pivotal image about halfway through the performance. In the midst of the exhaustion, the destruction, the spraying of quarantine lines, the action pauses and Matthew attempts, nonsensically, to grow a tree on his head, as if hoping to nurture a small oasis of fertility in a barren landscape. He empties a small mound of earth onto his crown and plants a seed in it from a small packet. He applies water from a watering can. He picks up and holds overhead a small, battery-powered hand-lamp, to shine a few watts of light onto his allotment, and a dictaphone, to encourage his crop with music. New life powered by machinery. A composition called "Goon Gumpos," by the Aphex Twin, pipes out on the dictaphone's tiny, low-tech speaker. Sounding strangely like a faraway orchestra of strings being plucked and bowed, the music is nevertheless entirely synthesized, using synthesizers, as fake as the overhead sunlight. Yet something about the dictaphone's primitive, retarded sound quality transforms this image, with time, from the ridiculous to the heartbreaking. As Brian Eno has observed, the moment a form of sound technology becomes obsolete—the vinyl record surrendering to the compact disc, for example—the particular qualities of the obsolete medium become a source of nostalgia; hence the vinyl crackle we hear as an effect on so many CDs. This is, perhaps, a *resistant* nostalgia; a querying of the march of machinic progress; a sense that the very flaws in the technology make it *more like us*. To err is human.

Fast rewind again to an obsolete *body* in *How Dear to Me the Hour When Daylight Dies*; another pivotal image about halfway through the performance. Slim-built Karen Christopher portrays Mike Walker, once the fattest man in America. A wooden table with foldaway metal legs is placed at a 45 degree angle to the floor, with two legs tucked underneath, and Christopher lies with her head on the floor, her torso sloping up the table, and her lower legs dangling over its top edge. She wears a curious white bonnet, a khaki shirt, an almost diaper-like pair of baggy white shorts, and a man's black shoes and socks. An old-fashioned metallic microphone, attached to a stand which also carries a busker's amplification box, is directed downward at her mouth, and into it she slowly recites Mike Walker's words of self-recrimination, lifted from a 45 r.p.m. record which he made as a warning to others to avoid his fate. At first glance, this (re)construction seems like a coy joke, an ironized quotation of pop-cultural debris. Yet something about Christopher's delivery is so pained and so sustained in its attempts at precision that the audience's initial impulse to laugh quickly peters out. A silence. Her awkward, amplified breathing is accompanied only by the whir of an oscillating desk fan, placed adjacent to her on the floor as if to relieve the heat suffered under this gross body mass. A sucking sound as Christopher forces herself to ingest large quantities of liquid through a plastic tube, in mimickry of Walker's own feeding regimen. Slowly, perhaps, the traumatic "reality" of this forgotten figure's situation begins to make itself felt, not through acted emoting but through the very awkwardness of this abstract-machinic assemblage. It is almost as if the ghost presence of the dead Walker were being conjured up by Christopher's robot-like divestiture of personal charisma, by the very absurdity of her painstakingly careful attempts to represent him.

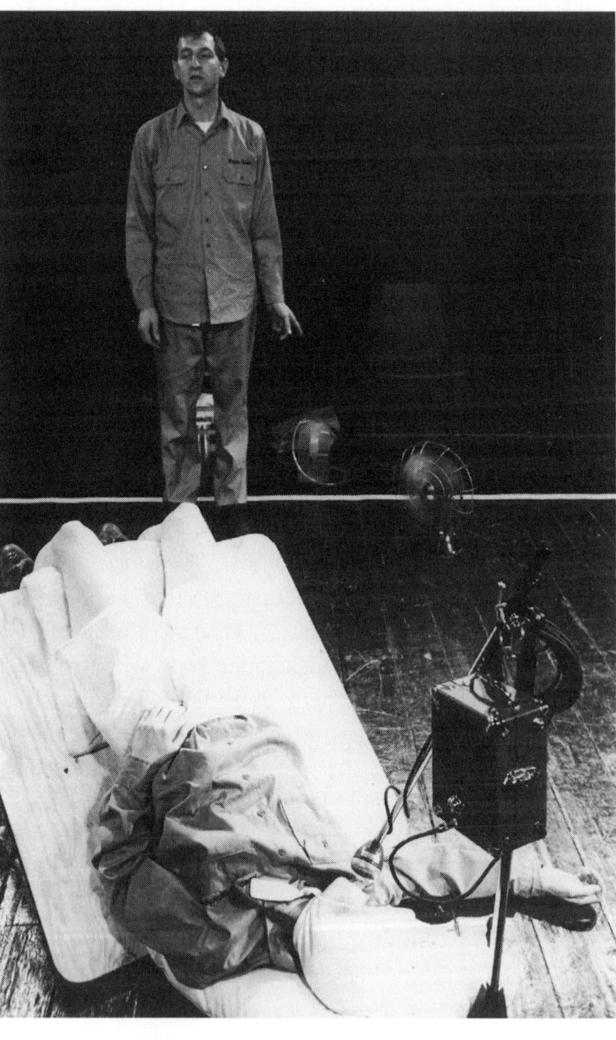

10 *How Dear to Me the Hour When Daylight Dies.*
Photograph by Alan Crumlish. Centre for Contemporary Arts, Glasgow, 1996.
Pictured top to bottom: Bryan Saner, Karen Christopher as Mike Walker

I was like you once. In Korea, I weighed two hundred pounds. Then, in medical terms, I suffered a severe psychological effect which brought latent neuroses to the surface, mine being strong suicidal tendencies manifesting themselves in a compulsive eating symptom. In plain, everyday language this means I gave up and tried to destroy myself by gorging myself with food. I ate constantly, getting larger and larger, until I reached the unreal weight of one thousand one hundred and eighty-seven pounds. I am unable to walk. The doctors have given me only a few months to live. I now see how I have wrecked my life, and also affected the lives of ones dear to me, my wife and my son and my mother. I have decided to place myself on exhibit in an effort to discourage the public, especially teenagers, from wrecking their lives the way I have wrecked mine. If I can stop one person, then my life has some meaning. On the other side of this record you can hear my song, telling you more about my problems and my physical condition.

Iowa farm girl seriousness Karen Christopher

Carol Burbank, a reviewer for the *Chicago Reader*, once described my performance in Goat Island's piece *It's Shifting, Hank* as projecting a sense of "Iowa farm girl seriousness." I would have to guess what she might be referring to. I have driven through Iowa once.

In Goat Island, we have never tried to adopt a particular performance style. We seek instead to be open to the incorporation of disparate elements and fragments and multi-vocality. Each of the voices we incorporate needs to be heard on its own terms and not written over by some attitude of our own. Yet perhaps because of this determination to honor the material we have stolen, there is in Goat Island's work a kind of earnest intentionality that gleams through and instructs the audience how to take it all in. Our seriousness (also present in humorous moments) informs the material, so that even when the content is wide open to interpretation, it is the focus and intentionality of the performers that supply a through line.

Most people writing about our work veer away from analysis of performance style. In the world of contemporary performance, it is mostly content and structure that the critic focuses on. The same is often true of practitioners. Lin, as our director, is not so much concerned with directing individual performances as she is with adjusting volume and speed and sequence. If she does not like the way a specific part is being played it is taken away. In the absence of directing from an acting point of view the performers look to each other for adjustments and inspiration. One function of our collaboration is the way in which we watch and listen to each other: if one of us alters our delivery or attitude in a certain moment, the others must respond to that accordingly. To maintain balance in the system, we are constantly calibrating. Yet this is not something we discuss. In fact other company members may not see our process in the way I do. When I say "acting style," all the hairs on their heads stand up.

Why don't you see anyone crying or laughing in a Goat Island piece? What is it to play a character in a Goat Island piece? It is acknowledged once in a while that we are "stoic" or "straight-faced" onstage. And yet after initially describing me as "neutral," one respondent in a work-in-progress discussion followed that observation by asking why there was so much anger in my performance. And so we might ask: how can a performer be neutral and project anger at the same time? In any given moment of the performance, someone just entering the room might see no emotional inflection at all in the delivery of a particular sequence, but for someone bringing with them a chain of connections, built up by the preceding events, that same sequence might seem full of expression.

When I play a character I play a series of gestures and sounds. I repeat certain positions and cadences and rhythms. I am not trying to repeat the person, only their motion and their sound. What we do is task-based and we do not "pretend." Sometimes we are falling in and out of roles and voices in rapid succession. In our piece *When will the September roses bloom? Last night was only a comedy*, I move from Paul Celan to Simone Weil-as-Lillian Gish to the howling landlady of Thomas Bernhard's *A Party for Boris*, and then to Simone Weil all on her own, and then Karen (myself) as a performer moving in front of spectators. These changes have to be something. They are part of the event happening in front of the spectators. They have to be sharp and fast and the differences between portrayals must be distinct. Never in the course of all this switching am I attempting to cause the audience to cease to see *me* in front of them. Yet it is not enough to say that we are "simply playing ourselves" as we perform this multi-vocality. It is a specific thing I do when I complicate myself with more than one voice. Like a series of transparencies sliding over each other, we are trying to enact a kind of simultaneity of being. I am neither a representation of Simone Weil, nor am I solely myself.

The architect Zaha Hadid uses a variety of styles to render ideas about the structures she designs. In documenting her plans for buildings, through sketches, models, and paintings, she attempts to demonstrate dynamic qualities within the structures she envisions. These images attempt to illuminate the buildings' lives in four dimensions—including movement through time as well as movement and energy flow through space. She traces trajectories of human traffic, the reverberations shapes will create in space, the inter-active relationship of a building to its surroundings. Her paintings may appear to consist of abstract shapes placed formally in space but there is a narrative involved. They may not be entirely legible or may take some time to absorb and to understand, but they are expressing more than simple walls and floors. The elements depicted have moved or doubled in response to environment, context, and interaction with transient elements. Hadid's paintings suggest a simultaneity of information and sensation.

In our 1996 piece *How Dear to Me the Hour When Daylight Dies*, a number of historical figures are represented. Among them are Mike Walker, the fattest man in America, and Amelia Earhart, the first woman to fly across the Atlantic. Amelia disappeared during an attempt to circumnavigate the globe, shortly before the US got involved in World War II (some say she was involved in military intelligence gathering). Mike, an American soldier in the Korean war, consumed so much food after returning to civilian life that he could no longer walk, so he placed himself on show as part of a traveling carnival. These two icons are portrayed by the same performer (myself), so as to combine them in ways that merely placing them next to each other could not. As Amelia disappears, Mike Walker appears and appears and appears. We see them as echoes of each other, linked in some way we can't quite articulate. Mike lies on his back, still wearing Amelia's little white cotton flying helmet, as if reduced to infancy.

After performing *Daylight Dies* in Zagreb, Croatia, I was walking back to my hotel room late at night when three young women started shouting at me from across a grassy park. They ran to catch me only to say that when they had seen the show they had seen me as Mike Walker, but when they remembered it they remembered an enormous man. They took great pains to explain the change that had gone on in their minds: the alchemy of the image, plus thought, plus time.

Just as Zaha Hadid might show a solid wall as transparent in order to give an understanding of relationships within the space occupied by a building, so we are seeking to layer one representation over another without obliterating or covering the first. Where Hadid uses paintings and drawings to represent buildings, our materials are our presence in time and space. Our bodies are mobile units, houses in constant motion.

Watch Lin Hixson (2000; Goat Island 1999a: 25)

I watch. Keep time. Stay awake deliberately.
I look for the sudden turn of a foot that catches me without warning;
Evidence of imagination pointing beyond itself.
I watch for low speed. Slow tempo.
Registering a time behind and below the correct one.

I watch for evidence of problems forming—not through characters in a play, but in actions of necessity. Trials as testimonies. Karen falling over again and again. Matthew and Mark running until their breath seems to go. Bryan hunched over a microphone for too long of a time.

In the seventeenth century, in early western natural philosophy, in trials of public performances, experimenters offered their bodies in evidence. They looked for long periods at the sun, inhaled powerful gases, and rubbed themselves with flint until bits of metal jumped toward them. These reporters of artificial experience were using their bodies, watched by others, to search for some truth.

In Southern Italy, it was said that poisonous spiders stung human beings. To be cured, those stung would dance for hours like spiders, on their stomachs, on all fours. Sometimes they were hung by ropes from trees and swayed in the wind, like spiders on a strand. This spinning or swaying extracted or exorcized the tarantula poison from their bodies.

In *The Sea & Poison*, Mark Jeffery sits at a school desk and is fed half a glass of white milk. He stands, walks to an empty space sprinkled with dirt, and falls into spinning cartwheels. Round and round he goes, only his legs are bent, crunched close to his body like a spider ball. And he's moving too fast, so he collapses when his weight gets thrown too far to one side. He can't get up. He can't get his feet under his body because his head spins and his body spins in his head, out in the space, even though he lies still on the ground. And eventually he's up again, at it again, a human ball turning round and round and round until his knees bend and he collapses over his feet, onto his arms, onto his shoulders, his stomach in his mouth, his eyes still but his head on the ceiling, on the walls, on the floor. Eventually he returns to his desk and finishes the glass of milk.

Becoming animal Steve Bottoms

The body as a complex physical mechanism, stressed biochemically in particular ways. A testing, an ingesting of poisons (the white milk not the whiteness of innocence, but of *The Sea & Poison*'s quarantine paint, its chemical spray; perhaps the whiteness of the whale that Ahab pursues to self-destruction). The search for an antidote through the absorption of limited amounts of the poison? Synthesizing a vaccine? A vaccine of synthesized music piped on a dictaphone? The machine becoming human? The human becoming machine? Becoming poison?

The meditative dimensions of Goat Island's work—I would contend, on reflection —begin and end with bodies becoming *abject*. Becoming puppet, becoming cog, becoming dirt, becoming obese. A renunciation of human(ist) self-sovereignty. Never a becoming *man* (unless a fat man, already unmanned), because as Deleuze and Guattari stress, "man is a majoritarian par excellence, whereas becomings are minoritarian; all becoming is a becoming-minoritarian" (1987: 291). To embark on a process of becoming is to embrace flight or flow (a Bergsonian submerging), to become one with natural flux, rather than to become *one* (unitary, phallic, dominant over an *other*). And this micropolitical resistance is summarized, for Deleuze and Guattari as it is, perhaps, for Goat Island, in the idea of becoming *animal*.

The animality of bodies is present as a minor key throughout the Goat oeuvre. We loop back to Carol Becker's notes on *Can't Take Johnny to the Funeral* (1991), the performers as "wild dogs gnawing on each other's legs." By the time of *The Sea & Poison* (1998), the animal-becomings have become unavoidable. Preceding the impossible dance is an establishing prologue in which Bryan and Mark speak as one, a dual consciousness called George who finds he has given birth to a frog; a plastic frog fallen from the armpit of Matthew, whose arms and legs have become frog-like:

KAREN: Do you love it?
MARK AND BRYAN: It's our child, isn't it?
KAREN: Does that mean you can't love it?
MARK AND BRYAN: It's hard enough to love a frog, but when it turns out to be your own son . . .

(adapted from Edson 1994: 120–121)

The performers as a curious frog family; the Georges genetically linked (as are we all, through a substantial proportion of our DNA) to the creatures later seen raining in a great storm of bendy plastic limbs, bouncing off a theatrical thunder-sheet before coming to rest on the floor, evidence of ecological chaos brewing in the atmosphere.

In the same performance, as Karen begins to shrink to the size of an insect, Bryan lifts his shirt over his head and hunches his shoulders to become a bear. Yet this is a dancing bear, a lone animal forced to anthropomorphize itself; a reversal of the multiplying trajectory of the humans-becoming-frog-chorus. "It doesn't feel cruel. Just humiliating," Bryan notes reflectively, in a passage appropriated from Sam Shepard's play *Action*:

It's not the rightful position of a bear. You can feel it. It's all off balance . . . as though something's expected of me. As though I was human. . . . Performing. Without realizing it. I mean I realize it but the bear doesn't. He just finds himself doing something unusual for him. Awkward.

(Shepard 1984: 171)

Always the awkwardness. The bear, torn away from nature, becomes a cog in the entertainment machine. Yet as Siegfried and Roy's Siberian tiger proved in 2003 by mauling Roy live on stage in Las Vegas, even the performing animal is never quite "civilized." And while Deleuze and Guattari may object to house pets as doe-eyed, sentimentalized reflections of the way humans would like their relations with other humans to be ("*anyone who likes cats or dogs is a fool*") they also note that *any* animal may again become a part of "the pack or swarm . . . Even the cat, even the dog" (1987: 240–241). Especially the dog. The dog always on the verge of becoming cur, mongrel, wolf.

It is this ambiguity—the dog as servile, the dog as pack—which recurs throughout Goat Island's most animal of performances, *When will the September roses bloom? Last night was only a comedy*. Periodically, different performers leap inexplicably into doggy solos: Mark snuffling at speed on all fours along the floor, his scampering hand extended ahead of him as sniffing nose; Matthew circling awkwardly on hind legs, pawing at the ground with his feet. And right on the edge, in the zone between entertainment and mauling, Karen staring out at us with teeth bared, grinning, *growling*: "Rrrrrr. . . ." Periodically, the group becomes a pack, a choreographed co-ordination of dog-becomings, pawing, scurrying, and repetitively brushing at their own bodies as if washing themselves, doggy-style (cleansing their humanity?). Crucially, though, these are not "imitations" of dogs (attempts simply to make humans *look like dogs*), but human–dog hybrids, their actions somehow reminiscent of doggery while also remaining those of people (and always, but for Mark, on two legs not four). "It is not a question of 'playing' the dog," Deleuze and Guattari stress:

Becomings-animal are basically of another power, since their reality resides . . . in that which sweeps us up and makes us become—a *proximity, an indiscernibility* that extracts a shared element from the animal far more effectively than any domestication, utilization or imitation could.

(1987: 279)

For Bryan Saner, this in-betweenness links the dog-people with the figure of theologian-philosopher-factory worker Simone Weil, who also echoes ghost-like through *September roses*:

I think she had knowledge of herself as a hybrid. A human body between the world of the factory and the world of heaven. A hybrid between the thoughts of a laborer and the world of intellectual ideals about labor. She bridged the gap. She points us to that double world. She says: "May God grant that I become a dog."

(Saner 2005: np)

Karen-as-Simone speaks that line in the performance, in a watershed moment when impressions suddenly gather up and spill in new directions. A renunciation of human ego, an embrace of the abject, in a performance where the movement vocabulary is less urgent, less machinic, than in any previous Goat Island work. Where the performers, instead of bursting into urgent motion, are as likely to stutter to a stop. To get off the treadmill. To stand still on one leg, as Litó Walkey does for a count of 377 seconds. To suspend at least one ecological footprint and wait quietly, patiently, desperately, for the world to come around.

I'm saying the lines of Scott Carey, protagonist of the 1957 science-fiction film The Incredible Shrinking Man. *I tell Bryan he's not a dancing bear. Mark drinks a lot of milk. Matthew tries to grow a bean on his head. We are all becoming something else at any given moment. I walk into the spray from the can I have been carrying on my back. It turns my hair gray. Scott Carey walked past some trees that were being sprayed. He thinks he might have been sprayed with them. Now he is shrinking. We live in a world we have poisoned. What we do to others we do to ourselves in spite of what we intend. If we spray the trees we spray ourselves and then we become the trees.*

(Karen Christopher, Goat Island 1999a: 33–35)

Puppet show #2 Lin Hixson (Goat Island 1996b: 10)

Basil ran into the toyroom and we followed. Out the windows, the night lights of Fribourg flickered. It was an evening in late July, and our sojourn in Switzerland was about to end. We had just finished performing *It's Shifting, Hank*, and this seven-year-old boy was staging a puppet show for us on the evening of our day off. We gathered around the five-foot puppet stage. Adrian, our eighteen-year-old translator, perched on his knees next to the theatre. A green puppet appeared in a purple dress with gold trim.

"*Bon soir, Mesdames et Messieurs*," said the queen.
"Good evening, ladies and gentlemen," Adrian translated.
"*Bienvenue au theatre du marionettes*," she said, spreading her arms.
"Welcome to the puppet show," said Adrian.
"*Ne parlez pas pendant cette performance.*"
"No talking during the performance."
"*Ne fumez pas dans le theatre.*"
"There is no smoking allowed in the theatre."

Suddenly, behind the queen, an arm rose, its hand covered with a yellow furry lion. The startled queen lurched for a moment, then rocketed through the air towards the audience, striking my neighbour in the eye. "Ow!" yelled the startled spectator.

After a moment, the lion spoke: "*Cette performance va faire mal.*"

Adrian translated, "The performance will hurt."

B1.4 TIME

KAREN:
Wann,
wann blühen, wann
wann blühen . . . ja sie, die September-
rosen?

LITO:
When do they flower, when
yes they, the Septembers
the Seven ambers
Roses, when when

(*Silence*)

BRYAN: We'd like to apologize, we're missing the beginning.

BRYAN: I think there is a kind of repair of the culture that's needed. And part of it is about slowly re-educating ourselves about how we respond to violence, and to the loss of *voice* in our culture. It's a long process. I mean, I think it's like a hundred year process—if we survive that long.

(Christopher and Saner, 2003)

LIN: You know, I've never been interested in trying to replicate or even trying to compete with TV or film, but it's interesting how much that does inform the psyche, even if you think you're not doing it. I'm shocked when I go to see a lot of live theatre these days because it's trying to replicate that almost in an unconscious way. The director or the playwright don't think that they're doing that, but they've been so programmed with this kind of *timing* thing. Film, for years, really dominated my psyche. I was really moved by films, and I started to realize how I was being manipulated. For a while I was really taken with it and would go in there to *be* manipulated. So the large-scale performances I did in LA were kind of like film because we'd have fifty people out there creating the images.* But then, when I saw [the work of Tadeusz] Kantor and [Pina] Bausch, I felt they got through to another level, because they took their time to let things develop: they made you come to the work, instead of thrusting the work at you. It was a hard thing for me at times, but I felt they got to this level of connection; that there was an experience that happened in live work that you couldn't get anywhere else. So I became more interested in what happens when you get people together in this small room and see what can transpire . . . To have an experience together, it takes time. And for me that's why you have to let things in a performance take the time that they need to fulfil themselves. And I don't see that happening much in the larger culture; I just see things speeding up.

(Hixson 1997)

Ecologies of time Steve Bottoms

In his important article, "The Ecology of Images," Andrew Ross notes that, given the extent of modern media-culture's perpetual *recycling* of the same visual and narrative formulas, one might consider it in ecological terms. He points out, however, that such recycling, "both conservationist and conservative . . . runs directly counter to the ecological spirit of preserving and encouraging diversity. The result more and more resembles an image monoculture" (Ross 1994: 334). That is, the same crop is mass-produced incessantly, starving alternative vegetation of nutrients (though a few rebel weeds somehow, stubbornly survive). And if this sounds suspiciously like a metaphor, Ross notes the real knock-on in terms of the way that even "images of ecology" too-easily become part of this monocultured "ecology of images." Thus, for example, TV images of Iraqi oilfields deliberately set ablaze by Saddam Hussein's regime, during the first Gulf War of 1991, helped further fuel the fire of the American-led invasion, and the massive environmental devastation it entailed: "The oil slick and burning wells were the only images of ecological spoliation the [American] public did get to see, and the ones that the public remembers" (327).

Although we didn't set out to do a piece on the Gulf War, I think it ended up informing [Can't Take Johnny to the Funeral] *on many levels. Particularly the stories that we were hearing about children's nightmares after watching the violence on TV. And how parents responded to that by saying, "You've got nothing to be worried about. It's not on your soil. It will never affect you." We grow up almost from the beginning being educated in denial.*

(Lin Hixson 1992)

---

* Hixson's early directorial career in Los Angeles was chiefly notable for expansive, spectacle-based performances such as *Hey John, Did You Take the El Camino Far?* (1984), which playfully manipulated iconography from movies and popular music. According to critic Jacki Apple, "no one, except perhaps Rachel Rosenthal, had a greater influence than Hixson on the direction LA performance art took in the '80s" (Apple 1991: 28).

A capitalistic subjectivity is engendered through operators of all types and sizes, and is manufactured to protect existence from any intrusion of events that might disturb or disrupt public opinion. . . . Therefore, it endeavours to manage the worlds of childhood, love, art, as well as everything associated with anxiety, madness, pain, or a feeling of just being lost in the Cosmos . . .

(Félix Guattari 2000: 50)

For Paul Virilio, the most insidious aspect of today's wraparound media culture is the way its very speed of communication foreshortens our concept of space. When instant broadcast or web links allow us to "be" almost anywhere in the world without ever leaving our homes, a critical form of myopia ensues: "When the *time depth* of instantaneity once and for all elbows aside the *field depth* of humanity's space, what 'optical layer' is there left to speak of?" There is now a fatal perceptual confusion, between "the visible horizon against which all 'scenes' stand out and the deep horizon of the imaginary" (Virilio 1997: 66).

The passage of time itself becomes polluted through the virtuality of "real time" telecommunications, Virilio suggests, and as this impacts directly on our concepts of space, so it must also pollute our relationship with the earth itself.

11 *Can't Take Johnny to the Funeral.*
Photograph by Eileen Ryan. Wellington Avenue Church, Chicago, 1991. Pictured left to right: Greg McCain, Karen Christopher

As teletechnologies begin to act as prosthetic extensions of our eyesight, so we lose actual, physical contact with the world so viewed: "the presence of a prosthesis further accentuates the maimed person's perception of a limb that has in fact gone. *Has Mother Earth become humanity's phantom limb?*" (Virilio 1997: 66)

There is, Virilio suggests, a "grey ecology" at work here, as opposed to a green one; grey because, when colours spin past us at speed, they all blur into that one (non-) colour. The real world has become virtual, through the virtuality of "real time" broadcasting; the sheer speed of information technologies and televisual narrative induces a kind of static passivity in the subject, which makes us "more easily controlled" (1997: 66). "The loss of material space leads to the government of nothing but time" (Virilio 1986: 141).

How then, to retrieve and repair time from this terminal acceleration? Another impossible cause, perhaps, but one which Goat Island pursue nonetheless, by insisting on what Virilio calls "life-size presence" (rather than the shrunken, sped-up presence of the small screen), and by obstinately exposing the awkward progression of time itself. Rather than the seamless sequencing of past time, via deft edits, into one rapid, homogenized present of cultural memory, Goat Island's work constantly references a past which is somehow lost, irretrievable, yet vital to the (re)constructive work we must do in the present. Even the colour schemes of the shows sometimes seem to locate them in another time and space than that of the perpetual technicolour now: the sepia-toned *How Dear to Me the Hour When Daylight Dies*; the monochrome black-and-white scheme of *When will the September roses bloom? Last night was only a comedy*. Fragments from old films, old records, old TV shows, old advertisements, appear reproduced in the onstage present, afloat like flotsam—detached from the conveniently linear cultural narratives they are assumed to be part of, or retrieved from the ashcan of the discarded and forgotten. Instead, they are stitched together with each other, allowing connections to be made between them, but only if we work actively to bridge the yawning gaps between them, by placing them against Virilio's "deep horizon of the imaginary."

How Dear to Me the Hour When Daylight Dies *is a collage of memories of the century —what flashes before the eyes of the dying, perhaps. . . . The piece asks what would happen if you folded time and squeezed it into one small space. One answer is that things separated in linear time butt up to each other and seem, by virtue of this proximity, to have a relation which they never had in "real time," or the time of history. This replicates, of course, the accidents of memory itself where events are elided and combined. Another answer is that some of that continuum will run backwards and some forwards and any one slice through that sponge—that Viennetta ice cream of time's folds—will co-ordinate points in forward and backward progress. Thus, there are pre-echoes of the piece's material which appear early in the running order but are only explained, as it were, when they arrive in their "original" context, much later in the show. They are memories of the future, or echoes without an origin.*

(David Hughes 1996: 32)

Memory model Karen Christopher

We can only measure past time by absence, using our memories, which are mutable and unreliable. The construction of a performance piece is the conscious act of constructing a memory model. We seek to suggest rather than to reproduce past experience or historical memory: an old idea of person or place is created anew in a liminal space before an audience. It is not an attempt to produce an illusion, but rather to suggest an avenue of thought.

When people sit around with a few drinks and tell stories about the past, they take a step out of the present and suspend their consciousness of now. Yet taking a trip back in this way also alters the sensation of the present: old thoughts and feelings return, and the filter-of-the-moment blends with an old filter with which the world was once viewed. Historical and personal memories combine to activate a process in the mind. A performance must stimulate this mechanism of memory somehow; it must take the audience to a place where something new or unexpected can happen; it must wake them up to their own uncovered thoughts.

Repair in process Philip Stanier (2005: 37–39)

I first encountered Goat Island's *When will the September roses bloom? Last night was only a comedy* at a work-in-progress showing in 2003. Split into two blocks, the audience faced itself across a space divided into small rooms by tape on the ground. The company wore high, starched collars reminiscent of Puritans, and had their limbs supported by cardboard crutches, standing for long periods with their legs lifted into the air. I remember company member Bryan Saner, falteringly explaining the principles of clockwise and anti-clockwise with the aid of a giant cardboard wheel. As I watched, I imagined the performance to be a creaking wooden house, carrying the traces of everything that had once occupied it, and so worn down by the wind and full of gaps that it was a performance that you experienced by passing through. Goat Island had been making *September roses* for a year, and they would work on it for another year before I would get the opportunity to see it in its completed form in 2004. By then I had only partial memories of what I had already seen.

This extended process of creation and contemplation is vital for Goat Island and any audience engaging with the work. A year on from my first viewing, *September roses* had evolved into a piece now designed to be watched twice, over two nights.

The material of the performance was densely layered, with sequences of movement and text having evolved from the company's gathering and arranging of sources ranging from the writings of Paul Celan, Simone Weil and W. G. Sebald to James Taylor songs, minimalist music, and the Lillian Gish silent movie *The Wind*. Yet the first night's viewing was for me a difficult, fragmentary and faltering experience, punctuated and interrupted by numerous silences, absences and voids. The performance negotiated the tension between the dense, overflowing material and the silences, by having some voids resist being filled by the audience's thoughts, while others invited the instigation of memory or the imagination. As the evening progressed, scenes were declared missing, uncomfortable silences occurred, blind spots in vision were demonstrated and at one point an imagined exchange between Paul Celan and Edmond Jabès was referred to: "I will not translate you," Celan explains, "our silences are too different." All of these moments slowed my experience and comprehension of the performance, and I was compelled to repeatedly contemplate the event in retrospect.

On reflection, it seemed as if the extended making process of *September roses* was present in its enactment, but always flickering from visibility to invisibility. I was periodically aware of sequences that seemed changed or unchanged in relation to the work-in-progress showing I had seen, and also conscious of the echoes of previous works making their presence felt—my memories of earlier Goat Island performances I had seen, or only read about, being triggered by the event I was involved with. As such, the experience of the first performance was one of many contesting durations, amounting to a slow evening, not so much for its pace but for my unavoidable negotiation of these durations.

The starting point for *September roses* was to question our place in a damaged world and our aptitude at repairing it. Not the accelerated cycle of replacement common within capitalist culture, nor recovery wherein the original state of being is restored and the fault or loss is forgotten, but rather repair which leaves your awareness of the fault in place. The inclusion of the poet Paul Celan in the piece, as a source and as an enacted presence, is thus fitting given his interest in repairing language. Celan's poetry and Goat Island's performances both labour to restore language or experience from the remains of destruction, and via the negotiation of the voids left behind, which must either be filled or left as they are. In a statement on poetry, which I think is equally applicable to the performances of Goat Island, Celan wrote:

For a poem is not timeless. Certainly it lays claim to infinity, it seeks to reach through time—through it, not above and beyond it . . . Poems in this sense too are underway: they are making toward something.

(Celan 2001: 396)

After watching the first performance of *September roses*, I had a fitful night's sleep as my mind tried to process the dense event along with the rest of my life. I thought about the performance through the following day, and that night I expected to find the experience much as I had found it the night before. I was tired and not expecting my second engagement with the material to be radically different. On the second night, the piece unfolded and blossomed in front of me, and it was as if the performance had repaired itself overnight. The experience flowed and material was approachable, familiar and open. To watch the performance was now a comfortable and pleasurable experience. The move from night one to night two was like moving from the resignedly impossible attempt to repair, and towards hopefulness.

This change was the result of switching the order of the two central sections of the piece, other smaller changes to the content and structure, and my contemplation of the piece overnight. In retrospect, it feels as if the two parts of the performance now framed the intervening night and day, dovetailing together and engulfing and making a void of them, as if that time had been annexed into its own separate duration, away from the rest of my life's flow; as if the performances were a respective inhalation and exhalation leaving the space of my life in between. Paul Celan had a technique of creating word aggregates, one of his most famous being *atemwende*, or *breathturn*.* Matthew Goulish interprets this as "isolating the space between the inhale and the exhale, the microscopic void that touches death in each moment of life" (Goat Island 2004b: np). As a concept, *breathturn* sits at the root of inspiration—which comes from the Latin *spirare*: to breathe.

I now consider my experience of *September roses*, from the work-in-progress showing in 2003 and through both nights in 2004, as a single event with three manifestations: a prologue, first part and second part. Moreover, the year between the prologue and the main event, and the night and day between the first and second part are as vital and as much a part of the performance as any of the silences and voids that occupy the event itself. In those extended intervals the audience goes home, but the performance does not stop; it is carried and contemplated until the opportunity arises to encounter the next part.

The rain, the school, the cabbage patch, the movement of the next door neighbor's dog. They are like so many broken boats drifting inside me in bits and pieces. From time to time the boats gather, speak, and consume the darkness.

(Hijikata Tatsumi 1985)

---

* "*breathturn*" is the translation chosen by two leading Celan translators, John Felstiner and Pierre Joris.

Safe Sara Jane Bailes (2001: 48)
The first time I saw Goat Island's work in the school hall of a briny town on the coast of Wales, I quietly, comfortably, fell asleep. Actually, it was a slip into a mild state of reverie between sleeping and waking: a threshold where, if lucky, we sometimes retrieve our dreams. I felt safe, secure, utterly seduced. I've since had to wonder about what happened that night, for in years of making and watching performance, this had never occurred. Fading in and out of *The Sea & Poison* that night, I swooned into the unfamiliar folds of a strange language. Perhaps this is an accurate way to describe what the company brings to the spectator—the gift of a different language. They describe a world unfamiliar but logical, difficult to understand but beautiful to behold. In their performances the members of Goat Island release expression from the burden of meaning. Time expands; something shifts; the world is not the same place afterwards. That night I awoke to find myself in a hall full of people, hushed and transfixed, as a small man meticulously planted a bean on his head, and nurtured it lovingly with a rain shower from a watering can.

Sleep to remember, sleep to forget Matthew Goulish (2000b: 14)
For two hours every night, sleepers make jerky eye movements. Nathanial Kleitman discovered this, and named the activity Rapid Eye Movement: REM. He awoke his subjects during REM sleep and asked them what was happening. I was dreaming, they said, and they described the dream. Nathanial Kleitman concluded that REM sleep is the sleep of dreams. He had made an error.

Sleepers dream constantly, but non-REM sleep dreams lack imagery. Instead of pictures, they involve words, ideas, emotions. They repeat the patterns of thought. One could say non-REM sleep dreams are thoughts. Upon waking the dreamer forgets them, and also forgets that they occurred. But they did occur.

Allan Hobson believes that dreams transition perceptions from chaotic short-term memory to stable long-term memory: we dream about things worth remembering. Francis Crick and Graeme Michison believe dreams eliminate overlapping memories: we dream about things worth forgetting. Owen Flanagan, neurobiologist philosopher, believes that dreams replenish the brain. They stockpile fresh neurotransmitters, the lack of which prevents many brain activities from properly functioning, and these activities include memory.

There is a rhythm here to the jumping. You can go to sleep in this section and wake up later and not have missed much. Remember your dream because it is important to understanding the work you are doing.

(Bryan Saner 1999a)

Rain Fall Lin Hixson (2002a: 99–103)

Bryan bends over and speaks the words of butoh dancer, Hijikata Tatsumi (1985), into a microphone:

I sat on the verandah and watched the rain fall into the cabbage patch. How important the verandah is to me, I would think. The rain falls without beginning or end. As it falls, time and space become mixed and entwined, until no distinction remains between the two. And then I too deteriorate from the center, like rotting cabbage.

An artificial hand on a long stick, held by Mark, hovers over Bryan's head while he speaks.

When passerine birds find an owl, the discoverer sends out alarm calls and soon a mob of birds surrounds the owl . . . They hover over its head, flick their tails and wings, and make vociferous sounds. (cf. Heinrich 1987: 197, 199)

In contrast, the hovering hand over Bryan's bent body hangs quietly. And as Bryan repeats the words of Hijikata over and over again, I cannot imagine these words being said without the presence of the hand watching over this man.

12 *It's an Earthquake in My Heart.*

Photograph by Rebecca Groves. Mousonturm, Frankfurt, Germany, 2001. Pictured left to right: Bryan Saner, Mark Jeffery

There's a someone who I'm longing to see
I hope that he
Turns out to be
Someone to watch over me.

It rained often when I was a boy. I sat on the verandah and watched the rain fall into the cabbage patch.

It rained often when I was a girl. I sat on my porch and watched the rain fall on the willow tree. How important this tree is to me, I would think. I was a freshman in college. My stepmother asked me to come home for a party. How odd, I would think. The rain falls without beginning or end. I had just left for college two weeks earlier. Everyone was on the porch when I arrived. Except Dad. He was in the shade under the willow tree with cancer.

Nein, das tast du nicht. "No, you're not to do that." . . . these words come from a figure that time has almost effaced . . . all that remains is a presence . . . that of a young woman sitting back in an armchair in the lounge of a hotel. I must have been five or six, and the young woman had been engaged to look after me . . . I can't make her out very well, but I can distinctly see her work basket on my knees, and on top of it, a pair of scissors . . . and me . . . I can't see myself, but I can feel it as if I were doing it now . . . suddenly I grip them in my hand . . . heavy, closed scissors . . . I aim them, point upwards, at the back of a settee covered in a delightful silk material with a leafy pattern, in a slightly faded blue, with satiny glints . . . and I say in german . . . Ich werde es zerreisen . . . I'm going to slash it.

(Nathalie Sarraute 1984: 4)

How odd, I would think. In Zagreb, on a late afternoon in July, everyone circles in and out of the plaza boutiques. I ask our volunteer where people are getting the money to consume in such expensive stores. He says, "Watch them go in. Now watch them come out." I watch. They have no bags going in. They have no bags coming out. They are searching not buying. How important the verandah is to me, I would think. These people are returning, looking for something they've left behind.

It rained often when I was a boy.

Karen stands in the performance space. She has big wooden blocks on her feet. She holds in each hand a long stick with a wooden bird's foot on its end.

I sat on the verandah and watched the rain fall into the cabbage patch. How important the verandah is to me, I would think. The rain falls without beginning or end. As it falls, time and space become mixed and entwined, until no distinction remains between the two. And then I too deteriorate from the center, like rotting cabbage.

Karen stomps through the performance space. As she walks, she bends over and moves the wooden bird's feet so they step along in front of her. Then she stops and says, "I am not afraid. I am not afraid." Now I am afraid because Karen has stated she is not.

It rained often when I was a girl. I sat on the porch and watched the willow tree. How important this tree is to me, I would think. It sits on the ground like Anna's skirt in *The King and I* and blows open in the rain. As it falls, time and space become mixed and entwined, until no distinction remains between the two. And then I too deteriorate from the center like my father's stomach. My heart was always thumping like a dog. Thump, thump, thump it would pound.

Ich werde es zerreisen. "I'm going to slash it" . . . I'm warning you, I'm going to take the plunge, leap out of this decent, inhabited, warm, gentle world, I'm going to wrench myself out of it, fall, sink, into the uninhabited, into the void. . . . "I'm going to slash it" . . . I have to warn you, to give you time to stop me, to hold me back . . . "I'm going to slash it" . . . I shall say that to her very loudly . . . perhaps she will shrug her shoulders, lower her head, look thoughtfully at her work . . . Who takes it seriously when children indulge in these provocative, teasing acts? . . . and my words will waver, dissolve, my limp arm will drop, I shall put the scissors back in their place, in the basket . . . But she raises her head, she looks me in the eyes and says strongly stressing each syllable: *Nein, das tust du nicht* . . . "No, you're not to do that" . . . exercising a gentle, firm, insistent, inexorable pressure, the same pressure I later perceived in the words, the tone, of hypnotists, of animal tamers . . .

(Nathalie Sarraute 1984: 5)

On a fall day
the air
turned the leaves stumbled
before Christmas and
a pinecone stopped in mid-air
I am remembering forward

As we take . . . a general view of the wonderful stream of our consciousness, what strikes us first is the different pace of its parts. Like a bird's life, it seems to be made of an alternation of flights and perchings. The resting places are usually occupied by sensorial imaginations of some sort, whose peculiarity is that they can be held before the mind for an indefinite time, and contemplated without changing; the places of flight are filled with thoughts of relations, static or dynamic, that for the most part obtain between the matters contemplated in the periods of comparative rest . . .

(William James 1981: 136)

It rained often while I was a boy. I sat on the verandah and watched the rain fall into the cabbage patch. How important the verandah is to me, I would think. The rain falls without beginning or end. As it falls, time and space become mixed and entwined, until no distinction remains between the two. And then I too deteriorate from the center, like rotting cabbage. My heart was always racing like a dog's, "thump, thump, thump" it would pound. I was possessed by the thought that if I didn't break the world apart, if I left it alone, somehow disaster would strike. I paced around and around and around. Hail would fall, and it would make no difference to me. So various things went on like this, events that occurred and those that didn't. They were all there. When I think of them I get carried away by the image of myself in grammar school, pattering down the long corridors like a sperm.

Mark holds a small artificial Christmas tree flocked with fake snow. He faces Matthew and they walk into the performance space from opposite sides. Karen, holding a speaker, walks between Mark and Matthew. Mark begins turning in circles holding the Christmas tree. Karen circles Mark. The sounds of children's voices playing outside on a fall afternoon come out of the small speaker. In the distance, a piano is heard.

Though I don't let anyone see, tears pour down my face when I recall my youth.

A hole Adrian Heathfield (2001: 19)

One can think of Goat Island's work as a kind of physical testimony, but one that side-steps and comments on the foundations and pitfalls of contemporary testimonial culture; the belief that we can return through a cathartic telling to an authoritative version of a traumatic event, the belief that in this telling we might arrive at an essential or truthful version of our selves. . . . In Goat Island's work this final truth remains forever inaccessible. This is the hole that takes the name of "earthquake" in *It's an Earthquake in My Heart*. And Goat Island are at pains to point out that earthquake is just a word for it, like "rain" or "broccoli," or whatever word you choose. Earthquake is a good name, but the hole itself remains unspeakable. Their silence enables *you* to bring an idea to fill *their* hole. Perhaps your hole is an actual earthquake, or a forgotten event, a lost love, or a car crash; you can rest assured it will be welcomed here.

Coincidences Steve Bottoms

Like many people, I can vividly recall watching the events of Tuesday September 11, 2001, unfold "live" on television. What I recall most clearly is the sense of utter seizure in the normally uninterrupted flow of TV images. The terrorists had neglected to give the media advance warning. The cameras weren't ready. At first, all the stations seemed able to show us was the same shot—taken from some way uptown—of an airplane coming from right of shot and disappearing "behind" one of the World Trade Center towers. Then a burst of flame from the other side of the tower. We watched this same shot again, and again, and again. Like the evidence of trauma in the system itself. In between, we cut to ostensibly live images of the towers burning, while the crawl at the bottom of the screen told us that both had collapsed. Cut again to Washington and long, empty shots of the sky from the White House roof, as we waited expectantly for something else to happen that never did.

Within days, of course (hours?), a complete televisual narrative of the attacks had been constructed from footage taken from the many cameras, public and private, that had, after all, been in the vicinity. Normal service had resumed. The interruption had not occurred. The events of September 11 were summarized, narrativized (heroes here, villains there), and instantly assigned to history as a movie now ended. Title: 9/11. Three digits to hide a hole behind. We waited for the sequel: *The Empire Strikes Back*.

The following week, September 20, I found myself in Bristol for the British premiere of Goat Island's *It's an Earthquake in My Heart*. Here, in a performance completed months before the previous week's events, there was nowhere to hide the hole. It was not simply a matter of the eerie coincidences: "Part 1, Tuesday morning," and a scene apparently taking place in an office building; "Part 3, Tuesday evening," in the shellshocked aftermath of some unnameable disaster. Nor was it just the unnerving way in which Part 1's calm sense of quiet routine was shadowed throughout by intimations of crisis—Karen's hand repeatedly tracing the meandering fall of a leaf from sky to ground; a piercing blare of car horns; Bryan's circular Hijikata monologue suddenly punctuated by new lines: "A noise came from the sky." All of this somehow laid the groundwork for what really got to me. "Part 2: 53 years earlier." A total displacement in time; a traumatic timeslip from the unutterable moment itself. The previously markedly verbal performance suddenly overcome by acres of mute silence, dreamlike intimations of some lost era of childhood innocence, and then a piece of muted brass music (somehow, in the context, seeming almost unbearably poignant), and bursts of strange, catatonically repetitive movement. Matthew tearing back and forth, slapping his foot at each turn. Karen, motionless with head to the floor, both legs jutting like a steeple into the air. Mark and Bryan running, jumping, diving. Then, Bryan and Karen swapping role and gender as they change into dripping wet clothing to become ghosts of each other. Part 2: A great, big performative hole. For me, emotionally, just about everything fell into it.

Eighteen months later, seeing *Earthquake* again in Glasgow in March 2003: the Anglo-American invasion of Iraq imminent. Suddenly, Part 3 rushes into fresh relief; the aftermath of the disaster; a fragmented landscape of strategies for coping. A radio host ranting; bursts of old-time hymn-singing; advertising rhetoric playing on fears

13 *It's an Earthquake in My Heart.*
Photograph by Rebecca Groves. Mousonturm, Frankfurt, Germany, 2001. Pictured left to right: Bryan Saner, Karen Christopher, Mark Jeffery, Matthew Goulish

for the future; calls to patriotic unity—"Are we brave? Are we true? Have we the national color?" (Gertrude Stein). And throughout, a punishing sense of the avoidance of the real trauma; the refusal to *take time* to mourn. Matthew repeatedly, bruisingly forcing Mark back down to the ground as he tries to stand (stay dead! No ghosts!); then repeatedly propping Karen up as she begins to topple (no time for weakness!). And the final, haunting lines: Matthew turning out to be a ghost himself, enunciating words adapted from Hal Hartley's 1998 film *Book of Life* as if speaking up (in a tone of faint irritation) for the forgotten dead.

Did they remember who we were?
Did they remember what we said?
Maybe somebody else came along and said pretty much the same thing.
Did anybody notice?

Did we have to go to work every morning?
What kind of cars did we drive?
What sort of houses did we live in? . . .
Did we have parents?
Did we mean well?
Did we think life was sacred?
Did it matter?

Do we matter?

This is all, of course, a very specific interpretation of highly allusive material, in relation to specific historical events. "That whole tour that we did with *Earthquake* in the fall of 2001 was so hung over by September 11 that it predetermined a lot of how people looked at it," Karen Christopher notes: "With the benefit of time, I think it's open to a lot more readings" (Christopher and Saner 2003). This is unquestionably the case, and yet for me the performances I saw remain indissolubly linked to the moments I saw them in, and I'm not so sure that this is a problem. In opening up real time and space for meditation on a catastrophe unhealed, *It's an Earthquake in My Heart* was the only truly meaningful, empowering theatrical response I saw to the post-9/11 crisis. And though it was never intended to *be* a response to that crisis, what it did consciously reflect on was the theft of time in order to manufacture fear in the name of security. As Matthew asks of an imaginary sales seminar in the performance's very first line (adapted from Harun Farocki's 1990 film *How to Live in the German Federal Republic*):

What would your family do if you did not come home last night?

There's a time warp in the very sentence, a projecting into the future of a past event that has not occurred. This, the dialogue tells us, is so as not to make the client unduly anxious: don't say "if you didn't come home tonight" (suggesting, say, an imminent car crash); say "last night" (because you know you *did* get home). And yet, paradoxically:

Let us articulate clearly, what it is we wish to take from the client. Yes.
Fear?
Exactly.

The client must live in perpetual fear of the future, by being kept hostage to an erased past that didn't really happen. Past trauma is past. We must act to protect ourselves now. Last night was only a comedy.

Remember we are in America, where art never fits, where we copy to disappear, to not die of forgetting.

(Matthew Goulish, Goat Island 2001a: 12)

If *Earthquake* deals, presciently, with the immediate aftermath of a disaster—the debris in the storm's wake—it seemed logical enough that the company's next piece should address the question of how to begin to repair. The conclusion they came to seems to have been that one must first expose the damage rather than simply covering it over—just as Paul Celan's attempts to "repair" the German language after World War II necessitated, for him, an exposure of that language as broken, fragmented, shattered; a weaving together of those shards into stuttering poetry.

So too, the urge to remember, to memorialize, makes *When will the September roses bloom?* Goat Island's most consciously "difficult" work to date; with time experienced as a raw nerve, an acute emptiness, a series of gaps in the performance where "nothing" happens. Except, of course, that nothing never happens.

Like with my standing on one leg for so long in this new piece, for the duration of 377 seconds. The leg image is from the Quay Brothers' movie Institute Benjamenta [1995], *and this idea of a figure practising attentiveness in his time off. So when I do it, I'm really attempting to project a sense of total focus: "I must practice; do not waste time." For me, that's a very intimate moment in performance. There's no other action that's distracting, and yet at the same time there's a lot of action going on in that stillness. I think there's often a lot of focus on my face, for instance. Physically I always respond to being watched in that sequence, because I always shake in performance, whereas I don't shake in rehearsal. My body responds to it, involuntarily. There's a space in me that gets filled up with other people.*

(Litó Walkey 2003)

As John Cage discovered in his search for total silence, the very *least* you can hear is the blood pumping inside your own head. Life goes on—until it stops: the most elementary of ecological principles. And every moment in a life is already imbued with the residue of the moment preceding it, and the spectre of the moment to come—just as the Fibonacci sequence of numbers that is embedded in the time structure of *September roses* gathers up its past into its spiralling future: 1, 2, 3, 5, 8, 13, 21, 34, 55, 89, 144, 233, 377. Each step forward also a faltering step back. *You get bigger as you go*, sings Bruce Cockburn: *Bales of memory like boats in tow.**

Stuttering Matthew Goulish (2004a: np)

A stutter is a moment that overflows. It arrests itself in its overflow, its quality of being too much. The arrest makes time itself stutter—move forward haltingly, if at all—and thus become apparent. Bryan stutters when addressing the audience. Stuttering movements interrupt the flow of the dances.

Wann,
wann blühen, wann
wann blühen . . . ja sie, die September-
rosen?

(Celan, in Cixous 1998: 64)

The stutter makes progress impossible. It replaces forward movement with crystalline rotation.

* Bruce Cockburn, "You Get Bigger as You Go," from the album *Humans* (Sony, 1992 [1980]).

Silence is a memorial Karen Christopher (2005)

At the beginning of our performance *When will the September roses bloom? Last night was only a comedy*, no sooner do we start the action than Bryan Saner enters to announce that we are missing the beginning. This announcement is followed by 55 seconds of silence in which those of us on stage wait motionless for the time to pass.

As part of our effort to approach the idea of repair, *September roses* attempts to perform incompleteness, to force a kind of fracture that does not automatically heal itself. Goat Island performances have always played with time and perception, but whereas in past pieces we may have done this by using repetition and duration of action, in *September roses* we are using empty space, silence, and dislocation. Our task is to make clear that irreversible rupture has taken place. And yet our theatre is not a theatre that dramatizes rupture. Rather, it examines states or conditions that are the evidence of this rupture. By this I mean we are not going to show you the way it was rent, only the evidence of that rending.

If we are in a state of disrepair, then something must be missing. Missingness equals loss and in turn equals mourning. We stop everything to absorb the loss. A moment of silence. Two minutes of silence. Let us observe a period of silence for our fallen brothers, for the murdered girls, for the countless millions who have suffered. Silence is a prayer. An offering. A gift. But also: because words cannot express my anguish, because I am at a loss for words, because I can't think, because it demonstrates the void I feel, because it is a sacrifice.

There is a healing quality to silence—especially group silence performed willingly. Why then is it a provocation in performance?

A book can present a blank page. A film can freeze on a single frame. Music can cease suddenly. But it must be impossible for bodies in front of an audience to stop time or to alter it or to stop the forward motion of the piece before it has come to its conclusion and the performers have left the space. Yet with the participation of the audience we make this attempt. In a work-in-progress performance in Bristol, England, there were several missing scenes. In the moments in which we stood still without moving or speaking the audience began to feel an assortment of altered states. In the post-show discussions, some people expressed discomfort with the pauses in action. They were holes in the performance, a breach of etiquette, a social gaff, maybe even an amateurish inadequacy. Because it was a work-in-progress some people thought that the blank spots were temporary. Others described their feelings about the holes or voids in the performance in terms of visceral experience, as something they had fallen into. For those who were paying close attention without blinking, the empty moments became the blank page on which they projected a kind of mental afterimage.

Human beings hear echoes. We see absences. It seems that we are always striving toward wholeness. A mending process begins the moment our skin is broken, as an automatic process of the body. It does not require thought. The brain/eye duet that produces images where they are not is what allows the still pictures of the cinema to appear to move, and allows us to miss the space between the stillness that is void. Our nature is to patch the gaps. Our entire organism is working to fill in the voids that we encounter, or to distract us from them, to instill a comfortable sense of continuity.

I met a man who is writing a book about waiting. He says that waiting is the most terrifying thing that we do. He defines waiting as a time when a person is doing nothing at all. You are not truly waiting if you are, for example, in the doctor's office reading a magazine while you wait for an appointment. He says in this case you are reading a magazine. If a person is truly only waiting, he claims, it is a terribly destabilizing existential crisis. We are faced with questions of our own existence and the nature of being if we do not have something to distract our minds from them. Busy hands and busy minds are protection from idle moments in which we might begin to doubt or fear. This is why the doctor's waiting room has magazines.

I'm on stage, waiting. No magazines. I sit still and try to soften my gaze. The tiny hairs on my face are ecstatic. They straighten out from my face and waver in the air around my head. I am not allowed to move: to scratch to twitch to sigh. It's just a piece of time, a duration, a moment of blank. In these moments, doubts creep in, questions, queries, desires: have we lost control of the performance? Yet also in these moments we are being watched more closely than before. Small signs become important, the quivering of the flesh, the pumping of the blood, the rise and fall of breath, the effort to remain still, the impossibility of the attempt, the readability of our faces, our postures, the futility of our intentions, the interconnectedness of people in a room, the multitude of death we represent in the form of our ancestors, the reality of our collective survival after years of struggle.

In 1985, John Cage wrote a piece for piano called *ASLSP*, or *As Slow as Possible*. It was supposed to last twenty minutes or so, but for years musicologists have deliberated over just how slow "as slow as possible" really is. Right now a performance of it is taking place in the German town of Halberstadt that will take 639 years to complete. The performance began on September 5, 2001 and is scheduled to last until 2639. Since the composition begins with a rest, the first year and a half of the performance was in silence. The first chord began to sound on February 2, 2003. On July 5, 2004 two more notes were added. An organ was specially made for this performance and the keys are held down by weights. The John Cage Organ Foundation agreed on the figure of 639 years to correspond with the number of years since the construction of Germany's first single-block organ.

14 *When will the September roses bloom? Last night was only a comedy.*
Photograph by Ivana Vucic and T. J. Kacunic. Kampnagel, Hamburg, Germany, 2004. Pictured left to right: Mark Jeffery, Matthew Goulish, Bryan Saner, Karen Christopher

The performance has been presented as the ultimate antidote to a fast-paced world. As organizer, Michael Betzle, has explained: "The long period of time is supposed to form a contrast to the breathless pace of change in the modern-day world." He also said: "I am 57 years old. I have to accept the distinct possibility that I shall die before the concert is over."

Being in Waiting Sara Jane Bailes (2004: np)

Performance grants us the permission to build not only death into the work of life, but to develop a poetics that acknowledges death's presence in all things and then hovers around it, making room, making time. . . . Performance is the articulation of time through space, [and in] Goat Island's work especially, the orientation of each moment's precise articulation depends upon and even calls attention to these two coordinates. During one of several Fibonacci sections in *September roses*, all five performers are huddled in a spiral, rocking, each independently, slowly, unevenly, intently. Time is the thing I am watching though I am not aware of it, only because it does not declare itself visibly. I pay attention to space, with or without bodies moving through it. I watch emptiness. I watch bodies. Yet even as it is willing to depend upon these two, Goat Island's work seems to want to resist the constraints time and space suggest, to loop themselves and us out of this assumed imposition just enough that we might *sense* those operatives at work (*now! here!*), and know how to perform small impossible feats within them, perhaps long after in our own lives. . . . Through performance we can understand how to resituate, or create intimate exchanges that last seconds or hours and walk away from them unhurt. We can become exhausted and recover, make time sensible through repetition and cessation, compose images of repair in thin air, dig deep, extend a hand, describe the way vision occurs, interrupt, change direction, dance impossibly, remember through our fingertips. We can build what [Gaston] Bachelard calls *felicitous space.*

I am moved along by the audible and the unheard; the broken, and the murmuring effort to mend. *When will the September roses bloom?* is on one level an enquiry into the effects of trauma—that peculiarly a-chronological event that instills in the individual the often devastating awareness of a missing (but unforgettable) memory, a memory that can involuntarily prey upon the subject—and an exploration of the generative human instinct to repair that lies deep within us. Simone Weil says, *Make it so that time is a circle and not a line.* Imagine what existence would become if we lived in a circle of time. Would we still say that night follows day?

The closing dialogue of *How Dear to Me the Hour When Daylight Dies*, adapted from Akira Kurosawa's *Dreams* (1990):

MR MEMORY: Private Noguchi. . . .

NOGUCHI: Captain, is it true? Was I really killed? I—I can't believe I'm really dead. I went home. I ate the special cakes my mother made for me. I remember it well.

MR MEMORY: You told me that before. You were shot. You fainted. Then you woke up. I was tending you, and you told me that story. It was a dream. You dreamed it while you were unconscious. It was so strong, I still remember it. But after five minutes, you died. You really died.

NOGUCHI: I see. But my parents . . . don't believe I'm dead. (*pointing to a far away light.*) That's my home. My mother and father are there . . . still waiting for me.

MR MEMORY: But it's a fact. You died. I'm so sorry, but you died. You're really dead. You died in my arms. . . . I understand how you must feel. Nevertheless, you were all annihilated. I'm sorry. . . . I sent you out to die. . . .

. . . I have only one more thing to say. It's important, but I'll try to be quick. As I look at you, I fear that the entire world is turning into stone. Now. Now is an unhappy time for the dead. But returning to the world like this proves nothing. A time will come. A time of wisdom. When the dead will be happy. Please, believe me. Go back. The day begins at dusk.

15 *When will the September roses bloom? Last night was only a comedy.*

Photograph by Ivana Vucic and T. J. Kacunic. Kampnagel, Hamburg, Germany, 2004. Pictured left to right: Mark Jeffery, Bryan Saner, Litó Walkey, Matthew Goulish, Karen Christopher

B2. PROCESS

2.1 Environment

2.2 Response

2.3 Body

2.4 Time

B2.1 ENVIRONMENT

A Letter to the Company Lin Hixson (January 2002)*

To my bosses, whose names are, in alphabetical order—Bryan, CJ, Karen, Litó, Mark and Matthew, on a first day of first days to come.

Four definitions from *A First Book of First Definitions*:

A watch is to hear it tick.
A lap is so you don't get crumbs on the floor.
A face is something to have on the front of your head.
A dream is to look at the night and see things.

(Krauss 1989: np)

You see time is passing. A watch is to hear it tick. And it is passing into first-ness. But before we go, I'd like to take some things from last-ness. Last, like being at the end of the line, say the one that started with *How Dear to Me the Hour When Daylight Dies* and ended with *It's an Earthquake in My Heart*,** and last, like a continuation, a lastingness we take along with us like the crumbs on our lap.

Which is all to say the following: I have notes that I will carry along like the face on the front of my head which you bosses have taught me.

The proof of creation is laughter.
To hear the sound of a bell struck off-center takes time and patience.
As we know how we know, we know ourselves.

---

* The date marks the outset of work on what was to become *When will the September roses bloom? Last night was only a comedy*.

** This reference is to a trilogy of works (the two cited and *The Sea & Poison*) co-created and performed by the foursome of Christopher, Goulish, Jeffery and Saner. At this stage in the company's evolution, it was felt that fresh input was required, prompting the invitation to Litó Walkey to join the group as a fifth performer.

The act of creation is not to fall back on childhood but to enter into it.
Our work does not coerce. It overreaches.
It oversteps, leaving space for others.

And when in rehearsal you run across the floor, throw your hand to the side and I cry, it is because I perceive the exactitude of what is happening independently of what is being expressed.

"Economics emphasizes competition, expansion, and domination; ecology emphasizes cooperation, conservation, and partnership" (Capra 1996: 301).
I like to think of Goat Island in relation to sustainability, but I need to look up the definition of conserve: "To protect from loss or depletion; preserve; to use carefully or sparingly."

We are fragile.
Speech breaks lives, creates enemies, and starts wars or
Speech returns life, hangs icicles from the edge of the nose, puts a child to sleep.
Actions break lives, create enemies, and start wars or
Actions hold lives, glimpse lightning and rub an old man's ears.

There is too much sorrow in the world.
Susan Howe has said, "Poetry is redemption from pessimism" (1985: 138).
Let's put our minds to it.

Pastoral Mark Jeffery (2000)

This one is during the summertime, just before the haymaking season, where John Deere tractors with mowers shave layers of grass from meadows. Harvest time draws near, hedgerows begin to bear their fruits of berries, twisted trees are heavy loaded with damson and sloes.

A departure in memory, spending time outdoors with five elder goats, creating birds' nests out of leftover grass cuttings and twigs—enticing pigeons, sparrows and finches to lay their eggs. One afternoon we took a Sunday drive to Dovedale, a National Park tourist spot in Derbyshire. There are stepping stones here, where people line up to cross the river, almost as if they are completing a crude theme-park ride every time they walk over the stones. Below, the water rushes past open toes: we carefully walk over the fifteen or so stones, tiptoeing from one side to the other.

Later the same afternoon we walked across two fields, over a stile, through a hedgerow and around the girth of an old oak tree. We finally reached a brook, a tributary leading into the river. This was a shallow part of the brook, but its width from one clay edge to the other clay edge was too wide to jump over. On the other side, a field filled with wild grasses and flowers ready to be picked. The middle elder goat instructed us what needed to happen. Large rocks were carefully placed one by one into the water, creating a pathway. A line for all six of us to negotiate.

In Chicago, in rehearsals, we meet three times a week for three hours each meeting. Here we exchange ideas in all weather seasons and respond to ideas given to us. A structure of living, of meeting three times a week, becomes engrained and gives us focus. We are not doing anything radical, and yet living within a hyper-capitalist world where structure and value are seen as individual commodities, we are making investments towards a non-capital market or language.

It seems as if once a structure is set, that once a sense of stability and pattern is established, that creativity within seeing and listening can begin. Where there appears to be an ever-increasing demand towards productivity, towards delivering agendas, we choose instead to exchange ideas over a long period of time—as seasons come and go, as plastic is tacked on and off our rehearsal room windows each winter to try and keep some sort of insulation and warmth. Through the slowness our work begins, of trying to understand and not understand what is around us.

Who are we? Lin Hixson (1995: 22, 1990: 18–19)

In 1979–1980 I attended graduate school at Otis Art Institute in Los Angeles. During my studies in the visual arts (which initially excluded performance), my instructors regularly asked me the question "Who are you?" (singular). This question presented the system used to shape my own identity as an artist. By examining it, I developed my own particular style and conceptual outlook and found the unique features of my work which differentiated me from others. Once I discovered these qualities, they were emphasized and honed. Through this education I gained a deeper understanding of my concerns and how I approached them creatively. However, a problem arose with the further definition of this path as my entrance into the artworld and my only method of artmaking. Discovering the particular genius within, articulating that creative talent, and marketing it in the commercial gallery system delineated the model for my success. This I found difficult in its exclusiveness and its limited notion of the artist.

At the same time, Los Angeles contained a vital, innovative performance community with the feminist performance art movement at its center. This movement problematized the solitary genius, a concept which dominated art history. In this sphere, artists posed a different question. Instead of examining oneself individually, the opposite vantage point prevailed. "Who are we?" was the question. By seeing oneself as part of a social construct, and by finding the collective conditions one shares with others, one comes to understand oneself as an individual. Many of these

16 Lin Hixson in conversation with the audience at a work-in-progress performance/discussion for *The Sea & Poison*, Wellington Avenue Church gymnasium, Chicago, 1998 (with Matthew Goulish to the left and Mark Jeffery to the right).
Photograph by Nathan Mandell

feminist artists collaborated to make performance work in opposition to the solitary genius image, considering collaboration to be a political act. The Waitresses, the Feminist Art Workers, Sisters of Survival, Suzanne Lacy, Leslie Labowitz, and Mother Art provided alternative ways for me to proceed with a form, performance, that was independent of the commercial gallery system. I also studied with Rachel Rosenthal, who taught me the process of using one's own experience as a way of formulating political analysis, by exposing the hidden and ignored and connecting it to the larger, public sphere.

I moved to Chicago to begin working with Goat Island, and in making our first piece together—*Soldier, Child, Tortured Man*—we had to create our own minute society. I was not conscious of this at the time, but looking back, I can see the societal structure we set up with its specific working agreements, language, ideals, and as a reaction, troubles. We tried to address and respect every idea brought into the group, but it was understood that once the idea was being explored by the group, it would change and no longer be "yours."

It was decided early on that each member of the group would make monthly contributions to a company account. This allowed us to produce the piece initially, keeping artistic control over it and helping us to understand all levels of production. We were also interested in performing in non-theatrical sites and finding a space to work within the community, where our rental money supported progressive projects. We found this at the Wellington Avenue Church in Chicago, which houses a homeless shelter, the Gay and Lesbian Task Force, and an affordable childcare center.

I feel it is important to be an activist in life in order to stay active in one's work. It is not a matter of doing "political work." It is a matter of internalizing concerns beyond one's own social sphere. When one digests the connection of his/her life with the lives of other people, whether it be political, cultural, economic, environmental, or spiritual, this knowledge in turn creates an art that is grounded in the personal and speaks out in the world. We begin each new collaborative work with our own particular experiences and continue working until relationships are forged with events and ideas outside ourselves.

Work Bryan Saner (1998)

Probably the greatest political statement that Goat Island makes is that it's a collaborative group. More than once I have come to rehearsals feeling inadequate with my contribution; in an uncertain, tentative and un-creative state; and still a small fragment of a poorly articulated idea is developed to its highest possible level. This is a group that appreciates the terrible fears humans experience in this life: the fragility of our bodies, the vulnerability of our confidence, the difficulty of our relationships and a dozen other burdens to be carried. This is a group that knows that collaboration is hard work.

I want to talk about work. I want to talk about what it is like to do this kind of performance theater work in the United States today and what we do for money. Except for the few exceptions, the work we make does not pay our rent or feed and clothe us. So we supplement our incomes and consequently divide our focus with other, paid work. When we have a chance to work full-time on our performances, we are either away from our homes working in other countries that do offer support for our work, or we are paying ourselves with United States money given to us through grants from local and federal governmental agencies, or through foundations that fund the arts. Those are diminishing sources and the application process consumes large amounts of our time. There seems to be an effort on the part of the US government to suppress creative thought and expression by cutting funding for the arts, while the military budget still increases even when our country is "at peace." Continuing to make our art in the shadow of these budget cuts by keeping our day jobs is for us a form of social and political protest. It positions us in solidarity with working people.

All of the members in Goat Island have day jobs. Most of us teach, or work professionally in the arts. I work as a carpenter. I have a small business making furniture and remodeling residential kitchens and baths. Some days I'm rehearsing or performing, some days I'm making furniture or demolishing a wall and scooping up plaster rubble out of a corner on my hands and knees. One of the hardest things about working this way is believing in myself. Because it's tempting to think that one kind of work is more important than another. When I have a healthy attitude (and it takes daily maintenance to stay healthy) I see artists' work as a holistic endeavor. The work I do to make money is a vital part of this goal. The idea for me is to find meaning and joy in life, to discover from day to day what my work is going to be.

Three things that I think happen in Goat Island to keep our heads above water:

1 We reject the thought that if an art or performance work is not commercially viable (i.e. not viable according to existing economic assumptions about buying and selling) then it is not important.
2 We try to maintain a slower paced time-line for our production. We take two years to make a performance. This allows us to do our work to make money and, perhaps more importantly, allows us time to listen to the work and develop the layers.
3 We collaborate. Not only in our performance work, but also in encouraging each other in the work we do for money. It's important to find meaningful day jobs, and it's important to keep a healthy attitude about them.

Like anything that is worth doing, this work can become unbearably difficult. At times I have wanted simply to quit; give up. There are many small companies like ours in the US that have quit. I don't know how or why but some days I have courage and some days I don't. I do know that often my courage comes from the other members of Goat Island, because they recognize the struggle, they recognize many different types of intelligence and skills and the importance of doing the money work. We encourage each other to pursue that task with dignity. I believe that the work Goat Island is doing right now is going to keep the world from destroying itself.

As a company, we are very insignificant. People know of us a little in Europe, but hardly at all in the US. Practically speaking, we've performed in Los Angeles, San Diego, San Francisco, Oregon, New York and Minneapolis. And Chicago, of course. But where else in the United States? It's nothing; there really is no money. We could go to more places if we could go for free, but we can't really afford that, we're all poor people. What's happened with reductions in funding is not that the art isn't happening, but that people aren't seeing it, because it isn't travelling. So work is very, very localized. The very idea is absurd, really—of trying to position ourselves within a cultural context; of making this kind of politicized performance work; to think that we can make a difference by doing projects like this for these very, very few people. It's an absurd gesture, but absurdly, we keep on doing it.

(Goat Island 1999b: 82)

Economy/ecology Karen Christopher

Ecology: Relating to or characterized by the interdependence of organisms.

Traditional theatre usually follows an economically oriented model: it begins a project with a blueprint of the final version and measures success as fulfilling that plan exactly. An economic system works to fulfill an initial strategy that has forecast a desired outcome. Conversely, Goat Island's approach might be seen as more ecologically oriented, in that we are out to discover something we can't imagine at the point from which we start. We begin working toward a solution to a problem, task, or question—"How do you make a repair?"—but we don't know what the solution is. Instead, we are looking to discover as many solutions as we can find. We identify a sustainable working method, one that encourages proliferation and self-nourishment and we watch where it takes us. We find a growth pattern and follow it.

An eco-system requires complexity: it benefits from the interdependence of creatures and minerals and soil and air and water. By contrast, the cultivation of mono-crops requires a rigid controlling hand. Pests must be removed with poison. Fertilization and irrigation are also tightly regimented. Short-term economic requirements take precedence: a high percentage of seed is expected to bear fruit within a limited time frame. When an eco-system is subjected to the dominance of one entity in this way, it becomes unsustainable in the long run, because the habitat is starved of the various interconnected services that the different elements of a complex eco-system provide.

I see all this as similar to those theatrical contexts in which we might come to an early rehearsal of a new piece, and be confronted by a director who tells us exactly what we are going to do, and by what deadline, and then single-mindedly sets about achieving that goal. In the long run, performers working in this kind of system might well become jaded and worn out. In Goat Island's working process, we try to ensure that the elements and ideas that come in over the course of a long performance-making period are as interconnected as the elements in a complex eco-system. Such a system is not dominated by one element or another but includes different kinds of plants, insects, and animals who all follow their own natures while playing a part in the sustenance of an environment that thrives precisely because of its diversity. In much the same way, we attempt to work within a non-hierarchical structure, and to allow multiple voices and multiple meanings to emerge simultaneously, with each participant sharing control of the outcome. The material we contribute to rehearsals will not all play a part in the eventual performance work, but the process of turning it over is essential, as we cast about looking for the pieces of our performance. Of course, we could start with a specific goal in mind and go to the library to look up and study the topic of our thought. Alternatively, we can step out of the room and walk in any direction and let the street lead us somewhere. We can take cues from observation, from doing something. Goat Island attempts to begin with activity, rather than talking. Action or activity can be a way of coming to thought from a point not of thinking but of doing. The thought surprises us from within the action rather than coming first to inform or create the action. The results seem, for want of a better word, organic.

In their book *Cradle to Cradle*, William McDonough and Michael Braungart tell the story of a community forbidden from planting cherry trees in public land, because the local authority complains that they will drop a mess of debris upon the walkways of the neighborhood (2002: 85). The cherry tree is not a tidy or efficient tree. It creates hundreds of buds and flowers which may never end up seeding a new cherry tree. In the same way, through our working process, we generate much more material than we will actually make use of in the end. Rehearsals can seem a little aimless at times, and we can feel lost in the mire of it all, until we reach a point of breakthrough. To the economically minded it might look like a lot of wasted time. But in taking our time, we have created an abundance of material that feeds the development process, lends itself toward the proliferation of further ideas, and, equally important, is pleasurable to those who engage with it—just as the cherry tree's blossom brings color to its surroundings. It takes faith in the process to keep moving forward without always understanding what the next step will be. Eventually the work begins to make itself; the accumulation of material begins to suggest certain directions. This method is not at all efficient in an economic sense, and yet no part of it is superfluous.

If nature adhered to the human model of efficiency, there would be fewer cherry blossoms, and fewer nutrients. Fewer trees, less oxygen, and less clean water. Fewer songbirds. Less diversity, less creativity, and delight. The idea of nature being more efficient, dematerializing, or even not "littering" (imagine zero waste or zero emissions from nature!) is preposterous. The marvellous thing about effective systems is that one wants more of them, not less.

(McDonough and Braungart 2002: 76–77)

* Text adapted from the Busby Berkeley movie *42nd Street*, dir. Lloyd Bacon (1933).

Many-Headed Lin Hixson (1999)

1 *Backdrop*

One story goes like this: Avalokiteshvara emptied himself of himself. With this action, he crossed the final threshold and stood at the entrance of nirvana, that boundless state beyond worldly fears and frustrations. About to enter, he was interrupted by a cacophony of sounds. The painful outcries of the world surrounded him and overflowed his intention to proceed. He vowed he would not enter nirvana until all others had crossed before him. His head burst into eleven heads all looking in different directions. His arms multiplied into a thousand arms for ceaseless activity. Once connecting with others, Avalokiteshvara multiplied.

I have been in the performance group Goat Island since its inception in 1986. I am the director in the group. I find the word collaboration inadequate to describe what we do, but then I would find any single word problematic. In fact, I can't even start with words to describe my experience in Goat Island. I can begin with a physical sensation; my head enlarging to six heads; my legs jumping up and down with twelve feet; my body restricted by five other bodies.

While researching for our sixth performance work, *The Sea & Poison*, Karen gave us a text which we read, about the 1904 Edison Company film, *Deaf-Mute Girl Reciting the Star-Spangled Banner*. In the film, a woman clothed in a simple country dress performs elaborate hand and arm movements against a cloth backdrop (an oversized American flag). The title of the film lets the viewer know that the woman is in fact using her body to sing—or rather, to sign—the national anthem.

At another early rehearsal for the piece, Bryan lays down a white sheet, kisses a pile of dirt, and is rolled up in the sheet by others. When he is pulled out, the sheet is held up behind him as a backdrop, like the backdrop behind the singing woman. Later, two green velvet curtains are found at a flea market in Totnes, Devon, while we are in residence at Dartington College of Arts. We replace the sheet. One white sheet grows into two velvet curtains. Because they are curtains, we hold them up like curtains. Bryan is rolled up, this time in two cloths, and unrolled by two performers, spinning quickly until he lies still in a small pile of dirt framed by a green square of velvet curtains held up by two performers.

Mark goes to Home Depot months later in Chicago. At this point in the process, we are discussing artificiality and nationalism. AstroTurf is on sale. He buys a roll because it looks like imitation grass. Once getting it to rehearsal, we replace the velvet curtains with AstroTurf and decide we want to make a big flag like the backdrop flag in the Edison film. We cut the turf into four rectangles and the struggle begins. It is difficult for one person to hold up a piece of AstroTurf and even harder to get four people together holding up pieces of AstroTurf flat enough to look like a flag. We put them on the ground the way they are intended to be used and start moving on them. This creates a smaller stage within our designated stage. But the AstroTurf rectangles do not stay flat or together to make this stage when we move on them. We decide to have professionals sew Velcro to the edges of each piece of turf to hold them together. This, in itself, is a test for the group as we attempt to make a sewing pattern showing which edge of Velcro sticks to which edge of Velcro.

The AstroTurf rectangles are sent to be sewn, and in time they are returned to the group with their Velcro edges. We begin to rehearse with them. The piece becomes not about a flag and what it represents, or about making a smaller theatrical world within a larger one, but about Velcro-ing AstroTurf together. We eliminate the Velcro AstroTurf, buy AstroTurf with pre-finished edges, and forget about sticking them together.

Now when Bryan is rolled up early in the performance, it is in two rectangles of green AstroTurf and not two velvet curtains. When he rolls out, he lies in front of a green AstroTurf backdrop held by two performers. Karen bursts through the backdrop, separating the AstroTurf curtains to make a theatrical entrance and identifying the backdrop with the small world of the theatre. Later, the backdrop of two multiplies to three AstroTurfs and becomes a stage within a stage when we lay it on the floor for what we call a school play, a play that moves from letters being read, to hair being cut, to children being born, to a *Hamlet* scene being performed. Finally, at the end of the piece when the AstroTurf is gone, when the little world of the theatre vanishes and the stage is bare, Matthew lies down. A tiny yellow flag is placed in his hands. A patriotic tune gone awry plays loudly over the speakers. Matthew lies still and in this stillness, he sings with his body an anthem.

For me, creating with Goat Island is like chasing a tail, catching it, holding it for a moment, losing it and beginning again in a new location. Only the tails keep multiplying and I, in turn, multiply with them. For I visit places I never imagined. I would never buy AstroTurf on my own. It would not occur to me to roll up in a curtain and spin out of it to start a play. I would not venture into *Hamlet* and Shakespeare alone and I would not think to shrink the image of the woman in a simple country dress to Matthew on the floor with a tiny flag. Only I do create these events. I create them not with my singular self but with my multi-headed and many-armed Goat Island self.

The place of human beings in the world can scarcely be conceived apart from their bodily and imaginative participation in it. The backdrop is a small example of Goat Island's bodily and imaginative participation in the world of making a performance. This multi-bodied movement of chasing, connecting, diverting, and disappearing informs all of our attempts at creating. The resulting performance works are much like the phenomena that physicist David Bohm describes in his book *Wholeness and the Implicate Order*. "All phenomena are to be understood, not as independently and permanently existent, but rather as products that have formed in movement and that will ultimately dissolve back into movement" (1980: 14).

Until the eighteenth century, the word individual was rarely used without explicit relation to the group. "That individuals die, his will ordains; the propagated species still remains," writes Dryden in 1700 (Williams 1983: 163). But all this changed. Sometime during the seventeenth and eighteenth centuries, in logic and mathematics, the individual began to be asserted as the entity from which all other categories, especially collective ones, derived. The medieval individual as a single example of a group, not to be parted as husband and wife, indivisible and unified as in the Trinity, was overtaken by the individual as a fundamental order of being —solitary, personal, and singular.

2 *Bridge*

Another story goes like this: Chang and Eng, the Siamese twins connected at their breastplates by a short, five and one-half inch ligament, were said to be the first to chop down trees by using the "double chop" method. This involves two men hitting a tree trunk alternately with axes. One wields his axe slanting one direction. The second wields his axe slanting the opposite direction. Back and forth the blades hit opposing one another. It is a fast and efficient way of chopping wood. Chang and Eng discovered it out of necessity.

The perfect unanimity and synchronicity of Chang and Eng, in the mid-nineteenth century, amazed their observers. Passengers on the American sailing ship *Sachem*, which brought the Siamese twins to America on their first voyage, relayed how the twins, being chased on deck and running at full speed, glided over an open and deep hatchway. Had either hesitated, leaving the other to move forward or leaving the other to fall behind, they most certainly would both have plunged to their deaths. In the report of the first medical examination of the Siamese twins, Dr Warrren of the Harvard Medical School states:

> The slightest impulse of one to move in any direction is immediately followed by the other, so that they would appear to be influenced by the same wish. This harmony in their movements is not the result of volition excited at the same moment; it is habit, formed by necessity. [Yet] there is no reason to doubt that the intellects of the two are as perfectly distinct as those of any two individuals who might be accidentally confined together.
>
> (Wallace and Wallace 1978: 57–58)

Chang and Eng were distinct persons but bound by more than a ligament. An autopsy, performed on the twins, found their two livers connected by a vascular string. Most likely, they would have died from bleeding had their band been cut.

In Goat Island we were not born together and we have not been confined together accidentally, although at times it feels that way. We made the choice to work together. And having made that choice, we formed habits out of necessity. I learned early, for example, the danger of bringing completed thoughts and intentions into rehearsal. The attachment and preciousness that come from perceiving a movement or a text as mine halted the group process with its inability to let others in and my inability to let things go. We formed a habit out of necessity; bringing in bits of ideas, half-empty movements, fractions of texts, and under-developed schemes. The completion of an idea, of a movement, of a sentence comes from uniting a half-empty fragment with someone else's half-empty fragment. Karen, in rehearsal, makes a fountain out of her mouth by spitting yellow milk into the air. Matthew brings in a text adapted from Richard Edson's poem "The Bridge" (1994: 173). Karen speaks the Edson lines in the completed performance of *The Sea & Poison*. "Dear Mother, guess what? Just now I am at the foot of a bone bridge. I shall be crossing it shortly. . . . I'll write to you from the other side if I can; if not, look for a sign." She takes a drink of water, squirts it into the air while squeezing two plastic orange fish. Water streams out of all three mouths. The Karen-fountain and the Matthew-found-text combine and complete one another. This is our habit of completion, stringing the incomplete with another's incomplete. Perhaps, at times, Chang and Eng reached synchronization in the same way.

The comedy begins with the simplest of our movements, carrying with them every inevitable awkwardness. In putting out my hand to approach a chair, I have creased the sleeve of my jacket, I have scratched the floor, I have dropped the ash from my cigarette. In doing that which I wanted to do, I have done so many things I did not want to do. The act has not been pure for I have left some traces. In wiping out these traces, I have left others. . . . We are thus responsible beyond our intentions.

So states the philosopher Emmanuel Levinas (1996: 4), who argues that we cannot understand human existence without basing it on our fundamental relation to others. He calls this relation, ethics. In writing on the philosopher, James Faulconer says:

For Levinas, the ethical relation is not to be understood as something *I* do. It is not, for example, a matter of generosity. Instead, the other breaks in on, and, thereby, breaks up my otherwise solitary intentions, including any intention to do good. . . . When I intend another person, that person overflows my intention, marking that intention inadequate and, by that, disrupting it as an intention.

(Faulconer 2002: 113)

17 *The Sea & Poison.*
Photograph by Nathan Mandell, Wellington Avenue Church, Chicago, 1998.
Pictured left to right; Mark Jeffery, Matthew Goulish, Karen Christopher, Bryan Saner

Anyone who works in a group knows the frustration of inadvertence or the anger that comes when your aims are challenged. We, in Goat Island, have the objective of making performance works in an agreed atmosphere of trust and support. But the unintentional and intentional sit alongside this desire. Cars break down. People get ill. Children charge into rehearsals when they are scheduled to use the gym at the same time as we are scheduled to rehearse. Someone loses their money-paying job. Someone brings in serious material but we think it's funny. Someone, not in the group, walks through rehearsal and because the atmosphere is so open, suggests changes we should make in the work. Someone has last-night syndrome where they witnessed a line Robert DeNiro said in a movie and now wants us to do it. Someone has a headache. Someone has a heartache. Someone speaks and hurts another unintentionally. Someone speaks and hurts another intentionally.

Thus there is intention, rupture, and overflow. These others are constantly interrupting what I have intended and fill me over the brim with their beings. There is an inevitable awkwardness as my personal and solitary designs adjust to accommodate these changes. It is a rude awakening, at times, for this awakening by the other signifies a responsibility. The banks of my original intention widen and I am accountable with the others for what flows between. I often know not where I begin and where the others end. But perhaps a bridge, over the overflow, offers some perspective.

The German sociologist and philosopher Georg Simmel, in speaking about the bridge, says:

> The bridge symbolizes the extension of the volitional sphere over space. Only for us, the banks of the river are not just apart but separated; if we did not first connect them in our practical thoughts, in our needs and in our fantasy, then the concept of separation would have no meaning.
>
> (Simmel 1997: 171)

Chang and Eng's bridge was a five and one-half inch ligament. The twins sought surgical separation from one another later in their lives. The surgery was never performed for fear of death to both of them if they were parted. Eventually, they died. Chang ailing, and having bouts with alcoholism, went first. Eng died two hours later, from what one doctor characterized as fright.

Being in Goat Island has taught me to persevere when creating with others; to see lines that connect us before seeing the spaces that separate us. Like Chang and Eng, I carry another when I move alone in the group. And when we go together, I go with six heads and twelve feet.

❖❖❖

Date sent: Thurs, 29 Sept 2005 15:19:06
From: Matthew Goulish
Subject: Johnny's new home
To: Goat Island

Hello everyone,

The purpose of this email is to tell you the little I know about Johnny. He is from Colombia, a painter, speaks very little English, and is currently living in the upstairs space of the side room of the Wellington Avenue Church gymnasium. Maybe Bryan can fill in some of the details, but it is my understanding that Rev. Dan Dale has helped bring Johnny here from Colombia and installed him into what was formerly our storage and dressing area. I suspect Dan's involvement means Johnny is a political exile of some sort.

I went to the gym before Venice to pick up program folders, and found our things in total disarray. Slightly panicked, I told Lin who called Bryan who said he would check with Dan about what was going on. We did not have a chance to discuss it again, but now I realize that was the first phase of preparation for Johnny's arrival. I returned to the gym last week to pick up some support materials for the Illinois Arts Council final report, and discovered the lock had been changed on the door between the gym and the back room.

I found Johnny downstairs in the kitchen cooking his lunch. He took me up the back stairs. He apparently has managed to do something unprecedented in the history of Goat Island: arrange all our stored things in an extremely organized and systematic fashion—props, trunks, publications, all of it. The shelves had been brought downstairs and our materials sorted in such a way as to remind me of a large filing cabinet. Maybe Bryan was involved in this move before Venice? In any case, Johnny gave me a tour of the new arrangement. Then he invited me upstairs to what is now his apartment.

He has a bed in the back room, the one I used to change in, and he has divided the large front room into a sitting area and a painting area. He showed me several medium-sized canvasses in a Van Gogh-like style (I noticed two books on Van Gogh on his shelf) "expressing" as he said, the political "violence" in his home country. My favorite was of an emaciated dog in a desert landscape with a human skull on one side and a bullhorn on the other. He also showed me two photographs of a woman, apparently his partner, who is still in Colombia.

He had our rehearsal boom-box on his shelf next to his Van Gogh books, maybe for music to work by. In his sitting area, his chairs were arranged around one of the Astroturfs from *The Sea & Poison*, and in front of his easel sat one of the green camping stools from *Can't Take Johnny to the Funeral*, waiting for him to take his place in it and start painting.

The other, as the philosophers might say, enters our lives as that which we could not foresee, to bring us what we did not know we were lacking. I recommend that we accept whatever inconvenience this arrangement may cause us, and welcome Johnny into our lives, and into his new home.

See you soon,

Matthew

P.S. We will need to get keys to the new lock.

B2.2 RESPONSE

We are wrong to believe that the true and the false can only be brought to bear on solutions, that they begin only with solutions. This prejudice . . . goes back to childhood, to the classroom: It is the school teacher who "poses" the problems; the pupil's task is to discover the solutions. In this way we are kept in a kind of slavery. True freedom lies in a power to decide, to constitute problems for themselves. [As Bergson writes:] "Discovery, or uncovering, has to do with what already exists, actually or virtually; it was therefore certain to happen sooner or later. Invention gives being to what did not exist; it might never have happened."

(Gilles Deleuze, *Bergsonism*, 1991: 15)

Everything we do, we do by invitation.

(CJ Mitchell, Goat Island 2001a: 1, quoting John Cage 1992: liner notes)

A first starting point Matthew Goulish (2000a: 9–10)

We began on Thanksgiving Day, 1986—Lin Hixson, the brothers Timothy McCain and Greg McCain, and I. On that first day, when the four of us met in my apartment on West Caton Street, Wicker Park, Chicago, we did not know we were beginning a performance group or even that we were beginning a performance. We only knew that we were beginning. We agreed that we would share a kind of impossible problem from which we would generate material individually, and then come together: a starting point.

Choose a specific incident from your past. Find a historical event that occurred at approximately the same time.

Create an environment and/or a performance expressing the feeling of the memory in relation to the historical event.

We had no idea where this would lead us, or when it would lead us there. We simply agreed to begin, and then went out for Thanksgiving dinner.

A bed is surrounded by black plastic with a window cut into it. Through the window a man is seen gagged and tied to a chair. Greg McCain reads an accompanying text. It describes his hospitalization with pneumonia in 1968, when he was nine—the trouble he had breathing, a dream of a young girl dying, and the Chicago Eight trial which included the gagging of Bobby Seale. The trial began the same week Greg was hospitalized.

This and other responses to the initial directive provided the structural and conceptual foundation for Soldier, Child, Tortured Man. *Greg becomes the "child"—the witness in the finished piece. He repeatedly rocks up and down, breathing hard almost to the point of hyperventilation.*

(Hixson 1990: 13)

Over the years we began to work many times, directionless except for our starting point.

Describe the last time you had sex.
Create an event of bliss / create an event of terror.
Why were you in pain in such a beautiful place?
Create a shivering homage.
Invent an arrival.
How do you say goodbye?

I feel thankful now for this collection of beginnings. Each one allowed us a kind of simplicity, as though each movement, or cell of movement, were a physical fact. We could align the physical facts with the facts of words, ideas, or music—the simplicity of facts: their selection, expression, and arrangement. There are oceans of facts.

Minor repair Lin Hixson (2002b)

Lipstick smears the upholstery.
Hair plugs the drain.
Tiles break under the bathroom rug.
Water leaks through the wall.
Dust falls down on the blackened church.
Tar hangs on the rain.
Mud soils the tools of the executioner.
Urine flames the wind.
Grease blinds the shaking dog.
Chocolate spots the sky.
With a few essential tools, you can make any minor repair.

1 *Repair*

This is how it happened. I was in Aberystwyth, Wales staying in a physicist's apartment in November, 2001 by the sea. There were nine books on the shelf in the living room. I read from two—a doctoral thesis on solar wind and a British repair manual from the 1970s called *Around the Home.* I particularly liked the instructions in the repair manual on how to re-grip a tennis-racket handle and how to re-face a table-tennis bat. Small acts of repair. Calming the hands in a troubled world. Restoring damage to renewed use. Wiping a stain with a cloth. When I returned to Chicago, I went to the bookstore chains searching for repair manuals. I found few. Today we buy new and discard the old. But in the basement, in Michigan, at my in-laws, I found the 1957 *Better Homes and Gardens Handyman's Book.*

A first directive to begin Goat Island's eighth performance work:

A two part dance.
Part i: Create a foot phrase dance from the following flush tank repair instructions:

- a Lift cover off flush tank and pull upward on float rod.
- b Shut off valve that feeds the water into the tank.
- c To adjust float position, slowly bend float rod.
- d To position float, loosen setscrew, slide collar up or down until water shuts off at the right level on the overflow pipe.

Part ii: Alter Foot Phrase Repair Dance with an Al-jabr Operation.
The word al-jabr appears frequently in Arab mathematical texts. There were two meanings associated with al-jabr. The more common was "restoration," as applied to the operation of adding equal terms to both sides of an equation so as to "restore" a quantity which is subtracted from one side by adding it to the other.

Consider the restorative use of the word "may" by Gertrude Stein, initiated by Alice B. Toklas who, after discovering that Stein's *Stanzas in Meditation* was an encoded love poem to May Bookstaver, insisted Stein "repair" the text by removing the word may. Stein sometimes changed the month of May to another month; she sometimes inserted an n into the word, changing "may" to "many"; and she sometimes changed "may" to "can."

I can I wish I do love none but you.

(Stein 1994: 216)

To describe the early rehearsals of Goat Island, change the month of May to the month of Can and submit it to an al-jabr operation. Subtract four days of impossibility from May and add 96 hours of possibility to Can and we have restored, recovered, repaired, brought under observation again May to equal Can. We can become Lillian Gish in *The Wind*. We can grow geese feet and wipe them in a field. We can do a Fibonacci sequence dance accompanied by James Taylor, the Beach Boys, data taken from plants, heartbeats, applause and laughter, Melt Banana, Howard Skempton, a cuckoo clock. In first rehearsals, everything is possible. But with possibility comes a sibling, impossibility. And as we move with the possible we know we are stepping with its sister.

John Cage said in 1983, "We're now surrounded by very serious problems in society. We tend to think that the situation is hopeless, that it's just impossible to do something that will make everything turn out properly. I think that this music, which is almost impossible, gives an instance of the practicality of the impossible" (Cage 1993: liner notes).

Once we could not imagine: a dirigible; synthetic diamonds; poodle skirts; waterwheels; freezing foods; fascism; novocaine; school prayer; the Nile; a bridge made out of concrete. Today, what was once referred to as impossibility is being redefined as some kind of natural law, something that cannot be changed in any way. "The impossible has, so to speak, lost its rights," says philosopher Alenka Zupancic (2001: 75). Can we lift the stain from the upholstery; scrape the tar from the rain; unplug the drain; and treat the urine in the wind? From the editors of *The Handyman's Book*: "Aside from saving money, working with your hands can keep you calm in a troubled world. . . . You should be warned, though, once you start, you'll never finish" (Meredith 1957: 4).

2 *To act in return*

This is how it happened. I gave each member of the group an alphabet letter from *Orbis Sensualism Pictus*, the first-known alphabet picture book, written in 1658 (see Crain 2000). I said, "Construct a response to the picture for another member in the group to perform."

Rr er er er. The dog grinneth.
Litó constructs a response for Karen to perform.

Hh hah hah hah. The mouth breatheth out.
Matthew constructs a response for Mark to perform.

O ooo. The carter cryeth.
Karen constructs a response for Matthew to perform.

Our process could be described as a series of directives and responses. We curve forward, like whirling dervishes calling back and forth. I produce a directive. The members of the group present responses to the directive—acts in return.

In response to the responses, I produce more directives, combine material into sequences, submit my own performative material, or do some combination of these. The performers, in turn, may present new material in response to the new directives, the old directives, the sequences, or other responses, which serve then, a secondary function, as indirect directives.

Hh hah hah hah. The mouth breatheth out like the wind.
Mark sits in a chair with a large funnel in his mouth.

"I got this start lying in my bed in the log cabin, hearing the wind blow between the criss-crossed logs. The winds in the winter could be ferocious; there would be blizzards, and you couldn't see a hand in front of your face. I tried to come to terms with that at the age of two or three. It wasn't as if I could turn off the wind, like somebody would turn off the radio; when one of those storms came it went on as long as it was going to last. And I found it to be very profound and awesome," says composer LaMonte Young brought to rehearsal by Matthew as an act in return (Schwartz 1996: 16).

Karen bares her teeth. She runs in circles. Round and round. She stares out at me the entire time even as she rounds the corner of the circle, her head turned back, her mouth plastered in a grin. The dog grinneth but I have forgotten the alphabet, the books, the pictures, the directive I gave Litó to make this action for Karen. Deliberately. In order to see what moved in front of me in that moment—say 1:15 on a Saturday afternoon on the thirteenth day of the month of Can—I deliberately forget. The intention of the performer, the source of the gesture, history and meaning, are set aside.

LITO: *Instead of understanding what we're looking at as we go, I'd say with Goat Island there's a level of unconsciousness—things aren't over-explained. If anything, it's unexplained, like for instance why somebody is bringing something in, in response to a particular question or stimulus. They might give you a few reasons, but you don't get into a whole discussion about it. You let that one part that you're bringing in speak for itself, and then let that fire off to another place. Almost like a drop in the sea—it finds its own place. It does have a significance, yet you can almost drop that significance and pretend that it's just arbitrary: you can just say, OK, it's this move, and not get too caught up in "but what is that move doing there?" At the same time, though, we know that the move came from a particular source, and that it does have some meaning, that it isn't just being completely arbitrary. So there's a doubleness there which is interesting, I think.*

(Walkey 2003)

Questions Matthew Goulish (Goat Island 2005b)

Plant a question in a garden; define it without preventing it from flowering. Take it literally; take it allegorically; take it as a preface; take it as a mystery to decode.

Compose responses that do not annihilate the question's delicate ecology; avoid the answer that kills it, and seek the response that disarms and multiplies it. One method is this: let somebody else answer, and from a place of unknowing; namely, the past.

A question does not express a lack, but a creative force: propose, disarm, multiply. This is a form of escape. From what are we escaping? I will leave that as a question.

Research Karen Christopher (1998)

As a starting point for Goat Island's fifth piece, *How Dear to Me the Hour When Daylight Dies*, we assigned ourselves an ordeal. We chose to go together to witness and take part in a pilgrimage up a mountain: Croagh Patrick in Ireland. This pilgrimage is no longer sanctioned by the Pope, but thousands of people undertake this ordeal once a year on the last Sunday in July. There are plenty of people who do it as a secular event, so we felt it was something we could participate in rather than being merely spectators. The process of the pilgrimage is very similar to the process of a Goat Island piece. Participants go through an ordeal in order to break down the everydayness of their lives, to reach a new state of consciousness; to be in that place where hard work has broken down barriers and free thought and association are possible. Or, as many people responded on the mountain when I asked them why they undertook this journey: "for the crack."*

Of course, I can go on a trip and just have a good time. But I can also go on a trip and say I will be collecting sounds. Then all things to do with listening and sound will stand in relief; will catch my attention. And so it was, knowing this as a rule, that five members of Goat Island set out on a journey, a pilgrimage, a research trip, with assignments each to collect a certain kind of information: one of us was collecting texts, one of us was looking at spatial arrangements, I was gathering sounds, and so on. In this way we provided ourselves with filters for the information we came across. Rather than seeing the world as a mass of generalities,

---

* *Crack* [krak] is a word in common usage in Ireland and in some parts of Scotland meaning fun, enjoyment, or good times, often in the context of drinking or music. [www.wikipedia.org]

we looked for specifics. It's a way of focussing, a way of organizing the chaos of reality. But it is important at this stage that we were thinking formally, not thematically. That is, we were not saying, and nor do we ever say, "this is what our piece is going to be about, now gather information about that." Not at the beginning.

Many things which remain hidden in the background pop out when you are looking for something. When I was looking for yellow things for a videotape on yellow, everything turned yellow for a few weeks. Yellow began to perform for me in a way it never had. The other side of this is that the things that pop out at you may not be the things you were looking for. Yet you need a reason to go to the card catalog or the bookshelf, something to look for so that on your way you can find something, something else maybe, something that distracts you, something that you see out of the corner of your eye but that drags your attention to it. Maybe you need something to be distracted from.

I was in a small tea-room at Yeats's grave in Ireland with my tape recorder on. I wondered what the effect taping had on the way I was listening. At this point a bird flew into the tea-room. It flew around the room and then back out. What excites me is these moments of synchronicity that we find: on the trip to Ireland, the flood of sound and information about sound that I experienced made me feel intimately connected to the mass of material out in the world. It was intimately ordered for me and paraded before me to pick and choose from. I felt privileged.

I heard the creaking rope of a rope bridge and the crashing of the ocean waves a hundred feet below.

I heard a thousand stones moved by a hundred feet grinding against each other like the gnashing of monumental teeth against mountainous bones.

I heard a man say, "He's trying to get a bit of punishment for all his wrongdoing."

I saw and heard a man climbing muddy down a rocky mountainside on hands and heels, dragging his bottom along the slippery wet stones. He can no longer walk upright on his feet.

I heard over a loudspeaker: "Lamb of God, take away the sins of the world. Lamb of God, take away the sins of the world."

This material came into the eventual performance piece in different ways and at different stages. Sometimes a bit of information or material doesn't enter the piece directly but as an element that leaves an imprint in our minds. It leads to something else, maybe, or maybe it just keeps us moving while something else has a chance to brew in the backs of our minds or in the collective storm over our heads. The piece reveals itself to us in various ways. What is important is to keep our minds in open and active mode, so that we can see and hear it.

Scavenging Steve Bottoms

Unlike trees or their roots, the rhizome connects any point to any other point, and its traits are not necessarily linked to traits of the same nature; it brings into play very different regimes of signs.

(Deleuze and Guattari 1987: 21)

From the outside, Goat Island's early working process may appear dauntingly amorphous, particularly as regards their appropriation of materials from external sources. Why bring in this text and not that one? Why copy this movement and not another? What happens if the "wrong" selection is made? The group insist, however, that experience has taught them to trust John Cage's precept that "each and every thing in all of time and space is related to each and every other thing in all of time and space" (Cage 1961: 47). Pursuing *any* line of enquiry far enough will render provocative connections between whatever other lines of enquiry are being followed simultaneously, however unrelated they might appear. Unlike Cage, though, Goat Island make no attempt to remove human agency from the creative process, acknowledging that the connections which exist between any two points are often very personal, intuitive ones—lateral, rather than linear. It is here, perhaps, that the "why this and not that?" question finds its answer—or rather, another question: what is the most resonant response for the individual respondent? Subsequently, the appropriated material that survives the ongoing winnowing process will do so because it somehow resonates with others, or connects with yet another brought-in element.

As I have watched Goat Island's workshop participants bring in objects from the streets to construct installations, it has occurred to me to see them and us as scavengers—like seagulls cleaning the beach, or vultures settling over dead, discarded things—devouring the waste, making new use, transforming, digesting, and re-gifting the world with a new twist on old matter.

(Karen Christopher)

Early work on *How Dear to Me the Hour when Daylight Dies* was significantly influenced by a seemingly rather insignificant item discovered in the aftermath of the group's participation in the Croagh Patrick pilgrimage in Ireland. During a short visit to Belfast, Lin Hixson happened upon a postcard depicting a dripping-wet man in a Speedo swimsuit, kneeling before a shrine to Mary. The card bore the caption: "a shivering homage." Struck by this odd conjunction of spirituality and raw physicality, and sensing a link with the pilgrimage experience (the body's suffering as soul's journey?), Hixson used this line as a starting point for two instructions to the company when, on their return to Chicago, they began workshopping the new piece.

First, the performers were asked to begin generating movement sequences in response to the "shivering homage" phrase. Thus Matthew Goulish created a short solo, "a tumbling homage dance," by fusing together two movements appropriated from other performers. The first was a violent stabbing of oneself in the back, taken from Ed Harris's performance in Sam Shepard's play *Simpatico*; the second, a whirling, marionette-like movement performed by Dominique Mercy in Pina Bausch's dance piece *Two Cigarettes in the Dark*. Goulish had seen the Bausch and Shepard pieces on consecutive nights in New York in November 1994, and this was his way of paying homage to the key performers. His creation was then modified further by the group's (mis-)interpretation of it in rehearsals, evolving into what was eventually a key, recurring sequence in the finished piece, the "puppet jump."

Hixson's second, and more open-ended instruction derived from the "shivering homage" postcard was for each performer to assemble found texts or images to create a brief, personalized homage to someone or something of particular personal importance. Again, Goulish provided an early starting point here with his decision to attempt a homage to Wooster Group performer Ron Vawter, who had died from AIDS earlier in 1994.

The "found" quality of our work comes in part from looking at the Wooster Group—at Ron Vawter and Liz LeCompte and what they did, in appropriating existing texts and reworking them performatively. I think also, for me, Kathy Acker has been really important, even though she's working with novels. She talks about plagiarizing texts, but changing them as you're doing it, changing the words you don't like. So there's a combination of your own personal artistic will, and this other thing that you're forcing yourself to use as source material. That really made sense to me.

(Matthew Goulish 1997)

In his quest to memorialize Vawter, Goulish turned to "Mr Memory," a character in Alfred Hitchcock's 1935 film *The Thirty-Nine Steps*, who had long fascinated him (not least because Mr Memory, a real-life performer with the ability to recall thousands of random facts on request, had himself been "appropriated" by Hitchcock). Goulish transcribed a speech sequence from Mr Memory's performance in the film, and created a new performance of the lines using the speed-talking technique that Vawter had famously used in the Wooster Group's *L.S.D. (. . . just the high points . . .)* (1984). He also incorporated the gesture of slowly dabbing his forehead with a handkerchief; a key image from the first half of Vawter's solo performance piece, *Roy Cohn/Jack Smith* (1992).

18 *How Dear to Me the Hour When Daylight Dies.*
Photograph by Nathan Mandell, Wellington Avenue church, Chicago, 1996. Pictured left to right: Mark Jeffery, Matthew Goulish as Mr Memory

The funny thing is that, even before Lin introduced the idea of creating "a shivering homage" as one of our starting points, I was wanting to create an homage to Ron Vawter. I wanted to envisage the kind of work that he might have done if he had not died so young. And at the same time I was thinking about this man Mr Memory, from The Thirty-Nine Steps. *He was a real character, who had created this new "art form" of performative remembering. And so Mr Memory became a vehicle to create an homage to Ron Vawter. This was my only idea. I just didn't have any other idea at that time. Before Lin asked the question, Mr Memory was the answer. But the question is very important—how it's shaped, how it's framed, what parts you use, how you narrow it down. The question does affect the answer.*

(Matthew Goulish 1996)

Thanks to a typical connective leap, Goulish's introduction of *The Thirty-Nine Steps* led to the group becoming interested in the figure of the Master of Ceremonies, who introduces Mr Memory to his audience in the film, and whose words were also appropriated for Bryan Saner. Noting that almost all such performances-within-films seemed to feature a version of this organizing figure, the group began research into the phenomenon of talent shows, looking at everything from tapes of old Ed Sullivan broadcasts to an experimental video piece by Leslie Thornton, *Peggy and Fred* (1987), in which her seven-year-old nephew Fred is filmed spontaneously inventing his own "emcee" performance, with his sister Peggy as the "talent." At one point in the tape, Fred complains to Peggy that "you're talking too fast," an exchange which became an obvious candidate for appropriation, with Saner's emcee addressing Fred's lines to Goulish's Vawter/ Memory hybrid. Meanwhile, yet another avenue of enquiry was opened by Mr Memory's reference—in the portion of the film's text that Goulish had pirated —to Bob Fitzsimmons, the heavyweight boxing champion of 1897. Research by Greg McCain into the real Fitzsimmons revealed that he had been known as "The Fighting Freak," a fact which helped spark a sideways leap from talent show to freak show, thereby leading—eventually—to Karen Christopher's introduction of a voice recording by Mike Walker, once the fattest man in America, who had put himself on display as a freak, as a warning to others not to over-eat.

Christopher's initial response to the talent show idea had been to mimic film footage of the pilot Amelia Earhart displaying herself to the 1930s media pack as a kind of talking female puppet. Earhart had appeared in the piece thanks to Fred casting Peggy in that role in Thornton's video:

BRYAN: *Now we will introd . . . Now we will introduce . . .*
And now, Amelia Earhart will show us some of her acrobatic tricks.

A lateral link was soon established between Earhart and Walker: the former had disappeared during World War II; the latter—as Christopher puts it—"appeared and appeared and appeared" out of the Korean War, his over-eating seemingly a result of post-traumatic stress. Double-back links of this sort proliferated further as the various, divergent lines of enquiry were pursued: "the laws of combination increase in number as the multiplicity grows" (Deleuze and Guattari 1987: 8).

Date sent: Fri, 15 Nov 2002 18:39:11
From: Lin Hixson
Subject: Re: A starting point . . .
To: Steve Bottoms

Dear Steve,
So nice to hear your thoughts on *Earthquake*. I will be curious to see how the work will read in February, 2003. I have a response to your questions. It is not fully formed but I hope a start.

The directives and responses made in the first six months of rehearsal begin to form a neighborhood through the process of placing divergent responses next to one another. There's this process for about six months of just letting anything come in, and seeing what the connections are. And we do allow all these diversions and accidents to happen, but then we start sequencing the material, and you have to make choices, and a lot of things have to start falling away in order to construct some meaning out of it. And there is a point where that process for me feels sad. Because a lot of material has to go off to the periphery, to be left behind. And yet, at this same point you've got something very multi-layered happening, and you start following each of the threads or themes you've established.

In any case, after six months or so, boundaries are delineated around the neighborhood or district of material generated. We stop bringing material from outside the neighborhood and begin the investigation of who is living next to whom and what is happening in this place. And it is here (and for the next year and a half) that we engage critically. Experimentation is happening all the time. New things are being tried. Sources get mixed up with other sources. But there are limits and I think the audience senses this, for we do have a perspective on the material we present. On the other hand, our images or movements or texts are not dominated by singular referents. There are interwoven threads but not authoritative themes. I think this allows for multiple readings in the neighborhood; for different ways that a spectator can navigate its streets.

We're looking to create something that "makes sense," but in a multi-voiced, polyphonic kind of way—coherent but not unified. Making sense here often has to do with the surface structure. Coherence may be sought through repetition or a deliberate musical or literary form. Choices are made to sequence material horizontally, lining up one thing after another in time; or diagonally by making hybrids or skewing one thing into another. Examples: for our new piece, I wanted to work with Simone Weil—specifically with Karen as Simone Weil. I was interested in the idea that she was seeking ways to bring new life to awkward, abused, over-used words like love, goodness, justice. Earlier, Paul Celan had been brought into rehearsal by Matthew around the idea of repair—Celan took on the project, through his poetry, of "repairing" the German language after the holocaust. We also looked at the silent movie *The Wind*, starring Lillian Gish, as a response to the alphabet directive H—Hah Hah Hah—"He breatheth out like the wind." So from this I decided to bring in the idea of Simone Weil "playing" Paul Celan and Simone Weil "playing" Lillian Gish. That's what I'd call a diagonal structuring device.

We do our first work-in-progress next week. It feels slightly out of control. We'll see.

Much love to you and Paula.

Lin

Palindrome Matthew Goulish (Goat Island 1996a)

Any pattern the second half of which repeats and reverses the first half is palindromic. From the Latin *palin* (to return, to repeat), and *dromos* (to run), it is that which runs back again. Our interest in palindromic form arose as a result of our interest in pilgrimage, at the start of our work on *How Dear to Me the Hour When Daylight Dies*. Stated at its simplest, a pilgrimage involves patterned movement: departing from one place, traveling to another, and then returning to the starting point. This journey represents a palindrome in form if the return mirrors the departure, if the route reverses. The Croagh Patrick climb, County Mayo, Ireland, has this kind of structure: ascend the mountain halfway (a), circle station 1 (b), ascend the second, steeper half of the mountain (c), circle station 2 at the apex (d), descend the mountain's steeper upper half (c), re-circle station 1 (b), descend to the bottom (a). This journey may be represented by the following simple palindrome: a-b-c-d-c-b-a.

We began structuring our material, as we generated it, around a loose palindromic form in which the second half did not exactly reflect the first, but rather whole blocks of time reflected as units. If the piece were to begin with a monologue (one person speaking to three) followed by a silent movement section (unaccompanied by music), the piece would then conclude with a similar block of monologue followed by silent movement. Next, working in toward the center from both ends, would come a group movement section, followed by a theatrical scene, followed by a "dance" section, and concluding at the center with another monologue (Mike Walker's testimony).

Once we had sketched in the first half of the piece and arrived at the center, we found that the compressions and interruptions required by the timing, rhythms and content of the material, and also by the spatial organization of the piece, necessitated substantial departures from the strict palindromic structure. We began working instead with either total freedom from any strict structures, or with micro-structures employed to organize small blocks of material (as with an Indonesian poem form used to assemble the moves in the central dance sequence we perform to Japanese techno-pop music). As the process neared completion, a third structural phase appeared during which palindromic solutions again suggested themselves as a means of resolving the conclusion.

DAUGHTER: Do we have to keep the little pieces of our thought in some sort of order—to keep from going mad?

FATHER: I think so, yes. But I don't know what *sort* of order. . . . "What sort of order should we cling to so that when we get into a muddle we do not go mad?" It seems to me that the "rules" of the game is only another name for that sort of order. . . .

DAUGHTER: But Daddy, do you also change the rules? Sometimes?

FATHER: I change them constantly. Not all of them, but some of them. [Because] the whole point of the game is that we do get into muddles, and do come out the other side, and if there were no muddles our "game" would be like canasta or chess—and that is not how we want it to be. . . . The point is that the purpose of these conversations is to discover the "rules." It's like life—a game whose purpose is to discover the rules, which rules are always changing and always undiscoverable.

(Gregory Bateson 2000: 16, 19–20)

Construction Lin Hixson (1996: 92–94)

The word "construction," amongst architects in the mid-nineteenth century, according to Joseph Gwilt's *Encyclopedia of Architecture*, "is more particularly used to denote the art of distribution, distributing the different forces and strains of the parts and materials of a building in so scientific a manner as to avoid failure and insure durability" (Gwilt 1982: 1180). I've often felt when discussing or reading about the contemporary notion of deconstruction that our process in Goat Island, when making a performance work, runs in the opposite direction. Rather than starting with something built and tearing it away, we begin with a nail and a board and build outward, attaching beams and trusses that eventually collapse if they are not structurally sound. We use specific exercises to do this, many of which we employ when teaching. It is much like a horizontal version of the game JENGA, in which players first stack wooden blocks (approximately ¾ inch square by 4 inches long) into a solid tower, and then pull individual pieces out from the center, sides or bottom. This is done delicately with the intention of keeping the tower balanced, tapping the wooden block out until it is free. This freed block is placed on the top. If the tower falls by one of your moves, you lose. And so we begin when teaching or rehearsing by building:

Block 1: Write down an impossible task.
Block 2: Exchange this task with your neighbor.
Block 3: Make a performance with three others performing these impossible tasks.
Block 4: Why were you in pain in such a beautiful place?
Block 5: Respond to this question by writing about an event.
Block 6: Construct a report of this event from your writing. Include a list of the date, time, place, and one sentence from your writing about the event.
Block 7: Integrate these reports into the impossible task performances.

This continues. Next we rearrange the blocks, carefully pulling them from the center, the sides, and the bottom, all the while attempting to maintain a precarious balance.

Take the least interesting moment in your performance.
Pull it out.
Expand this moment into a full performance piece.

Gaping holes appear and the structure teeters. Eventually the unwieldy object topples. For Goat Island, the art of distribution is explored not so as to avoid failure and insure durability, but in order to reveal fragility, fluidity, and the moment when things fall apart. The point of failure is something we study. When the object topples we note the breaking point and how we got there. The repeated constructing, teetering and falling become a template for the performance. Each toppling is an ending that is also a beginning. Meaning emerges in the cracks. This decentering expansion divests the work of an absolute author. Instead the precarious structure takes its shape from the absence of a master builder.

To me, the ephemeral, moveable architecture of all live performance is one of its main strengths and should not be underestimated. As James Hillman warns in *The Soul's Code*:

> Hitler's own greatest passion was neither the German Reich, nor war, nor victory, nor even his own person. It was architectural construction. Megalomaniac emperors, from Nebuchadnezzar and the Egyptian pharaohs through the Roman emperors to Napoleon and Hitler, construct in concrete. . . . For this reason, megalomania haunts the actual architect—as the Bible warns with the story of the Tower of Babel, which is not only about the origin of language but also about the megalomania inherent in all attempts to make concrete the grandeurs of fantasy, especially in architecture. Tribal peoples are usually careful to keep their sacred altars moveable . . .
>
> (Hillman 1996: 242)

Sometimes a great notion   Matthew Goulish (Goat Island 1994: 20)

During the process of creating Goat Island's fourth performance piece, we were working on an idea of developing different stations of a movement, one of which was a sort of human pyramid. Four of us were seated in chairs and we each changed positions until all were seated one on top of the other. Out of the bottom of this pile, in a low, guttural whisper, came the phrase, "It's shifting, Hank!"

We never perfected the human pyramid because whenever we rehearsed it, just as we'd get all piled up in position, Greg McCain—who was on the bottom—would start saying, "Hank! It's shifting, Hank! Hank!" This would cause his brother Tim to start laughing, and soon we would all lose our balance. Lin finally demanded a full explanation. They explained that the line came from a scene in the movie *Sometimes a Great Notion* (1970), in which a fallen tree trunk pins a logger (Richard Jaeckel as Joe Ben) to the ground in the shallow part of the river, and another character (Paul Newman as Hank) tries unsuccessfully to save him from drowning.

Lin then called a rehearsal to watch the movie, after which she asked me to transcribe the drowning scene dialogue. After various versions and experiments,

19 *It's Shifting, Hank.*
Photograph by Eileen Ryan, Wellington Avenue Church, Chicago, 1994. Pictured: Timothy McCain as Joe Ben, Matthew Goulish as Ezra Pound

she settled on Tim as Richard Jaeckel/Joe Ben, and Greg as Paul Newman/Hank. We forgot the human pyramid, but the distracting joke it prompted, the drowning logger scene, concluded the performance, and at Lin's suggestion we even agreed on the title for the piece: *It's Shifting, Hank.*

> Sometimes I live in the country.
> Sometimes I live in the town.
> Sometimes I get a great notion
> To jump in the river and drown.
>
> Irene goodnight.
> Irene goodnight.
> Goodnight Irene, Goodnight Irene,
> I'll see you in my dreams.*

* "Goodnight Irene" words and music by Huddie Ledbetter and John A. Lomax. TRO – © Copyright 1936 (renewed) 1950 (renewed) Ludlow Music, Inc. New York, New York.

B2.3 BODY

A proposition Bryan Saner (Goat Island 2005b)

We propose to make a small contribution to the transformation of culture.
We will do this with our bodies in performance.
But first, we propose a transformation of lifestyle.
Nothing will change until we change.
We will have nothing to perform until that revolution occurs.
The best tool for change is our own body.
We will be placing our bodies in the path of mindlessness.
We propose riding a bicycle.
Position the body on a bicycle.

I like to play a game with cars in traffic when I ride my bike. For every car I pass I get a point. If a car passes me I lose a point. On an average day while biking from my house to the Loop in Chicago, I receive a positive total of 65 points. In the past year I've earned about 16,900 points while passing the average commuter traffic jams with my bicycle.

We propose that the following facts become common knowledge for anybody planning to make performance work:

- Only one fifth of the world's people live in industrialized countries, yet they consume more than two thirds of the planet's resources.
- With less than 5 percent of the global population, the United States accounts for about one fourth of global consumption.
- A child born in a developed country will consume and pollute more over his or her lifetime than thirty to fifty children born in low-income countries.
- Resources extracted from countries other than those in which they are consumed create environmental damage far beyond local and national borders.*

---

* Source: wwww.sierraclub.org/population/consumption.

We are participating in an unsustainable lifestyle. We will pay with our bodies. We cannot live this way unless we take resources away from someone else. When we resort to violence to "protect" the American way of life we are actually trying to perpetuate this lifestyle of consumption. We propose stopping. Position the body off of the war machine.

> We can blame our leaders for the state of the world, but we propose blaming the car.
> The car and ourselves who drive cars. We propose that there are too many cars and they are rapidly destroying the world.
> Stop Driving.
> If you must drive, drive slowly. Drive 55 mph.
> We are forgiven.
> If we could just first change our minds—then we will have a performance.

Body Intelligence Karen Christopher (1996: 75–79)

When Goat Island were in Cardiff to perform, I went for a walk around the city and ended up walking near some large government buildings. The lawns were carefully manicured leaving a patch of wild in the middle, in an oval shape. Tall grass with a few weeds and some wild flowers grew in these patches. They were patches of ground left wild and set off by the trim lawns surrounding them. I had never before seen that kind of lawn design.

I want to point out intuition and body intelligence and suggest using these forms of knowledge as guides during the creation of new work. I don't think people generally give credence to our body's response to thoughts and emotions. We think about things and work with our mental and emotional responses. But there are sense memory and blood memory. There are body signals that originate in the body as well as the brain or the mind or the psyche or the universe. There is consciousness under the skin. The various aspects that make up the person comprise totally different forms of intelligence. In the early stages of creating a new work we, as members of Goat Island, don't insist on knowing intellectually where we are going. We acknowledge that there are more than the usual ways of seeing and understanding.

In 1994 I was diagnosed with insulin-dependent diabetes. In getting used to my new body, I found new ways in which the body speaks to the mind. Because I'm now on insulin, there is concern that my blood sugar level could dip too low, which would cause my brain to cease functioning properly, and if it got low enough I could slip into a coma. This isn't likely to happen while I'm awake because there are certain warning signs, certain signs the body sends to the brain. One of them is a chemical which has a very simple message: panic. This panic is purely chemical, and has nothing to do with the rational mind. It is not a response to external stimuli. The remedy is sugar, something I normally have to avoid. Once sugar or food that can be turned into sugar by the body is eaten, the situation reverses itself and the body comes out of alarm.

But what if my blood sugar gets too low in the night while I'm asleep? The body continues to use up sugar, but the body doesn't eat any more food. After I was first diagnosed, this was a real fear for me. How would the body tell the mind that it was crashing? I spoke to another diabetic about this, and she said: you wake up. You just wake up. I thought: OK. That sounds good. But I only partly believed it until the first time it happened to me. I woke up in the middle of the night. It was four in the morning and I was suddenly, peacefully, wide awake. I lay in bed wondering why I was awake and started thinking about the dream I'd just woken up from. I'd been dreaming of a large bowl which had several different kinds of syrup rolling down its sides. As I looked into the bowl I saw that there was maple syrup and honey and corn syrup and a couple of others—all syrups I can no longer have. One trickle was rice syrup, and that I can have, so I reached in and took a fingerful of that. As I lay there thinking over this dream it became clear to me that I was awake now because I had low blood sugar, though I had no feelings of panic or weakness. I took a blood sugar test and it was 30. Very low. So I ate the tangerine I'd placed on the bedside table before I'd gone to sleep.

As a diabetic I have to trust that my unconscious will protect me. I have to believe that there are different forms of intelligence at work in my life and that I can trust intuitive connections.

The warm-up Goat Island does before rehearsals and before performances operates in several ways:

- it loosens and aligns our muscles;
- it prepares us mentally for creative work;
- it brings us together through the performance of a series of simple actions;
- it lays a foundation of agreement: we agree to perform these movements together; we agree to breathe in unison.

It is a transition and a ritual. Performing this ritual each time we get together creates a trigger, over time, so that even under pressure—in a crisis, when tired—this activity provokes a response in us and the response is the one we have endowed it with. We create the power this ritual has over us. And this transition is a very important one and one in which we have to remain present—not just get through it to the other side. Each time the exercises are performed we are focused on the task: the stretch, the breath, the relaxation of muscle—the mind wanders from time to time but the main focus is the task at hand and its purpose. There is no void time.

When someone says, “I'm in transition,” this usually translates as “I'm not normal right now. I'm different, but don't worry, this will pass.” It means: “I may not behave as I should or as I usually do.” It is a time not to be trusted: movement, flux, change. Just as our heads want to remain what we believe to be vertical, our minds want to grasp something solid, stationary, reliable. But we in Goat Island try to be comfortable with change, constant fluid change, and to be content without creating meaning or facts during the early creative process. We try to work with all of the various intelligences that make up a person and be open to what might happen.

Warming up Lin Hixson (1990: 17–18; 1997)

From the outset of our work as a company, our primary way of speaking artistically has been physical. In working on our first piece, *Soldier, Child, Tortured Man*, we became fascinated with physical exertion in performance. No one in the group had extensive movement or dance backgrounds, but the main connection Tim and Greg McCain had with performing was in terms of sports; they had both done athletics in high school; wrestling and football.

When we started out, we didn't have a space, so we worked in a living room. We didn't know what we were doing yet, but we did a warm-up every time; the one consistent thing we did was this warm-up. Then, when we began working in the gym at Wellington Avenue Church, we discovered that the warm-up was the most interesting thing. The gym was so big that, when we were doing the warm-up, I said “well, run between these different places.” And that was really interesting. You could see the body getting tired; you could hear the involuntary breathing of a performer after running. As director, I found this visible commitment to the performance of physical tasks to be very powerful. So we said, OK, well this is going to be physical.

While we were working on *Soldier, Child, Tortured Man*, the group was volunteering at the Chicago chapter of CISPES, the Committee in Solidarity with the People of El Salvador. We didn't set out to do a piece on El Salvador, but this CISPES work directly influenced the piece. I began studying photos from El Salvador (1980–1985) and developed specific movements from them. These movements were combined with physical drills that were brought in by Tim McCain, and formed what I thought of as the “training” section of the piece. The three men, struggling repeatedly through this rigorous movement series, resembled what one does to prepare for a football game or to go into battle.

20 *Soldier, Child, Tortured Man.*
Photograph by Dona Ann McAdams. PS 122, New York City, 1988. Pictured top to bottom: Matthew Goulish, Greg McCain, Timothy McCain

MATTHEW GOULISH: *The physical training for* Soldier *was constructed around five permutations of movement that were stated and then repeated with variations. Five was decided on for formal reasons. Lin tried to construct it so that by the end we were so tired that we couldn't do a sixth repetition. As we got in better shape, we didn't tire so easily, so Lin made the piece more difficult. She put the hardest stuff right at the end.*

TIM MCCAIN: *It would end when we couldn't do it anymore. I know there were times when we finished the fifth repetition and I couldn't go on. I was dying. I was so glad we were going into the next section.*

(Goat Island 1991a: 67–68)

As a woman directing the piece, I decided to view this material as something to be watched. I had never participated in this level of training and only knew it as an outsider or an observer. The audience was seated on all four sides of the space and watched properties you could observe such as group precision, speed, efficiency, and physical conformity. It was the kind of training necessary for one to go through in order to perform such inhumane acts as the bombing of El Salvador. This process of "rehumanization" was what we felt our policy in Central America is predicated on. I felt that we, the spectators, in the act of observing and in the judgement of this activity, were equally complicit in this process of rehumanization.

Triggers Steve Bottoms

Goat Island's work on *Soldier, Child, Tortured Man* established the group's concern with exhaustive physicality, and their practice of generating extensive movement sequences during the foundational stages of creating any new work. Movement seemed to offer the potential for a non-verbal performance vocabulary that was rich in possible meaning, and yet less easily reducible to simplified interpretation than an aesthetic dominated by language might be. Words became, and remained, a performance element treated with great care by Goat Island—textual passages often being introduced quite late in a creative process, at a stage when the visual and physical elements were sufficiently well-developed that they could not be simply contained or explained by the words being juxtaposed with them. For similar reasons, though, the company swiftly moved away from the tendency—visible in *Soldier*—to create movement sequences that overtly referenced recognizable activities such as military drills. Rather than expecting movement work to illustrate a consciously held, socio-political concern, Goat Island looked increasingly to generate more abstract or ambiguous movement, detached from any easily agreed-upon reference points or emotional content.

In pursuing an intuitive physical creativity whose outcomes were not predetermined by rational objectives, it was hoped that the performers could, instead, learn from the feelings and sensations arising from their bodies' attempts to perform unfamiliar, often unusual tasks. This cultivation of "body intelligence" would then allow meaning to emerge or be extrapolated *from* movement, rather than vice versa. It also held out the possibility to the performers themselves of a "rehumanization" very different to the one undergone by soldiers in training. Hixson's choice of this word, rather than the more familiar term *de*humanization, seems to me significant: soldiers are not, after all, turned into monsters, but they may well become different kinds of people than they once were—their bodies attuned to the gun, to the impulse of pulling the trigger, even when they can see the whites of the eyes of those in front of them (it might just save their lives; though it might also take an innocent's). The question, then: what kind of person might a performer become, if her or his body is constantly challenged to experience previously foreign sensations of motion, to *feel* things from another perspective.

Unfamiliar tasks Matthew Goulish (Goat Island 1994: 12, 23)

We used sports photographs to generate movement for the first time in 1990. While on tour in Glasgow, Scotland, Lin found an old book in a thrift store, *Rugby Football for Schools*, by J. T. Hankinson (1948), priced at 80p. It was a small, rust-colored hardcover book full of photographs demonstrating drills, catches, tackles, kicks, foot positions, and team formations, captioned with titles like, "Demonstration of Loose Scrum Formation at the Line Out." While still in the store, Lin showed me the book and said, "I'm going to photocopy these pictures and make dances for our next piece."

The photographs produced much of the movement for our third piece, *Can't Take Johnny to the Funeral*. Lin reproduced the pictures, arranged them on sheets of paper, repeating and alternating images, and glued them down. She gave each performer one of these "scores" from which to create movement solos, duets or trios. Pleased with the outcome, Lin went on to present us with photographs of lacrosse maneuvers, Frisbee tricks, and water polo diagrams. Most of these sports images derived from games we had never played or even watched. One rugby photo showed a man in a trenchcoat backing away from a uniformed younger man holding a ball. Our outsiders' viewpoint prevented abstract interpretations of the movements. We re-enacted them as accurately as we could, then accelerated the time. The results seemed to suggest human activity under extreme stress, dictated by specific but hidden rules, with no apparent objective other than survival.

For our next piece, *It's Shifting, Hank*, Lin again introduced photo images into rehearsals. Various images generated the moves for the dance/movement sequence featured in the first half of the piece—including pictures or drawings of dancers, actors, athletes, and kama sutra subjects. Sometimes one figure's upper body inspired an unusual movement, but the lower body seemed vague and generalized, or vice versa. In rehearsals, we began to fold the pictures and paperclip the mismatched halves together. Lin started to cut out the photocopied figures, rematch the body halves or parts, and create collaged figures for us to interpret, particularly to give the sequence more leaps and falls. An office supply store had drawn her name out of a box, and she had won a home Xerox copier and 100 reams of paper, which tremendously speeded up the collage process.

Task texts Lin Hixson (Goat Island 1996a)

One of the ways we generated movement for our fifth piece, *How Dear to Me the Hour When Daylight Dies*, was through the use of phrases of text that I brought into rehearsal. An example might be:

Create four movements from the phrase "shy hands."
Create a jump from the words "call on death."

When the group asked me my criteria for choosing these phrases, I realized I hadn't given it much thought. But reflecting on it now I see that the process of choosing texts reveals some of the attitudes toward movement, and the way movement functions, in our work.

The actual process of finding two phrases that I think will work can take over an hour of my scouring poetry books and novels. Some of the authors I've used are Michael Ondaatje, Anna Akhmatova, Patti Smith, and Miguel Asturias. I seldom find

21 Lin Hixson: body collages for *It's Shifting, Hank.*

a phrase unless I am in this concentrated state of searching for the sole purpose of generating movement for the piece.

When I look, I look for phrases that are corporal or physical, and that relate to the body:

quiver in time with your gait
a fish slaps back your face shake out shake out

I look for phrases lacking in obvious emotion to avoid abstract illustrations of feelings. I hope instead to find emotion where I least expect it:

bless your hot mouth
pelvic wind up

I look for phrases that can be performed as task. Viewing movement as a piece of work, or as a difficult or tedious undertaking gives us, who have little formal training in dance, a way into the physical; a way to draw from the everyday, the familiar, and the mundane. I look to task for metaphor, for taking the familiar and using it to designate something else, to leap across meanings, to criss-cross ideas. I look for words that require assemblage—the gathering of parts and the fitting together, what I call constructing.

When the group was in Belfast at the Linenhall Library, I found a photo of a man in a speedo swimming suit, dripping wet, who was kneeling in front of an altar to the Virgin Mary. The picture's caption became an instrumental phrase in the creation process for *Daylight Dies*:

A shivering homage.

The impossible (a dance) Matthew Goulish (Goat Island 1998a: 17–21)
For our sixth piece, *The Sea & Poison*, we set out to construct an impossible dance. We would construct this dance from a series of unperformable individual movements. We divided the idea of a movement into its five most basic ingredients:

1 the part of the body or area of the body performing the movement;
2 the speed at which the body performs the movement;
3 the duration of the movement in time;
4 the repetition of the movement; and
5 the intention of the performer.

We then decided on two methods of generating individual movements: (a) from an image, and (b) from a phrase of text. Lin would supply these two starting points. She brought in *a lizard with its tongue out* (image) and *MAKES AN ECHO* (phrase). Each of the five basic ingredients Lin then assigned to a corresponding member of the group. We used a chart to prevent confusion, with two columns—one below the lizard and one below MAKES AN ECHO.

Working individually and using the starting point at the top of the column, each collaborator developed a specific possibility, or list of possibilities, to complete the designated assigned ingredient area on the chart. Each individual brought in a complete fragment of a single movement. The combination of those five fragments, in sequence, constructed one unperformable movement phrase in the impossible dance.

		**MAKES AN ECHO**
Body Part or Area	"Fire, throw, or propel an object from your mouth"	stomach
Speed	speed progression of slow to quadruple speed; fast to quarter speed 1 ◄——► 4	1. standing in a shallow brook 2. an airplane at takeoff 3. a hundred-step run up a castle tower 4. a typist at 60 words per minute 5. a machine in constant cycle 6. a person who breathes next to you
Duration	1. 74 completions 2. as long as it takes to sing the national anthem	(?)
Repetition	spinning thread around a small jewel-like object	repetition ratio of 1:2:3:4 Mark Bryan Karen Matthew
With the Intention of	a walking snake	stopping the spread

Our work on the initial Impossible Dance chart prompted two hybrid forms for generating more unperformable movements. In the first, Karen drew four phrases from her poison research, and gave one to each performer. She completed the remaining four ingredient boxes with selections from the first chart. Each performer generated an unperformable movement in this way.

In the second hybrid form, Lin (1) selected two phrases from poetry, and (2) photocopied a number of diagrams from a book on Scottish Highland Dances which Karen had found during a company residency in Glasgow.

Phrase	1. break up time (Karen) 2. keep it secret (Mark) 3. breathe past (Bryan) 4. avoid detection (Matthew)
Body Part or Area	stomach
Speed	68th through 82nd step in a 100-step run up a castle tower
Duration	one circulation
Intention	divide

twist and turn like a pig's tail in a summer night as thick as flies' milk smell flesh food in a baited trap from a distance of five miles

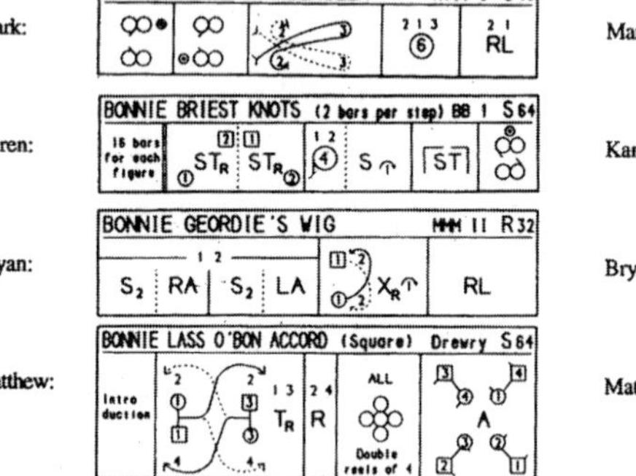

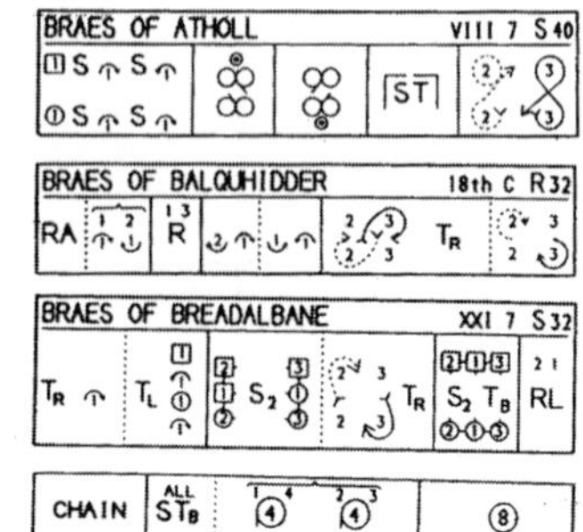

Each performer received a different unperformable movement. We had no understanding of the correct use of the dance diagrams, and worked backwards from their incomprehensible documentation, using them and the poetry phrase as imagination guides. Working in these ways, we constructed a series of impossible dances. Each impossible dance resulted from the assembly of four or five unperformable movement phrases into a series.

We decided to structure this assembly according to the 1:2:3:4 ratio found in the second column of the initial chart. In this way, using five different movement phrases, the four performers perform the same material at the same pace, but according to different divisions. Mark performs (or rather, fails to perform) each movement phrase completely from beginning to end. Bryan performs the first half of each movement phrase in the series, followed by the second half of each movement phrase in the series. Karen performs the first third of each movement phrase in the series, followed by the second third of each movement phrase, followed by the third third. Matthew performs the first quarter of each movement phrase in the series, followed by all the second quarters, all the third quarters, and finally all the fourth quarters of each movement phrase in the series.

The aspect of impossibility in the dances derives from both the oddity of each individual movement, and the complexity of the precisely timed structure of the assembly of the movements into a dance. The actual human performance results in a style of ongoing failure and adjustment during each moment of each impossible dance.

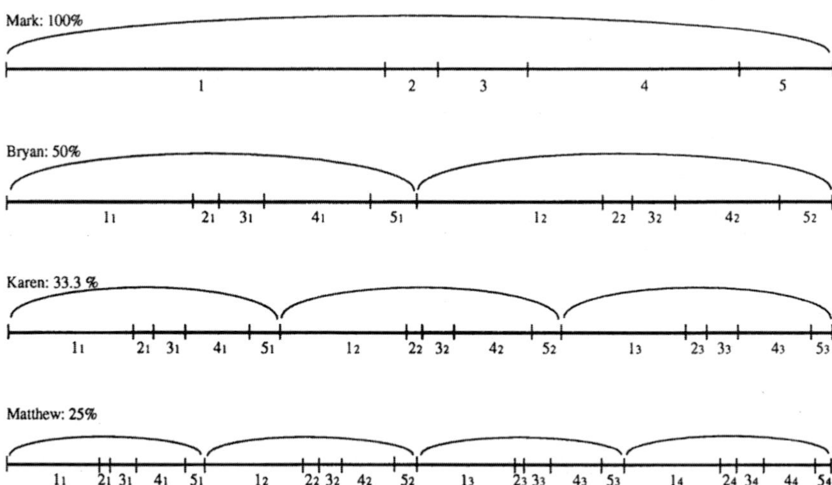

12 sentences Lin Hixson (Goat Island 2001b: 177–178)
In 1972, I majored for one semester in dance at the University of Oregon and failed. I could not point my toes properly and I could not copy and perform the complicated dance patterns in Belinda Cartwright's Intermediate Modern Jazz class.

In 1984, I saw Pina Bausch's company perform in the Olympic Arts Festival in Los Angeles. I was mesmerized by the personal, quirky styles of each performer; the varied physical types; the different ages; the many mother tongues.

In 1999, I gave the four members of Goat Island dance segments on video taken from Pina Bausch's company. I asked them to copy the movements and bring them into rehearsal.

In 2000, I watched rehearsals for our performance *It's an Earthquake in My Heart*. I was mesmerized by the failure of Bryan, Karen, Mark and Matthew to achieve the filmed version of Bausch's choreography. Each one seemed to be reaching for a gesture outside of themselves while performing the gesture with themselves—a process of self-quoting and citation from another source, simultaneously. I liked the idea that we would never get these movements right; that we were staging a failure. With the inability to succeed, we were given a stuttering. We were given fragility. We were given unstable possibilities.

Imitating Dominique Matthew Goulish (2000b: 6–12)
An international dance festival invited Goat Island to teach a workshop in Berlin. While we were there, we attended a performance of Jerome Bel and company from Paris, called *The Last Performance*. It consisted almost entirely of a series of imitations. Each of the performers took a turn dancing a solo, about four minutes in length, by the famous German dancer and choreographer Susanne Linke. Each performer wore a diaphanous white gown. Even the male performers, including Jerome Bel, wore this gown when it was their turn. Each performer approached the microphone and said, "Ich bin Susanne Linke."

I am Susanne Linke.

Then the performer would dance the solo to the best of her or his ability. Each time, the same music played. One could compare the imitations, if not to the original, at least to one another. Each attempt seemed like a collection of imperfections. At the end of the show, Jerome Bel and the other three performers stood on the stage and bowed. A woman dressed in white, and carrying four white lilies, leapt up from the audience and began to bow with the performers. She was Susanne Linke. She handed each performer a lily. They looked stunned.

In the lobby after the performance a festival organizer explained to us that the dancers, at Jerome Bel's instruction, had independently studied the same videotaped solo of Susanne Linke, and then tried their best to perform it. Lin said: In our new piece, I want each of you to imitate a dance like that.

Lin had appropriated the idea of choreographic appropriation. She liked how the imitation performed the gap between the attempt and the original, even when the original was absent. One struggles to perform the imitation well, yet the gap never totally vanishes. It is a kind of failure.

We turned to leave the lobby, excited once again about the future. I noticed that the theater door had been left open. Inside, Jerome Bel and his dancers, still in performance clothing and each holding a white lily, stood around watching as one of the performers danced a bit of the Susanne Linke solo on the floor. Susanne Linke stood beside them. She held the performer's lily for him, and dictated what appeared to be some detailed instructions about the position of the leg and foot. She seemed to be saying: Get it right.

The festival had housed Lin and myself at Fidicinstrasse 32a, the apartment of Martin Figura, a painter summering in southern Italy. Martin Figura possessed a massive, neatly stacked videotape collection. On our last night in Berlin, I noticed a tape labeled as a documentary on Pina Bausch and the Wupperthal Tanztheater. It contained a great deal of dancing choreographed by Pina Bausch. In America, video of this group is extremely rare. Why not imitate something from this video for our new piece?

I selected the most difficult dance performed by the male dancer whom I felt I least resembled. Dominique Mercy is a French dancer in Pina Bausch's company. He is older than most of the other dancers, and has medium-long blond hair, and a neat mustache. When Dominique Mercy dances a solo choreographed by Pina Bausch, he seems to perform the impossible, as if possessed, although without exerting himself too much. I selected a solo from a piece called *Die Fenster Putzer* (*The Window Washer*). On the video, Dominique performs the solo for about 45 seconds. I said to myself, I will learn this dance.

The first problem presented itself—I did not know where to begin. The dance progressed from one quick impossibility to the next. I could find no way into it. I would need to reduce my ambition. I focused on the first 30 seconds, and started again. After this cycle of discouragement and shortening had repeated itself several times, I decided to consider myself successful if I managed to imitate a single movement.

I paused the tape and examined the still picture. I could see that every part of the dancer's body seemed entirely foreign not only to my knowledge of movement, but also to movement in general. No still picture made sense without the syncopation of the rhythm—and the rhythm did not make sense without the still pictures. After watching a small portion of the tape 20 times I found I could get moderate results by imagining the following: myself combining with the dancer's body, like those skydivers in training who leap from airplanes tied face-to-face with their teacher —two bodies fused into one. I felt the dance movements then. I could sense a body (his, mine) moving as a result of a series of impulses of limited energy, microbursts, which produced each move in rhythm and detail—as though a small animal were learning to walk with the aid of a steam engine.

In this way, over the course of an hour that evening in Martin Figura's apartment at Fidicinstrasse 32a in Berlin, with the furniture pushed aside, I managed to commit to memory a relatively accurate imitation of four sequential beats of the solo—about three seconds in length. The foreignness of the movement forced me to make a double adjustment:

Adjustment #1:	that a hand, arm, head, torso, leg, foot, may move in this way.
Adjustment #2:	that a body may combine these movements at this speed and rhythm.

The wrongness of the feeling was not wrongness. It was "getting it right." The car I had been driving for 39 years had always had a gear between second and third, that I had only just now discovered: the 2½ gear, with a new sense of delicacy, possibility, fuel efficiency.

I showed Lin the four beats I had learned. She said: That's great, but don't roll your head back, it's too dancey. I have no choice, I said. That's how Dominique does it. I don't believe he does it that way, she said. And if he does, change it.

We were to leave in the morning to return to Chicago. But before going to bed, I made an announcement: I'm taking Martin Figura's videotape with me. I've only managed to learn 4 beats (3 seconds) of the dance. In Chicago, I will duplicate the tape, continue to study my copy, and return the original, with a thank you note, to Martin Figura.

That night I had trouble sleeping, nervous that I would not retain my new discoveries as a memory in the body. Yet I felt excited once again about the future. I had established a process, albeit slow, by which I could learn to imitate Dominique. It was a familiar process, although it took me some time to recognize where I had seen it before. I came to think of the process as catechism, with Dominique as catechist, myself as catechumen, and the dance the word handed down from above.

Back in Chicago, Lin made video clips for the Goat Island performers to imitate —one for Mark, a different one for Karen, a different one for Bryan—all from moments in various works by Pina Bausch. I received my assignment of continuing to learn Dominique's solo, building upon my initial four sequential movements, three seconds in length. Mark Jeffery offered to take Martin Figura's videotape to the Media Center at The School of the Art Institute of Chicago, where he teaches, so that a student worker there could duplicate it from PAL to NTSC so that I might continue my work.

At our next meeting Mark reported that he had returned to the Media Center at the designated time, to find not only that no NTSC transfer been made, but also that Martin Figura's original tape had vanished. Searches of the shelves yielded no results. Mark Jeffery related this grim news with the full knowledge of its implications. With a work-in-progress performance only a few rehearsals away, my dance solo had stalled at 3 seconds, my personal quest swallowed up in bureaucracy. Rehearsals continued, however, and I could not expect anybody to take much notice of my crisis. They had their own problems. They expected me to take care of mine without making too big a melodramatic deal out of them. And so I did. I made the following two adjustments:

Adjustment #1: I hoped that Martin Figura would not miss the single videotape that had mysteriously vanished from his collection forever.

Adjustment #2: I repeated, in performance, the 3 seconds of movement that I had learned until my solo accumulated the duration required by Lin's choreography.

Like a skip in a turntable record, my solo repeated itself through rehearsals and performances—because how lackluster it is to perform without inspiration—until the night of November 6, 1999. On that night Lin and myself as well as Goat Island members Karen Christopher and CJ Mitchell, and other friends, attended a performance at the Brooklyn Academy of Music of *Danzon*, a piece by Pina Bausch, performed by the Wupperthal Tanztheater including two solos danced by Dominique Mercy. We found our seats in the back of the second balcony. I would have only one chance—no rewind—to commit to memory as many new movements of Dominique's solos as possible to graft onto my 3 seconds.

I sat ready to engage the methods I had learned over the past weeks, and when the time came for Dominique to dance, I projected myself onto the stage and felt the strain and the rhythm of the choreography in my limbs as if I had already rehearsed it. As my body vibrated in my seat in the back of the second balcony, I felt obliged to acknowledge that now I am no longer the same man, that a new person is here beside me, adhering to me, amalgamated with me, a person whom I might, perhaps, be unable to shake off, whom I might have to treat with circumspection, like a master or an illness.

I realized then, as the twentieth century drew to a close, as TimeWarner and America Online prepared to merge, that memory is not a commodity, that I may watch a dancer, and that by watching a dancer I may change, and emotion appeared unexpectedly, blossoming like a raincloud not as a threat to memory's fragility, but because of memory's fragility, because I have changed by choice and not by habit, I have remembered, I have escaped.

I added seven moves to my solo.

In subsequent rehearsals, when assembled onto the original four, they gave the dance the quality of an ecstatic misremembered catechistic jumble—exactly what it was. After the performance on the night of November 6, 1999 in Brooklyn, as we stood in front of the theater exchanging opinions and interpretations about *Danzon* by Pina Bausch, I thought how strange, because what is criticism, where does it come from? I attended this performance in order to compose it.

And then a friend said something inconceivable. I see a connection, she said, between you and that one dancer, the blonde-haired guy. She was describing Dominique, the one who, some weeks earlier, I had selected as the dancer whom I felt I least resembled.

From this choice, what result? What has been made, and who has made it?

This could be what a conversation is—simply the outline of a becoming. The wasp and the orchid provide the example. The orchid seems to form a wasp image, but in fact there is a wasp-becoming of the orchid, an orchid-becoming of the wasp, a double capture since "what" each becomes changes no less than "that which" becomes. The wasp becomes part of the orchid's reproductive apparatus at the same time as the orchid becomes the sexual organ of the wasp. One and the same becoming . . . as someone becomes, what he is becoming changes as much as he does himself.

(Gilles Deleuze in Deleuze and Parnet 1986: 2)

Rehearsal directives Mark Jeffery (1999b)

1 Create a chase/pathway with your body. June 1999.
2 Create a circulatory chase. June 1999.
3 Re-create dance moves from Pina Bausch's *Café Müller* by way of a three-minute dance video. September 1999.

In a living room and a dining room, furniture is rearranged and moved to create a diagonal pathway. Crockery is moved into the kitchen. Shoes are taken off and put to one side. A TV is turned on and a video cassette is placed into the VCR. A person takes hold of the remote control and presses play. What he watches is the start of a scene. The scene progresses, activities are shown: a man falls off his chair, falling to the ground. He begins to run along a line back and forth. He falls, he runs, he pauses for breath, he runs. A man chases and follows him over and over, following his pattern, creating a pathway. Chairs are constantly removed, thrown to the side away from the man who is running.

A woman with red hair and high heeled shoes paces along with the man who is clearing a pathway for the other man who is running and falling. A woman in a dress sits at a circular table, takes off her full-length dress and lays her head and arm across the table.

Back in our living and dining rooms, people begin to re-enact these moments, this scene, over and over.

STOP FORWARD REWIND PLAY SLOW SPEED. . . .
This has happened before
This unlikely loading of our bodies towards sky
A redistribution of weight
Pulling up just under our arms
Lifting us.

Places of location and mobility, of moving until we cannot move or continue to go forward or back. Beats still continue in spaces we no longer occupy or places of memory where we momentarily say goodbye.

The heart jumps, creating a circulatory flow, an internal pathway, a segmentation we can't see. By running we play games, we chase one another, under and over, through halting breaks and U-turns, creating patterns of slip roads, highways and traffic lanes with differing speeds of transportation, and a mixture of cirrus clouds high above.

KAREN: *Matthew, especially, has really been studying dancers. You could see it in* Earthquake, *in his copying of Dominique Mercy—he's really wanting to be that kind of dancer. So I think with Litó [Walkey] joining the company for this new piece, there's a meeting there that's interesting. Because Litó is that dancer, already.*

BRYAN: *There's a physical precision in what she does that none of us ever had, or claimed to have. It's a really advanced kind of body sense. People who are trained as dancers often have trouble doing the kind of non-dancerly work we do, but Litó's solo work is like that anyway—and she brings a precision to it that you wouldn't if you didn't have the training.*

KAREN: *She's consciously non-dancerly. That's a conscious effort on her part, I think.*

(Christopher and Saner 2003)

Dog Matthew Goulish (2004a: np)

Rr—the dog grinneth

Early in the making of *When will the September roses bloom? Last night was only a comedy*, Lin assigned this alphabet directive to Litó, with the instruction to devise a solo for Karen to perform. Litó presented her response at rehearsal #5 on February 14, 2002: Karen walked in a tight circle, growling, periodically striking a posture with arms and hands stretched downward, wrists flexed, teeth bared.

Two years into the creative process, at a company meeting on April 14, 2004, Lin told us that the dog needed to start taking over the piece, and supplanting some of the other animals. We would all have our turns at playing dogs, and we would need to devise new dog movements. In simplifying the *animal* presence in the piece, we would clarify the *human* as well.

She showed us several early twentieth century photos by Jacques-Henri Lartigue —dogs; dogs with children; children in adult party costumes.

Lin and I had seen Robert Bresson's *Au Hasard, Balthazar* (1966), a film from post-war France, deeply influenced by Simone Weil's theology—by her statement: "I have become a beast of burden before thy face," and by her proposal of the meeting of the highest and lowest in the sacred (Weil 1992: xxiv). In *Gravity and Grace*, she writes:

He, on the contrary, in whom the "I" is quite dead is in no way embarrassed by the love which is shown him. He takes what comes just as dogs and cats receive food, warmth and caresses, and, like them, he is eager to obtain as much as possible.

(Weil 1992: 26)

The animal presence in the piece had prompted Lin to read Giorgio Agamben's book *The Open—Man and Animal*:

> if the caesura between the human and the animal passes first of all within man, then it is the very question of man—and of "humanism"—that must be posed in a new way. In our culture, man has always been thought of as the articulation and conjunction of a body and a soul, of a living thing and a *logos*, of a natural (or animal) element and a supernatural or social or divine element. We must learn instead to think of man as what results from the incongruity of these two elements, and investigate not the metaphysical mystery of conjunction, but rather the practical and political mystery of separation. What is man, if he is always the place—and, at the same time, the result—of ceaseless divisions and caesurae? It is more urgent to work on these divisions, to ask in what way—within man—has man been separated from non-man, and the animal from the human, than it is to take positions on the great issues, on so-called human rights and values. And perhaps even the most luminous sphere of our relations with the divine depends, in some way, on the darker one which separates us from the animal.
>
> (Agamben 2004: 16)

In Weil's theology, the dog appears as an image of the egoless human. Agamben's philosophy focuses on the unbridgeable divide between human and animal. Both of these writers carefully stated that these thought constructions located themselves entirely within the human. Gilles Deleuze, the philosopher perhaps known for most de-anthropomorphizing the animal, had confronted these questions differently in his writing on the animals and the flesh in the paintings of Francis Bacon:

> Sometimes an animal, for example a real dog, is treated as the shadow of its master, or conversely, the man's shadow itself assumes an autonomous and indeterminate animal existence. The shadow escapes from the body like an animal we had been sheltering. In place of formal correspondences, what Bacon's paintings constitute is a *zone of indiscernibility or undecidability* between man and animal. Man becomes animal, but not without the animal becoming spirit at the same time, the spirit of man, the physical spirit of man presented in the mirror as Eumenides or Fate. It is never a combination of forms, but rather the common fact: the common fact of man and animal. [. . .] This objective zone of indiscernibility is the entire body, but the body insofar as it is flesh or meat.
>
> (Deleuze 2003: 21–22)

Deleuze (through Bacon's paintings) links the gray zone of human/animal indiscernibility with the fact of suffering, and its terrible location in the flesh.

These passages resonated with texts we had been performing in the piece for some time: Simone Weil's plea, spoken by Karen, invokes a rending of the flesh to produce a void, to allow the presence of the divine.

Father, rend this body and soul away from me, for your use, and let nothing remain of me, forever, except this rending itself, or else nothingness.

(Weil 1970: 244)

In the passage I perform from *Austerlitz*, by W. G. Sebald, the speaker visits the prison cell in which, many years ago, Jean Améry had been tortured. In the room, the speaker inexplicably experiences a childhood memory of a butcher shop, and the unexpected overlay of the present and the past terrifies him. As Deleuze wrote of Bacon:

This is not an arrangement of man and beast, not a resemblance; it is a deep identity, a zone of indiscernibility more profound than any sentimental identification: the man who suffers is a beast, the beast that suffers is a man.

(Deleuze 2003: 25)

In response to Lin's second directive, we began devising new dog choreography. In early June, 2004, we had finished a complete sketch of the piece in both its versions, and now began to orchestrate it with dogness, replacing the moments that seemed unresolved or otherwise improvable. We gave the piece a sort of dog upgrade. At this time, Litó put her thoughts on the subject in the form of an email.

Date: Thu, 03 Jun 2004 15:37:26
From: litó walkey
Subject: dog notes
To: lin

hi lin,

these might not make sense, but they're the notes i have been working off for the dog. responding to our talk, the photos you sent me and the hunting dog texts from karen.

vibrations—shaking
leading with nose—smelling
staring at a spot—empty space—as if something were there
holding/grabbing presence (showing off)

performing without control, without any order
suddenly stopping in (its) track—frozen (by a smell)
tense and ready—frozen to attention—becomes a statue—a dog of stone
suddenly plunging, diving
looking up at owner/partner
systematically quartering the ground (back and forth)
jump—play (like toby in lin's lartigue photos)
standing and barking
'losing feet' to guard along ground
resting—holding down floor

all in contrast to thinking standing man—perhaps leaning man like in lartigue photo
wildness of animal versus sophisticated human movement

hopes these notes can help.

best,

litó

If flesh and suffering represented one zone of human/animal indiscernibility, another zone, our choreography proposed, might be behavior. We had approached some of our choreography based on the Preston Sturges movie *Palm Beach Story* (1942) through the idea of the *swarm*—the behavior that destabilizes distinctions between individual and group. Each individual follows the same small series of tasks, and in doing so makes the group appear as an individual, the way a swarm of bees appears as a single entity, a sentient cloud.* We now applied this strategy to some of the dog choreography, to mimic not just single dog behavior, but structural animal behavior, as a pack (or swarm). As Paul Celan wrote:

> Save it,
> before
> the Stone Day has blown dry
>
> the swarms of men
> and beasts, just
> as the seven-reed flute mandates,
> in front of mouth and muzzle.
>
> (Celan, qtd. Howe 2003: 71–72)

* I am indebted to Marc Luker for the swarm discourse.

22 *When will the September roses bloom? Last night was only a comedy.*
Photograph by Lin Hixson. Alfred ve Dvore Theatre, Prague, Czech Republic, 2007.
Pictured left to right: Mark Jeffery, Matthew Goulish, Karen Christopher, Bryan Saner, Litó Walkey

Testing Mark Jeffery (Goat Island 2005b)

The process of making a Goat Island performance is a process of connecting physically with appropriated, separated and broken contours or terrains that we carefully join together, six individuals rotating in a core. Sometimes we will try to engage a specific body part: an engaged back that becomes a public monument in mourning; an extended arm pulsating as if thorn and stem cut with shears two red roses from the garden; an extended torso as she stands on one leg, a beacon an anchor, headstrong. There are particular pressures placed onto the surface of the skin, a bone, a right arm or leg, overcome by inhabiting the behavior of an animal. This pressure, this connection, these multiple acts of imitation. In our long process we explore the limitations and extensions of each individual member of this collective.

B2.4 TIME

Duration Bryan Saner (1999a)

I want to talk about a few durational blocks of time, not forgetting that this bit of talking, at the 1999 Chicago Goat Island Summer School, has a duration of its own.

5 seconds. There is a short pause that happens after we walk single file out of the dressing room and before we set foot onto the performance space. Preceding this there has been a 30-minute warm-up and stretching. Preceding that there has been an hour or two of setting props. Preceding that was 2 years of making and rehearsing a performance work. Preceding that was a lifetime of maybe 30 years of dreaming and studying and thought and experimentation. Preceding that was the centuries of developing the performing arts as we know them. Preceding that are the millennia of human evolution. Sometimes I can see the whole scheme of events during this 5-second pause. I am stretched out and flattened and dematerialized and sent back and sent forward and rematerialized and comprehend some great and simple truth . . . and step onto the stage and begin the performance.

1 hour and 45 minutes. This is how long our current performance is. This is about as long as the average American will sit in one spot. We've learned to endure this length from Hollywood. We expect a conflict and a resolution toward the end. This is an absurd block of time to expect all that. Much too short unless things are carefully crafted to tell you what to think and feel. 1 hour and 45 minutes isn't enough time to give a proper account of 2 years' research. It is enough time perhaps to pose a proper question. But we need much more time to think about an answer.

3 years. We generally spend 1½ to 2 years making a performance work and then another year performing it. About 3 years to spend with the material. Producing one work over this amount of time is unusual for theater. During this time we also show several works-in-progress. This is another form of durational, perhaps interactive performance: an audience sees a question being posed and can respond literally through the feedback session immediately afterward, and then ponder the questions or forget them completely until perhaps a year later when we present another work-in-progress showing. Often the same audience members have the opportunity to look again at the work and think again about the questions. Perhaps another year later, they may return to see the "finished" work. 3 years is a very short time according to some time lines, but lots can happen to a person and a mind in this amount of time, and we can change our minds about things and allow events from our personal lives or events from the world news to layer our thinking about the question. 3 years does allow time for some things to settle, for some things to get edited out or confirmed as important. 3 years gives us time to make the money that supports us. 3 years allows the time to leave the material alone and do something else for a while.

11 years. In 1988 a friend told me to see the new performance group Goat Island, who were performing their first work *Soldier, Child, Tortured Man.* I didn't see the piece, but later I heard lots of talk about it as it endured in people's minds. I did see their next 3 performances over the next 7 years or so, and began working with the company on their fifth piece. We are rehearsing the seventh now. Lin says that the individual Goat Island works are markers on a long trail of events. An alternative to understanding a single work is to view the collective works as one long durational whole which is yet to be finished. A work in time that cannot be viewed without being conscious of the past and anticipating the future. This spring I saw a recorded performance of *Soldier, Child, Tortured Man.*

Another 5 seconds. In our gymnasium performance space in Chicago, I look out of a window as I pause during a rehearsal. I can see a condominium tower that I recognize because I saw it being built. It stands in a place that 15 years ago was a vacant lot where I played with kids. I think about things that were not but are now. I think about things that are now but will not be.

Longevity is not a goal. Survival may be overrated as a measuring stick for performance. There is no intention here to produce an epic life story of Goat Island's response to the world we live in. The intention is to follow a vision collectively that no-one sees or has ever had. Vision is an obstinate task master. We attain clarity for a brief instant and then lose it again for long hours and days and weeks before it returns to give us the inspiration to keep working. But these points of inspiration are not what keeps us going. That takes vigilance. We repeat with our bodies the actions over and over again: back out to the streets, back into the office, back onto the stage, back over to rehearsal, back to work. Often the revelations happen when we have forgotten the vision altogether. All we remember is that we have work to do. The work precedes the vision; creates the vision. The most profound guideline for our work is simply to follow what is in front of us. And as simple as that sounds, it is a humbling experience for me to realize that I often cannot see what is in front of me until long after it has passed.

❖❖❖

Reading back Lin Hixson (2002b: np)

The cormorant bird fishes for sweetfish at night. A metal collar rings its neck and a tightening leash hangs off of it. The long leash leads to the hands of its owner, the fisherman. On the boat hangs fire in metal cages. The fire attracts the fish. The fish attracts the cormorant. The cormorant catches his catch. The fisherman tugs hard on the ring. The cormorant stops swallowing. The catch hangs in the bird's mouth. The fisherman retrieves it.

Let's say it's March 23, 2003 in a gym, in Chicago, 18 degrees Fahrenheit outside. We are in rehearsal, rehearsing a performance in a later stage than a year ago. Acts of return, flush tank dances, James Taylor singing "I've seen fire and I've seen rain"—these have been combined into sequences. We say, "What is it?" I watch Bryan perform a lecture on nuts and bolts turning clockwise and counterclockwise. Unexpectedly, he pulls something out of his pocket and discloses a small, white paper cup in the shape of a funnel. Later, reviewing notes of the rehearsal alone in my study, I'm set off by the remaining presence of Bryan's funnel. I read back restlessly, over days and months of rehearsal material, searching for a sleeper to fetch in the tall seagrass.

Fires light the water. Stars whisper to one another. The performance rings my neck with a leash, its hands resting around the string. I dive under, knowing I have a long way to go. I pass spiraling yew trees, Z a poor Zany left in a lurch, consequences. A chirping cicada. A tangled strand of poetry by Paul Celan "daynightly the Bears-Polka" with a grinning man wiping his feet on sandpaper, and a Hah Hah Hah—the mouth breatheth out like the wind.

A tiny man named Mark in a tiny chair, clapping his tiny hands, floats across my feet. It is May, the month-of-Can, 72 degrees Fahrenheit. A huge, turquoise blue funnel juts out of his mouth. Invisible wind blows across broken seashells. Separating fibers, filaments, and strands in an unweaving process more akin to forgetting and re-collecting than remembering, I recollect Bryan's paper funnel cup and collect a sea-drowned Mark and the wind in my mouth. The neck ring tightens before I swallow. I carry back the recollection for the pulling hands of the performance.

Now the revived activity of Mark, retrieved from the long distance of stored time, sits next to the lecture activity of Bryan in the same performance space and the same performance time. Distance continues to separate the two, their origins coming from different lands and different times. Their divided two-ness united seems contrary and disruptive. I cannot absorb them together. I cannot make sense of it. I do not take it in like ink on thin sheets of paper; or receive it like the hit bumper on the car without reverberation. It recoils. It rebuffs. It refuses. It delays its meaning in my mind. And I travel longer with it.

"Speed is the enemy of difficulty," says Susan Stewart. "It tends to absorb or erase every other phenomenal quality" (2002: 330). The time system that governs my work schedule, my trips to the bank, auto repairs, food shopping, meeting with my friends, emphasizes speed. And yet when I dive it's for the difficult moment apprehended by the slow turn of the head, the pace of a heartbeat, the encounter when

HEARINGREMAINS, SEEINGREMAINS, in
Bedroom one thousand and one,
Daynightly
The Bears-Polka:
They re-school you, and
Once more we become they.

Hauntings Mark Jeffery (2005)

Haunting # 1: From the age of six until I left home, I was fortunate (living in a three-bedroom house with my parents and two elder sisters) to have my own small room. A room in the house where I was born. From the age of six until the age of eleven I slept on the bottom level of a bunk bed. No human being shared these two beds with me. Yet on some occasions during this period the bed shook for no apparent reason. I did not shake the bed. The bed would shake involuntarily without my consent.

I was very scared. My response to this action was to huddle in bed with the covers around my body and to shake the bed myself. I felt that if I engaged in this activity, if I learned to *be* the visitor which had rested itself above me on the top bunk, then I would not be so scared. I had to embody and to become the thing that had visited me.

Haunting # 2: I remember that one evening, while trying to get to sleep in that same bunk bed, I felt the breath of something blowing and whispering in my ear. From that point on I placed my finger in my ear when I lay in bed at night, going to sleep. Now I had not only to embody the thing that had visited me, but also to prevent it from entering my body. While shaking the bed, I would contain my body by closing my eyes, while keeping one ear next to the pillow and one finger inserted into the opening of my other ear.

Haunting # 3: The same bedroom had a window facing out onto the garden. One morning I awoke and heard my mother feeding the lambs outside. As I looked out of the window, the handle of the window turned itself up without my assistance and the window opened by itself. After this, when entering the bedroom, I would always make sure that the curtains were drawn far enough that I didn't have to see the handle of the window. When I was outside in the garden, I would always keep my eyes from looking up towards the window.

Haunting # 4: From the age of thirteen to eighteen, I would wake each morning at 6 a.m. and bike to the village where I delivered newspapers to the villagers. Each morning in seasonal light and darkness I rode two miles to the store where I was to collect the papers. Each morning I would ride past a barn at the top of the lane leading from the family home. The barn was on my right, and there was a slight incline in the lane before this barn. The barn had seen an incident many years before in which, supposedly, a woman by the name of Molly Morton had fallen to her death. She is said to roam the lanes I rode my bike on. Each morning as I rode past this barn and on my return home I would close my eyes and sing.

He learned that he had to protect the body and seal it off from a possible encounter. He learned how to embody fear and to attempt to control it. As if it had a skin, a surface. A point and place where it could absorb, summon and capture. An insular vessel that captured experience and repeatedly held it, caught as if suspended.

How do you absorb an experience?
How do you greet a haunting?
How can our experiences be stored and called upon?
How do you capture and reproduce a moment using your body?
How do you make of your body a ghost?

When Goat Island considers material that has been brought into rehearsal as part of the creative process, we must consider how it enters our bodies and jogs our memories. The material could be a question, a fragment of text, a physical movement, an object in a collection, a found fact that connects itself with a gesture that reminds us of an error, a mistake, a coincidence, perhaps long forgotten. As a moment of insight collides with a misunderstanding, so an investigation begins. It is our nature to physicalize our acts of learning, and to learn from our bodies' responses.

In exploring performance material—in turning it over, over time—we have to consider its relationship to ourselves, to its source, to its other self, in order for it somehow to be captured, physically. How do you take on a condition or instruction, how do you embody and absorb it, while also questioning and resisting that which is taken on? How can a body create resistance to itself? How do you resolve these gaps, hold these spaces in tension?

An act of recording ourselves,
Itself,
An event,
A memory,
A dwelling,
A childhood,
A trauma
keeps replaying itself over—if not in the body then in the fixtures of dormant walls and surfaces, where in the spaces and gaps of invisibility it appears, half woken, ready to emerge. How to open the doors, air out the rooms, exorcize the ghosts?

In absorbing and embodying new material, we may consider the words of the American installation artist Ann Hamilton: "Part of making work is to allow for those things that perhaps are always already there but are not visible to us, and to try and make them visible" (Hamilton nd.).

Or we may consider the words of French photographer Henri Lartigue, who when asked whether a camera is a trap for vision, explained that he had been trapping vision long before he had a camera:

> It's something I did when I was little. When I half-closed my eyes, there remained only a narrow slot through which I regarded intensely what I wanted to see. Then I turned around three times and thought that by so doing, I'd caught—trapped—what I was looking at, so as to be able to keep indefinitely what I had seen, but also the colours and the noises. Of course in the long run, I realized that my invention wasn't working. It's only then that I turned to technical tools for facilitating it.
>
> (qtd in Virilio 1991: 11–12)

These thoughts to me somehow address the value of performance in the world. Our attempts to look at situations, to listen to language, to recall memories, to ask questions, are given particular focus through our attempts to capture and embody these realities anew. How and why do we ingest a dance, a text, an object, a history, a figure who disappeared or is no longer with us? As Jean Baudrillard writes in *The Perfect Crime*:

> To recover the trace of the nothing of the incompleteness, the imperfection of the crime, we have, then, to take something away from the reality of the world. To recover the constellation of the mystery (secret), we have to take something away from the accumulation of reality and language. We have to take words from language one by

one, take things from reality one by one, wrest the same away from the same. Behind every fragment of reality, something has to have disappeared in order to ensure the continuity of nothing—without, however, yielding to the temptation of annihilation, for disappearance has to remain a living disappearance, and the trace of the crime a living crime.

(Baudrillard 1996: 3–4)

How to forget Lin Hixson (Goat Island 2001a: 6–7)

I watch a German documentary on TV. The filmmaker has taken fragments of 32 scenes from German instructional and training films and compiled them into one film:

How to sell insurance.
How to wash patients in nursing.
How to test beds for longevity with rolling metal bars.
How to test washing machines by repeated shakings.
How to test toilet seats by lifting them up and down over long periods of time.
How to do a striptease.
How to be sensitive to a senior citizen who has lost her keys.
How to resuscitate a victim.
How to live.
How to rehearse to live.
How to live the rehearsed taught by the professionally living.

I decide to edit together my version of the "How To's" taken from the German version of the "How To's". It is two minutes. I give separate videos of these minutes to each member of the group to watch in order for them to perform and re-enact the instructional enactments of the people and the machines in the film. In one part of this edit, an elderly actress in a community theater is being directed to perform the act of a woman who has discovered she has lost her keys. She moves to the wall, over to the door, catches her breath, and retraces her steps. This becomes "The Lost Keys" dance in our performance *It's an Earthquake in My Heart*.

In rehearsal, I watch Karen and Mark in our performance space try to recall the actress performing the act of memory loss. They are searching for the steps of the actress who has now learned the steps of an imaginary woman who has lost her keys. Soon, Karen and Mark will learn these steps too. They will have achieved the how to of losing one's keys. It will become second nature to them. They will not think before performing the steps. The act of loss will have been enacted, made into the unseen law of their bodies.

I ask myself:

- Are we all looking for something as though we've lost it?
- Have I lived my memories? Or did they come from some high-rise office on Lake Street?
- And if I could remember, keep forever, just one story, what would it be?

How to remember Mark Jeffery (2004b)

In his book *Sculpting in Time* the late Russian filmmaker Andrei Tarkovsky states:

> If you throw even a cursory glance into the past, at the life which lies behind you, not even recalling its most vivid moments, you are struck every time by the singularity of the events you took part in, the unique individuality of the characters whom you met.
>
> (1996: 104)

Action 1: I would like you to recall all of the objects that were in the living room of your family home when you were a child. Please write them down.

Action 2: What was the largest thing? What was the smallest thing? What was the largest thing made out of? What was the smallest thing made out of?

Action 3: What does / did your mother / grandmother / aunt or father / uncle / brother/ do for a living? What were the materials connected with their livelihoods?

Action 4: On a sheet of paper I would like you to draw the largest object associated with your mother's job, and the smallest object associated with your father's job.

These instructions are a way of focusing a group and of seeking to capture a certain kind of charged materiality. In my own personal history, the gathering of objects with specific associations becomes somewhat of a fetish or a way to recall and remember. How do we create a localized, personal vocabulary that comes from a certain place, tone, collection, archive? I often think the inhabited world of Goat Island is one in which we interact with objects that suggest a kind of temporal imprint; we try to find materials that will present themselves in the space with as much presence and charge as the performers. Somehow each element we use contains a trace, a remainder and a reminder of how it—or something like it—was once situated and framed, even as we resituate it, reframe it.

Matthew Goulish: *A repair gives an object a triple life, and makes that tripleness visible. A window has cracked. The custodian has applied a transparent plastic square to the cracked area with epoxy. This will prevent further fracture if the kids' basketballs hit the window. It also stays within the building's organization budget, which cannot afford to replace the window. Now when we look at the repaired window, we see: (1) the ghost of the original unbroken window; (2) the residue of an unknown force, in the window's crack; (3) the result of a thought process, in the clear plastic patch. We see three windows at once—whole, damaged, repaired.*

(Goulish 2004a: np)

Misconstruction Lin Hixson (2004: 130)

One of my tasks as the director of Goat Island is to hold distraction and attention together; to use an arising galaxy of forms, multiple histories, multiple bodies, and multiple ways of knowing; to keep the locality of site and remote vistas in the same room; to allow a constellation of situationally arising units, bound to time, accident, and circumstance.

Five performers sit on stools in the new performance. We travel to Glasgow for a residency. We do not want to take the stools. They are too heavy. We ask the producers in Glasgow to get stools. We arrive in Glasgow. There are no stools. Bryan Saner, a member of Goat Island and a carpenter, goes to the wood shop at The Royal Scottish Academy of Music and Drama to make them. Since we are re-making the stools, I re-make my idea of a stool. It should be one-legged so the performers have to balance themselves to sit. And while Bryan is at it, why not make a long stool for the arm of Simone Weil to rest on when she, as Paul Celan, says the following words:

> Pour the wasteland into your eye-sacks,
> the call to sacrifice, the salt flood,
> come with me to Breath
> and beyond

(Celan 2001: 387)

Bryan returns with the stools. The long stool looks nothing like a stool. It is, instead, a crutch. Simone Weil now rests on it. Damaged. In need of repair.

Travel. Weight. No stools on arrival.
A situationally arriving unit has given us a path of repair to follow.

LITO: (interrupting): *All right now everybody. QUIET, and listen to me.*
There is a hole in the performance.
We, the performers, must escape through this hole within the next 90 seconds.
This is not a drill. Fetch the hole and fetch the escape equipment.
Hurry. . . .
Show them the hole. . . .
Good. . . .
Get as close as possible to the hole. Cover your eyes.
I will count to seven, then we will escape together through the hole.
Failure to do so could result in irreparable damage.
Don't ask me to explain—the math is too complicated. . . .

STEVE: And now this is me talking to myself. There is a hole in this text. Something is missing and it's just here at this point in the edit. I know it every time I read it over. (How do you talk about time and process and make it cohere in a few thousand words?) So I just inserted the passage above, and now I'm going to pretend that I'm asking Bryan a question in an interview, but the interview was years ago and I just reconstructed the question in an attempt to plug the hole. So anyway, Bryan, there's one thing I still don't get. If the working process is so lengthy, if you keep following all these divergent lines of enquiry, or interrupting lines of enquiry to pursue others, picking up on accidents and misinterpretations and so forth, how do you ever know when the performance is actually finished?

BRYAN: think you know it's finished when you've looked at all the details and have at least asked and answered the questions. You might have doubts about whether or not you've given it the "right" answer, but you certainly know if you haven't answered the question. You look at what's in front of you, and if there's a detail that hasn't been dealt with, it's not finished. That's how I would finish a sculpture: if there's some curves or some lines that I haven't really paid attention to, then I need to. And when I've dealt with all that, all those textures and surfaces and lines, I'll say it's done. Whether it's perfect or not, that isn't the question.

(Saner 1997)

Date sent: Saturday, February 07, 2004 11:39 PM
From: Matthew Goulish
Subject: ecology question
To: Steve Bottoms

Dear Steve,

I took the day today, a cold Saturday in February, to write out my thoughts in response to your question about how ecology relates to our work. I have other thoughts on economy, and what has changed since we started, but this answer turned out so long, I thought I had better send it first.

Thanks as always,

Matthew

Ecology and compactness Matthew Goulish (2004a: np)

In work-in-progress conversations, people sometimes ask us how we know when a piece is finished. I think they ask this for two reasons. The first is perhaps that, in the absence of a clear linear narrative, people wonder what guidelines exist for finishing. The second, related reason is that it is difficult to grasp the process of creation as a search for an unknown, working at those edges where understanding first appears. Maybe ecology, as a system of enquiry, can help describe the character of this search.

Ecological thinking considers each eco-system it studies to be contained within certain parameters; not infinite, but limited, and subject to fixed rules. For this reason, ecologists prefer to devote their research to islands. One can draw an outline around an island, and determine where the island stops and the ocean begins. Darwin could trace the evolution of the creatures on the Galapagos more easily without the complications of migrating creatures passing through and disrupting trends. In the case of the island, one can immediately identify three ecologically closed systems: the island, the ocean, and the edge. We could say from the standpoint of our work, that the performance is the island, the audience is the ocean, and the edge (shoreline) is the shape of the performance space. Each has its own complex set of rules. I will try to say a little about why I think the performance itself is an ecologically closed system.

First, we have to distinguish between an open system and a closed system. Gradients, or pathways, characterize trajectories in an open system. For example, if one seeks something in an open system, one follows a path to its source. One finds faint tracks, and walks along them in the direction in which they grow less faint, until encountering the tracks' maker. Take the example of Fred Flintstone smelling his dinner. The cartoon odor of good cooking wafts out of the kitchen. The instant he smells it, his nose attaches to the scent and lifts him up. With a dreamy expression on his face, he floats through the air into the kitchen (the direction in which the odor grows stronger) and arrives at the odor's source, the dinner table.

Now imagine Fred Flintstone in a closed system: the dark inside of a giant beach ball. The sealed environment presents him with certain problems. When the odor of good cooking arises at dinner time, it arises everywhere. The entire interior smells equally of dinner. In no direction does the smell grow stronger. Yet it has a source. How does Fred find it? Rather than tracing a gradient, he must follow rules, such as: when you smell dinner, run as fast as you can in any direction until you bump into the kitchen table.

Gradients and pathways become apparent in open, infinite, and endless systems; systems made up of collections of systems. Closed systems, singular in nature, take on more mathematical characteristics. Ecology is the science of studying a system as if it is closed.

We may now return to the How-do-you-know-when-it's-finished question. Our work I think finishes when it closes as a system of thought or experience: when each moment in some way points equally to each other moment. It proposes its own logic, or set of rules. We arrive at this quality by following each subset of rules along the way, but each aspect of the piece proposes its own subset of rules. We need to search according to the rules that limit the search. A narrative is like a gradient: a line with a source and an endpoint. But searching in a narrative manner can sometimes mislead us.

Before we find the conclusive balance of the piece, there can be a great deal of confusion for audiences when they see a work-in-progress. They can confuse the relative significance of structures, sources, and concepts. They think one needs to know the sources in order to interpret the concepts correctly. It is difficult for us to communicate—or for that matter even to understand—the process of searching for a kind of equilibrium in which sources, concepts, performative moments, and even elements of structure and duration, all point equally to one another. But one way of thinking about it clearly is to consider it an ecologically closed system—an island—and to tailor one's work on it in that direction: working toward echo and return rather than toward resolution.

It was with this principle of working toward creating a closed system that we approached a particular dilemma which arose during the latter stages of working on our new piece, *When will the September roses bloom? Last night was only a comedy.*

We had proposed a piece in two different versions, to be performed on consecutive nights. On the first night, the introductory section "a" would be followed by "b1", then "b2", and then concluded with "c". On the second night, b1 and b2 would be performed in reverse order: a/b2/b1/c. As the piece advanced, we were able to run both sequences in rough form through the first three parts (a/b1/b2 and a/b2/b1), and also had a notion of what c might contain. After watching these rough run-throughs, Lin came to an uneasy conclusion. Late in our three-week residency in Columbus, she sat us down and announced that we had a problem. The piece, she said, adhering to this structure, always fails at the same point: halfway through whichever b section comes second. She explained that a/b1 works nicely, as does the transition into b2. But then halfway through b2, it becomes irreparably tedious. Conversely, a/b2 works nicely, as does the transition into b1. But then halfway through b1, the piece again becomes irreparably tedious. I was fascinated by her proposal: that a dynamic structure fails in a dynamic way. The failure seemed somehow to float beyond the material itself. It was instead a failure of duration, of the structure of the time. She proposed that something needed to "fly in" to the piece, the same disruption, at the same point, on both nights.

Her thoughts proposed a new fixed point in the structure, as a and c are fixed. Since we discovered it after c, we decided to call it d, even though it makes its appearance in the piece before c. The revised structure now looked like this:

> First night: a/b1/b2(start)/d/b2(end)/c.
> Second night: a/b2/b1(start)/d/b1(end)/c.

d supplants part of the section it replaces. In either case, the audience will see different material on the different nights. They will see the middle of whichever b section comes first, performed in a way undisrupted by d. The company seemed instantly pleased by this scheme, and they grew fond of referring to d as "the flying wedge." But now the question became, what is d? What performative material does it contain?

While we were in residency in Columbus, I had arranged a short math tutorial for myself with Professor Brian Rotman, who is on the Ohio State University faculty. For reasons initially unrelated to the piece, I had asked him a question about topology, and he had explained to me Goeddel's PhD thesis on *compactness*. I understood the concept as follows: one renders the universe as compact by proposing a point outside of it, and by including that point in the universe itself. Or one could say that by pointing to an outside, one defines an inside. I thought of this now in relation to the question of d in our piece. At the point at which this pointing outside arises, the concept of closure also arises, and the piece is finished. It becomes compact.

Back in Chicago, I asked for some rehearsal time for the presentation of a proposal. d, I suggested, could express the exterior of the performance itself: my half-idea for executing this was that each of us in turn attempt to "escape from the piece," and that the only route for that escape was the hole in the middle of the large cardboard disc that Bryan uses in the performance to give a demonstration of the principles of clockwise and counterclockwise rotation: he puts his finger through this hole to rotate the circle on its axis. Consequently, the hole was the only point on the circle that did not turn in either a clockwise or counterclockwise direction. It was the piece's exterior. In trying and failing to force our bodies through it, we would point to the outside of the piece's universe, and by doing so define all else of the piece as inside, ourselves (our bodies) included.

A tiny opening in time and space through which we attempt to escape the performance.

Lin asked us each to prepare responses to this idea. At the next rehearsal, Bryan passed Mark's "shadow" (rendered as a black thin plastic silhouette) through the hole. Mark attempted to cut away at the hole and widen it. Karen dribbled water from behind the hole, and inflated a white rubber glove through it. Litó performed a dance of getting sucked into the hole as into a drain. I whispered, "Help!" through the hole. Lin brought in a short speech from *The Poseidon Adventure*: "That's the only way out!" Subsequently, she began arranging fragments of these escape responses into a short, somewhat hysterical sequence.

With a sense of relief, we start to see how the creation process of the piece can draw to a close. Each time, I wonder whether we can actually accomplish what we set out to attempt. But the possibility draws closer, and I have great faith in the members of the group. This particular sense of relief also has to do with the feeling that the questions people ask at works-in-progress will start to subside, as will our incomplete responses. Proposals and interpretations will start to replace questions, and while the form may be strange to many people, they will recognize it as a form. The completeness of the experience of the piece will reveal the partialness and provisionality of our explanations of it. The set of fragmentary points of movement, text, structure, music, lighting, etc. will cohere into some enchanted shape. And while not every audience member will like what they see, they will recognize in it something tangible, some clarity beyond the intentions and abilities of those who created it, some aggregate of temporal structure and physical presence that animates into ghostly life. We could call that animation the appearance of the angel of form. Or we could simply call it compactness. Whatever we call it, we will welcome its arrival.

Now in the accelerated time of late capitalism that wags its finger and speaks its slogan that time wasted is money lost, I watch Litó in rehearsal waste time by balancing on one foot. All the past energy of repetition and endurance funneled into a balancing act of resistance. One foot on the floor, the other leg bent at the knee and lifted high like a show-horse. Her arms straight at her side, these too lifted but ever so slightly. Determined those arms, like oars in the sea, she weathers weather. Those arms serve as ballast in the wind and those hands point the way like a compass and the stars. Standing there on one leg her muscles move. The standing leg quivers. The whole body shakes again ever so lightly. But it whispers its firmness; speaks its resolve; calls out its decision to stand upright in a tremulous stillness to quiet it all; the all being determined by the length of two James Taylor songs—"Sweet Baby James" and "Fire and Rain"—that being 377 seconds, equalling 6 minutes and 17 seconds.

I think of the choreographer Yochiko Chuma, who in 1992 stood still in St Mark's Church in New York City and said, "I do not feel like dancing." It was the time of the Rodney King verdict, the first Gulf War, and the war in Bosnia. The writer

24 *When will the September roses bloom? Last night was only a comedy.*
Photograph by Boris Hauf. Alfred ve Dvore Theatre, Prague, Czech Republic, 2007.
Pictured left to right: Bryan Saner, Litó Walkey

André Lepecki (2000), when researching stillness in dance, was struck by the possibility that stillness emerged in moments of historical anxiety and could be seen as a body's response to those moments.

Sweet dreams and flying machines in pieces on the ground
Oh I've seen fire and I've seen rain
I've seen sunny days I thought would never end
I've seen lonely times when I could

discover in this act of a leg held high against gravity in the act of time passing away in the fullness of time an act of commemoration commemorating the unspoken, the unthought and the forgotten.

"Stillness is the moment when the buried, the discarded and the forgotten escape to the social surface," writes Nadia Seremetakis (1994: 12).

Litó stands. Perhaps the buried, the discarded and the forgotten stir beneath her feet.

C. TEACHING

A On pedagogy

B A workshop

C Letter to a Young Practitioner (2007)

A. ON PEDAGOGY

from **"Tenderness, for Lynda Hart"** by Peggy Phelan (2002: 21–25)

The Chicago-based performance ensemble, Goat Island, has a moment of exquisite tenderness in their work, *The Sea & Poison*. The performance is physically exhausting. The four performers do what they call "an impossible dance," a complex movement performance that involves a lot of jumping up and down in rhythm and then falling down on one's back and lifting the legs up and down with more rhythmic tapping and then up again on one's feet for more jumping. In between these long jumping and falling sequences, various narratives start and stall. The "plot" involves some toxic spraying, some remembering and forgetting, and some business with plastic fish; mainly there's a lot of water and dirt and a feeling of playfulness and exhaustion all at once. Then the performance pauses after about ninety minutes of physical sweating and running, and in that pause, *The Sea & Poison* finds its center. Matthew Goulish, who is slightly built, climbs onto the tall, strong Bryan Saner, lacing his fingers across the back of Saner's neck. Saner carries Goulish in a full body embrace around the circumference of the stage. In a fascinating discussion of this scene, Chris Mills remarks: "In a performance where much of the text is about contamination and malady, Goulish's combination of a nearly-comatose body posture, the psoriatic look of his lolling skull and his unfocussed stare all read as envenomed death or near-death" (Mills 2000: 5).

After several loops around the stage in this difficult embrace, Saner positions his burden in front of a microphone and Goulish creaks out, "What is the name of this field?" Saner then resumes his carrying but this time he rotates around the narrow circumference of the microphone and stops when he is positioned in front of the amplifier and Goulish's back faces the audience. Saner replies, "The field here is called The Scuts. This name shows how old dialect words are often crystallized in field names." After speaking, Saner picks up Goulish again and they repeat their circular track. Goulish, again facing the microphone, asks: "How do you mean?" Some laugh painfully in the audience. Again Bryan shoulders Matthew and around they go once more. Bryan, now with gentle patience, replies: "The word scut is a variation of the word scoot. A scoot is the triangle left within the headlands after a field of an awkward shape has been ploughed. Robert Savage referred to it as a box-iron piece, a piece of land roughly the shape of an old fashioned box-iron." Bryan appears satisfied, as if he has answered everything there is to ask about the field. But Matthew is indefatigable and once again Bryan carries him around the microphone's circumference. This time, Matthew asks, "What's a box-iron?" Bryan reverses their positions once more and replies, "It's an old-fashioned iron used for smoothing linen. And he [Savage] related that the old ploughmen used to refer to the plowing of this type of field as goring work. A gore or gusset is, in fact, another name for a scoot. That's how this field here came to be named The Scuts." Exhausted and sweating, the two reverse positions once more and Matthew, his voice now creaking with effort, asks once more, "What is the name of this field?"

Watching this scene I feel as if I am seeing pedagogy at its most elemental. Paedagogus, I recently learned, was the name of the elderly slave who gathered up the young boys and walked them to hear the lessons of Socrates and Plato and the other philosopher-kings. In classical Greek depictions of him, he has an enormous cock, a too eager grin: he's the quintessential dirty old man. When I saw his image I knew instantly (but for the first time) that he could not be the teacher; he was far too happy. As a slave, he was cast as the pedophile, the walker of the young boys who would learn how to become masters, and not only of philosophy. Looking at this Greek art, I felt a kind of relief. While I am now accustomed to the routine misogyny of academia, I am still startled by the violence of its class distinctions. Seeing the historical Paedagogus brings me up against the vastness of the various historical, economic, and gender displacements and continuities that have led us from the Greek's conception of Paedagogus, to our own understanding of pedagogy. Watching Matthew and Bryan perform their exhausted dialogue about the field, I realized anew why the Greeks prized the erotic bond between male teachers and students. Such bonds include both the tender love the aging feel for the young, and the resigned love the teacher has for the student, who will, because he must, make his teacher dust. This ambivalence produces a kind of amorphous tension often associated with erotic desire. In *The Sea & Poison*, the teacher carries the questioning student, knowing full well that the facts he proffers do not and cannot fulfill the student's desire, because the student wants a response that cannot be given by the other. (In this, the dialogue also echoes Jacob's struggle with the Angel, the quintessential story about the struggle to name and to be named by the beloved.) The student asks and the teacher answers once again and together they produce their repetitions. Some consider these repetitions love. As Matthew and Bryan circle the microphone, they retread the tracks that constitute the cycle of teaching and learning: the patient response to the question that cannot be answered fully produces the repetition of the same question, one

amplified by its own echo. Goat Island might be dramatizing the history of the field and its names, but they are also exposing the ways in which love itself provokes and provides access to questions and responses. Love, despite its toxicity and violence, can bring us closer to the softness of words, and therefore closer to the possibility of expressing human tenderness. If one is ambitious enough to want to create a shared history, then one must be willing to risk an impossible dance, one that pivots on a desire strong enough to outmuscle exhaustion, a desire alive to our wavering capacities to bestow and to receive responses, and an apparently insatiable desire to question these capacities and what motivates and blocks them, repeatedly. Watching Matthew and Bryan dance their impossible dance, I remember my own history as a student, endlessly curious, asking-asking-asking until I was dead on my feet, and I remember myself as a teacher going back around and around when asked, over and over again, *what is the name of your field?* The answer is not Performance Studies.

The Sea & Poison stages the poetics of exhaustion. In this, it speaks to our age—our age in the sense of this, our zoom-zoom accelerated cultural moment, and our age in the sense of the historical chronology of live art as such. Set against a loose narrative of toxicity and deterioration, *The Sea & Poison* exposes the attenuated, but still persistent, call of the life drive in a landscape overrun by the history of death. This is the field first ploughed by Samuel Beckett. In the distance traversed by live art between Beckett's *Waiting for Godot* (1953) and Goat Island's *The Sea & Poison* (1998), theatre has mapped the ever-dimmer prospects of theatrical plant life. Beckett's single tree does—amazingly—grow leaves, but Goat Island can only offer us a kind of Chia-pet tree literally growing out of Matthew's wet head.

While theatre historians have—for very good reasons—concentrated their energy on Beckett's two philosophical tramps Didi and Gogo, the more prescient achievement of Beckett's play resides in the character called, with perfect Irish wit, Lucky. One can trace Lucky's legacy in contemporary theatre and performance ranging from Caryl Churchill's *The Skriker* (1994), to Suzan-Lori Parks' *Venus* (1996). In creating Lucky, Beckett approached something transformative in our understanding of character after the catastrophe of World War II. This transformation in understanding is both prospective and retrospective; therefore, readings of Shakespeare's *Richard III* are as transformed by the catastrophe as are our encounters with Churchill's *Skriker*. Fundamental to these alterations is our own exhaustion. Faced with the recounting of the history of genocide begun during World War II and continuing in places such as Rwanda and Bosnia, we begin to lose our logic, our capacity to judge, our energy to follow the plots and counter-plots of a story whose point seems impossible to grasp. In this, we are latter-day Luckys. Having seen too many Pozzos posing as philosopher-kings, we stumble forward only to be hauled back and turned around, not so much by the urgency of Pozzo's bark, but more by the nagging dream of what it might have once sounded like. Lucky's impossible speech in Act One, a recitation that mimics the structure and rhythm of philosophical thought but conveys no discernible meaning, becomes in Act Two, a mute vocabulary of gesture, indeed an impossible dance. But the work of Goat Island reminds us that even after everyone falls down, limbs asunder and knotted in rags, something propels us to our feet, and to our exits and entrances, once more. This propulsive force is the life drive, and it is both fierce and tender.

Still looking for a master and still certain of (his) death, like Lucky we labor to carry the baggage of a history that everywhere exceeds our grasp and everywhere outpaces our capacity to learn from it. Aware of the impossibility of our situation but unable to transform it, we pivot in the repetitious rhythm of wanting to be alleviated of our hunger and, because we know such nourishment can only produce more killing hunger pangs, wanting not to want the bones.

It is here that theatre might begin to be approached as an epistemology of love, one whose value comes precisely from its intimacy with the fleshed bodies of players and observers. Beckett gives the bones to his tramps because he knows that the body clings to its appetites, despite having better wisdom, smarter plans. The bones won't save the tramps. But they might keep the play going a little longer. Love, in the end, will get planted in skin's soil because, like words, love approximates the thing it seeks. From such approximations, tenderness sometimes springs. A leaf appears before the final leaving.

Shakespeare's apparently intimate relation to love's approximations help him forge the poetry of exhaustion at the core of the sonnets:

> That time of year thou mayst in me behold
> When yellow leaves, or none, or few, do hang
> Upon these boughs which shake against the cold,
> Bare ruin'd choirs where late the sweet birds sang.

These yellow leaves are the ones that appear, so unexpectedly, in the exhausted tree of *Godot*, and get translated into the green clovers that curl across the lip of the Chia-pet tree planter that Matthew Goulish wears, so ridiculously, so heroically, so lovingly, and so jauntily on his head in *The Sea & Poison*.

B. A WORKSHOP

0: To begin

0.1: We come from a country that has made a fetish out of proving it can live without art.

(C. D. Wright, *Cooling Time* 2005: 7)

0.2: Surely one way to argue for the necessity of art in a democratic society is that it proposes change without violence, that it has the capacity to alter received relations between one another, ourselves, and the world without coercion; to allow us

to see differently
less afraid of what we do not know
to include that which is, those who are, different from ourselves.

(Ann Lauterbach, *The Night Sky* 2005: 157)

0.3: The absolutely foreign alone can instruct us.

(Emmanuel Levinas, *Totality and Infinity* 1969: 73)

0.4: The possibility of mutual transformation of both the observer and the performer within the enactment of the live event in unscripted ways is extraordinarily important, because this is the point where the aesthetic joins the ethical. The ethical is fundamentally related to live art because both are arenas for the unpredictable force of the social event.

(Peggy Phelan, "Marina Abramovic: Witnessing Shadows" 2004: 575)

0.5: . . . they are encounters, paths of a voice to a perceiving Thou, creaturely paths, sketches of existence perhaps, a sending oneself ahead toward oneself, in search of oneself . . . A kind of homecoming.

(*Selected Poems and Prose of Paul Celan* 2001: 412)

0.6: I say to students: write from the known into the unknown, as if on a journey. This is not a matter of forgetting everything so much as a coming upon the place where all belongings and habits and familiar surroundings are suspended, and you begin to move on, out, away, and what propels this movement, this *trajectory*, is a desire to find out what you do not yet know. As if language were a sea, buoyant, which will hold you up as you go along.

(Ann Lauterbach, *The Night Sky* 2005: 122)

0.7:

I will go into the ghetto: the sunlight
for only an hour or two at noon
on the pavement here is enough for me;
the smell of the fields in this street
for only a day or two in spring
is enough for me.

(*The Poems of Charles Reznikoff* 2005: 182)

0.8: There are no miracles except for the poor.

(Edmond Jabès, *The Book of Margins* 1993: 123)

0.9: To study is not to consume ideas, but to create and re-create them.

(Paolo Freire, *The Politics of Education* 1985: 4)

0.10: In art, and in painting as in music, it is not a matter of reproducing or inventing forms, but of capturing forces.

(Gilles Deleuze, *Francis Bacon: The Logic of Sensation* 2003: 56)

0.11: Let all the avenues be equal, not only so an idle eye might linger on the view, but because no other method gets the earth to give in matching measures and grants the boughs free rein and run of air.

(*The Georgics of Virgil*—instructions for planting a vineyard 2004: 51)

0.12: What I have learned cannot be generalized, but it can be shared.

(Hélène Cixous, *Three Steps on the Ladder of Writing* 1993: 7)

[LH, MG]

1 Introduction

1.1 *How to use this chapter*

We have assembled this chapter from documents and plans of actual Goat Island workshops. We intend it to function both as a teaching guide and as writing on the subject of teaching. We teach collaboratively, with company members rotating into and out of the role of teacher/leader. We formulate the shape and structure of the workshop in advance, and individual members often devise and detail the steps that they lead within that framework. For this reason, the initials of the leader/deviser appear after each step to reflect the balance of individual voices: Karen Christopher [KC], Matthew Goulish [MG], Lin Hixson [LH], Mark Jeffery [MJ], Bryan Saner [BS], and Litó Walkey [LW].

This chapter adopts the structure of a one-day workshop. It collects multiple versions of each step. One could assemble a workshop by selecting one version, or by mixing aspects of the variations. Some of the commentary by company members offers a level of detail and depth outside the possibilities of a one-day workshop. These derive from the three-week summer workshop presented annually at The School of the Art Institute of Chicago, and other similar, longer workshops.

[MG]

1.2 *Workshop introduction*

We aim here to provide a place for all of us to work and study together in a structured, creative, communal environment. We hope to guide you with some methods and ideas that we use when making work. We are, at the same time, guided by you. Each workshop takes on a very specific life of its own, driven by the people involved. All of you come from different backgrounds and practices. This workshop will focus on live performance. We will also examine writing, sound, structure, research, and other forms of expression. These forms are, at times, dictated by your interests as well as by our experience. This is also to say that you do not need any specific training in performance to participate in this workshop. We are interested in destabilizing the boundaries between disciplines and between creative and critical modes. Your differences and varieties of expression make this possible.

Creating community and understanding methods of collaboration are key issues presented and examined in the workshop. You will be working collectively as well as individually, and we will try to put you in as many different configurations as possible so you have a chance to work with many of the other participants.

In general, we will begin with an emphasis on doing and experiencing rather than on talking and discussing. This is deliberate on our part. We will reserve some time for conversation to conclude the workshop.

[LH]

2 Writing

2.1 *Version 1: interruption*

Prepare your writing materials, but do not begin writing yet.

Consider a time when you were **in motion**.

[The *you* does not need to be yourself. You may write autobiographically, or you may imagine yourself as another person, or as a fantasy, fiction, or dream. I will give you the instructions in this form, as if asking you to write from your own experience, because that is the clearest way to communicate the instructions to you.]

Consider a time when you were in motion: walking, in a vehicle, on a bicycle, flying in a dream—some form of motion, real or imagined, maybe the first one that comes to mind. Begin writing by writing about the motion, or in relation to the motion. You may write in any form: description, dialogue, fragments of language, notes to yourself. You do not need to write well. You will not have to share what you write with anyone. Write in detail in relation to the time when you were in motion—the speed, the quality, the intention, the duration, of the motion.

Consider **an interruption** to your motion. How was your motion interrupted? What interrupted it? By interruption, I mean that something stopped you, distracted you, rendered your motion out of sync, caused you to swerve, or intervened in some other way on your motion. Maybe this was a large and pronounced interruption, a radical break, or maybe it was a small, even microscopic interruption. Whatever makes sense for what you wrote in the first part. Write in detail about or in relation to the interruption to your motion.

Consider your **motion and interruption as a single event**, an aggregate, the two merged into one phenomenon or image. Write in detail about, or in relation to, the motion and the interruption as combined into one event.

Imagine **an impossible opposite** of the motion/interruption aggregate phenomenon. What is the opposite of that event, even if that opposite is impossible? Write in response to this question.

Take a moment to notice **a pattern** in the motion/interruption event that you have written about. This may be a pattern of your own devising or observation. Write to describe or to reflect this pattern.

Now imagine, or remember, **an interaction with a stranger** at some point during or after your motion/interruption event—maybe a spoken word or dialogue, maybe simply a look or a gesture, or some other form of interaction. Write about or in relation to this interaction.

Review what you wrote, and extract the following three elements:

question
answer
date, time, and place.

The question may have been spoken by you, or it may be a question that you have in relation to your event, or a question that appeared in some other way in your writing. You may or may not know the answer to it. The answer does not need to answer the question. It may answer a different question. Try to pinpoint the date, time, and place of your event as accurately as possible, even if you need to guess.

You will share these three elements with the other members of the workshop. Think of them as texts to be spoken aloud, by yourself or someone else.

You may begin by underlining selections from what you have written in response to these three elements. Extract those selections and recopy them onto a separate worksheet. You may rewrite them if you wish as you recopy them.

Outside of the workshop you may return to the rest of the writing that you did. For now, everyone will proceed out of this step with only these three elements.

[MG]

2.2 *Version 2: absence and presence*

Prepare your writing materials, but do not begin writing yet.

Consider a time when you noticed that something or someone was **missing**. This missing X could be an object, a person, a quality, an event; large or small, trivial or significant; real or imaginary, historical or personal. Maybe choose the first thing that comes to mind. Begin writing when you have a clear sense of this missing X, by writing about the absence. You may write in any form: description, dialogue, fragments of language, notes to yourself. You do not need to write well. You will not have to share what you write with anyone. Write in detail in relation to the absence.

Now write **three questions** regarding the absence—generated by your writing thus far in this first part. You may or may not know the answers. They could be questions simply in proximity of the absence, distillations or extractions from your writing. You will share these questions with the other members of the workshop. Think of them as a text to be spoken aloud, by yourself or someone else. Write the questions and underline them.

Now consider a response to the absence you wrote about, a response in the form of **a presence**. This could be an arrival, a repair, a substitute, a replacement, a return, a new memory; expected or unexpected, welcome or unwelcome. Begin writing when you have a clear sense of this response to the absence, by writing about the presence. You may write in any form: description, dialogue, fragments of language, notes to yourself. You do not need to write well. You will not have to share what you write with anyone. Write in detail in relation to the presence.

Now write **three answers** regarding the presence—generated by your writing thus far in this second part. The answers are lines of text in the form of statements, in relation to the presence. They do not need to answer your earlier questions. They may answer entirely different questions. They may be distillations or extractions from your writing in this second part. You will share these answers with the other members of the workshop. Think of them as a text to be spoken aloud, by yourself or someone else. Write the answers and underline them.

❖❖❖

Select one question from the three questions that concluded the first part of your writing, and one answer from the three answers that concluded the second part. Recopy your **question and answer** onto a separate worksheet. You my rewrite them if you wish as you recopy them.

Outside of the workshop you may return to the rest of the writing that you did. For now, everyone will proceed out of this step with only these two elements: a question and an answer. Keep your worksheet retrievable in a safe place. You will receive instructions later on how to make use of it.

[MG]

3 Movement

3.1 Version 1: tender and imperfect

Sit in the space so that you have a person on each side of you (like a circle). **Prepare** two separate blank sheets of paper and something to write with. Orient the sheets as "landscape" rather than "portrait." Write one line of text on each sheet, according to the following directives.

On one sheet of paper write down an action / task / gesture that you would consider **tender**.

On the other sheet of paper write down an action / task / gesture that you would consider **imperfect**.

Fold both sheets in two and very carefully tear each sheet in half. You now have four pieces of paper. Please name them as follows: **left tender half**, **right tender half**, **left imperfect half**, and **right imperfect half**.

Pass **right tender half** to the person on your left. Pass **left tender half** to the person on your right.

Pass **left imperfect half** to the person on your left. Pass **right imperfect half** to the person on your right.

Now reassemble your halves as follows: **left tender half + right imperfect half = new line A**; **left imperfect half + right tender half = new line B**.

Take a few moments now to generate and devise **two specific physical movements**, one from each of the hybrid lines you have received.

Focus Activity: Close your eyes. The workshop leader will say, "Start." 55 seconds later the workshop leader will say, "Stop." Try to become sensitive to the duration of 55 seconds. Concentrate, and try to retain the specific duration as if your body were a recording device.

One-minute solo #1 Divide the body as follows: head to lower torso / lower torso to feet. Perform your line A movement moving down the upper half of the body, from the head to the lower torso, in seconds 0–30; perform your line B movement moving down the lower half of the body, from the lower torso to the feet, in seconds 31–60.

One-minute solo #2 Maintaining the same body division, perform your line A movement moving up the lower half of the body, from the feet to the lower torso, in seconds 0–30; perform your line B movement moving up the upper half of the body, from the lower torso to the head, in seconds 31–60.

Now take a few moments to **generate a new line C movement**, as a combination of your line A movement and your line B movement.

One-minute solo #3 Perform your line C movement stopping and starting 6 times during 1 minute. Consider that at each re-start you must accelerate and catch up.

One-minute solo #4 Perform your line C movement with one body part making unbroken contact with a surface (wall, floor, furniture) for the entire 60 seconds.

One-minute solo #5 Take a moment to lie on the floor and indicate the space demarcated by the length of your body, from the bottom of your feet to the top of your head. Imagine a square floor space determined by this measurement. Perform any of the previous solos, or any combination of movements from the previous solos, for 60 seconds within this space.

[MJ]

3.2 *Version 2: impossible task*

Sit in the space so that you have a person on each side of you (like a circle). **Prepare** a separate blank sheet of paper and something to write with.

Take a moment to think of **an impossible task**, and write the task on your sheet of paper.

Pass the paper to the person next to you.

Take a few moments now to **generate and devise a movement** that attempts the impossible task you have received.

Construct the movement so you can **repeat it**, and simplify it so you can **teach it** to someone else.

One-minute solo #1 Repeat this impossible task movement for one minute.

One-minute solo #2 Perform the movement very slowly; one repetition per minute.

One-minute solo #3 Half of the group, stand shoulder to shoulder in a line. Perform your movement while taking one minute to move with the line from one side of the room to the other. (Repeat with the other half of the group.)

One-minute solo #4 Verbally describe the movement aloud while standing motionless.

One-minute solo #5 Perform the movement in reverse.

One-minute solo #6 Extract one sample of your movement. (For example, choose a ½ second section out of the total movement phrase.) Repeat this sample for one minute.

One-minute solo #7 Imagine your total movement is a piece of paper, and you can fold it or overlap it so that some things happen simultaneously or everything is compacted into ½ the space and time. Perform it this way twice over the course of one minute.

One-minute solo #8 Choose two body parts. One of them can be a body part that has been broken or injured. Use that body part as a miniature of yourself, and perform your whole movement with just that body part. The second body part will be a stage for your miniature self to perform on. Perform your movement using your new performance body on the miniature body part stage.

> If you do not understand the instructions, perform what you think you are being asked to try. Perform your confusion or misunderstanding with confidence.
>
> Questions for consideration:
>
> Does your movement have a front and back?
>
> How does the movement look when viewed from the other side?
>
> Do you see your movement as dance? choreography? labor?
>
> Does the movement remind you of anything new, not related to its source?

[BS]

3.3 *Version 3: falling*

Sit in the space so that you have a person on each side of you (like a circle). **Prepare** two separate blank sheets of paper and something to write with.

Take a moment to imagine or remember an **object that is falling**. On one of the pieces of paper, write down the object that you imagined falling. Fold the paper in half and place it by your right side.

Take a moment to think about the consequences that resulted from this object falling. Choose **three consequences** that you can describe as physical activities. Write three short descriptions of these physical activities on the other piece of paper, fold it in half, and place it by your left side.

Pass the paper by your left to the person on your right. Pass the paper by your right to the person on your left.

Unfold both of the papers that you receive. You should have **one object and three physical activities**.

Take a few moments now to **combine these elements, and generate and devise a short movement phrase with** a clear beginning and end.

Show this short phrase, as you've created it, together with half of the group for the other half of the group to watch.

Show your movement phrase with the following **variations**:

Perform it three times. Over the three rounds of repetitions, **start slow, accelerate, and decelerate to slow again**.

Perform it once **as if being moved by someone else**.

Perform it as many times as you can **while locomoting along the floor** from one end of the space to the other.

Perform it **standing still with small bursts of the phrase interrupting the stillness**.

Perform it **in longer bursts inserting short bursts of stillness**.

Perform it together with someone else who is also performing their phrase. Walk close to this other person and perform your phrase **as if whispering** to this person.

[LW]

3.4 Version 4: repair

Sit in the space so that you have a person on each side of you (like a circle). **Prepare** two halves of a blank 8½″ × 11″ sheet of paper and something to write with.

Take a moment to imagine or remember **something that needs a repair**. Consider a physical rather than a psychic or emotional repair. Think of the repair of a machine or object of some sort, perhaps something that you use every day that has broken or could break or simply malfunction.

Conceive of this **repair in five steps**. On one of your blank halves of a sheet of paper write down five steps that will effect the repair. Number them one through five.

Now identify your **most injured body part**. It may not be injured now, it might be that it has healed already, but it is the part of your body that, up until now, has been injured the most. Write the name or a description of the body part on your second half sheet of paper.

Pass the paper with your five step instructions to the left. Pass the paper with your injured body part to the right.

Take three minutes now to **make a dance in five parts**. Base each part of your dance on one step of your five-step instructions. Make sure there are five distinct parts and that you number them. **Use the body part identified** on your other sheet as the focus of your dance. I have called it a dance, but you may think of it as sculpture with your body, as a movement poem, or as a pedestrian task.

One-minute solo #1 Find a space in the room to perform your sequence from start to finish. Begin again if the time allows.

One-minute solo #2 Perform your sequence so that it lasts exactly one minute. If you didn't make it to the end, speed it up this time. If you had to repeat your sequence, find a way to lengthen it.

One-minute solo #3 Perform your sequence with the idea of fading. Take the idea of fading any way you like.

One-minute solo #4 Perform your sequence with the idea of expanding. Take the idea of expanding any way you like.

One-minute solo #5 Imagine you can cut up your sequence, rearrange it, and tape it back together, tightly or loosely, speeding up parts, slowing down parts, and using sporadic repetition. Perform it this way so that you still complete it in one minute.

Now take a moment to gather your thoughts about the various versions of your sequence. **Decide on a sequence or combination of sequences** that you will take into the next step.

[KC]

3.5 Version 5: attack and decay

Sit in the space so that you have a person on each side of you (like a circle). **Prepare** a blank sheet of paper and something to write with.

Take a moment to think of **a simple task**—simple in the sense of everyday or mundane—and write the task on your sheet of paper.

Exchange papers with the person on your left.

Read the task you have received. Think about how you can add to the task or alter it to **make it impossible**.

When ready, write the **altered task** on the opposite side of the paper. If you are adding to the task, make sure you write out the whole new altered task, not just the alteration.

Exchange papers with the person on your right.

Determine a 3-foot square area in the room to work in. Take 3 minutes to **construct or enact the impossible task in the 3-foot square**.

❖❖❖

We are now going to look at the tasks, and we will look at them for a specific length of time. We want to start with **54 seconds**. You may have an activity that is 4 seconds long, so you have choices to consider. You can repeat the activity for the length of 54 seconds, or you can extend one cycle of the activity to last 54 seconds. If you are repeating, consider the idea of a pause or stillness between the repetitions. You may have an activity that is 2 minutes long. In that case, you will need to edit or shorten it to fit within 54 seconds, or you may need to do it faster. **Perform your task for 54 seconds**.

> Focus. Where are your eyes during the activity? Are they focused on one point? Does the focus change while you are performing the activity? Consider this while performing.

Now we will divide the group in half so half can watch while the other half performs. Take 11 steps in a line out of your square. **Perform your activity traveling** this 11-step distance in half the time: **27 seconds**.

Now we will divide the group in quarters, and perform in four smaller groups.

Consider the dynamic of **attack and decay**: attack as a beginning, decay as an ending. Divide your 27 seconds into 2 parts of unequal length. For the first part, consider the dynamic of attack. For the second part, consider the dynamic of decay. You may attack aggressively or delicately. Decay can happen very quickly or very slowly. Perform your activity, still traveling the 11-step line, for 27 seconds, divided into part one: attack; and part two: decay.

Now borrow a gesture you have observed in someone else's attack/decay performance, and add this into your sequence as an **interruption**.

You now have a sequence containing a beginning with the dynamic of attack, a middle which is an interruption based on someone else's gesture, and an ending which addresses decay. Perform this sequence for **54 seconds**.

[LH]

4 Collaboration

4.1 *Duet*

We would now like for you to take some of the generated writing and movement material and combine this material with another person. We will place you into pairs by a chance operation. Please take one of the cut up dog shapes that I have placed on the floor. Once you have the found the person who holds the matching other half of your dog, please sit down with your "dog partner."

We would like for you now to construct a duet working with the following menu.

- Give the duet an exact duration of one minute and twenty seconds. Consider either an external or internal timing mechanism. You may have someone outside of the duet time you, or you can time it somehow yourselves. Make this duration part of the structure of your duet by using it as material.
- Begin the duet with one of you saying your first name and end it with the other person saying their first name.
- Include the Question and Answer from the writing exercise. Your duet will have two of these Q & A's to work from, so please consider working with all or part of both. We would like for you to speak these texts aloud.
- When combining the movement, consider emphasizing a body part; think about slowness, quickness and stillness; consider splitting a generated gesture across the entire body or across two bodies; consider how a gesture may migrate, fall and rearrange itself onto you and your new partner.
- Consider where you focus your eyes.
- Consider how you start and how you end.

You will have 20 minutes of work time and then we will see the duets.

Note on viewing: When we see the duets we will ask that each duet decides when they are going to present their 1 minute and 20 seconds. Once this has been decided and everyone knows where each of the other duets is in the room, then in silence the first duet will begin. Once the first duet has finished, I will gesture to the second duet, and so on until we have seen them all.

[LH, MJ]

4.2 *Quartet*

We have paired each duet with another duet. In the next 45 minutes, combine the two duets to make a quartet performance that is 3 minutes and 37 seconds long. You will be 4 people working together. Please include the following 5 elements.

Engage **structure** in two ways:
A. *Fixed*: devise your quartet in A–B–A form, so it is palindromic. The beginning and the end recognizably echo one another, and the middle is different.
B. *Floating*: include a moment of unison activity at some point in your quartet.

Think of **time** as one of your materials. You have 45 mins to make a 3 minute 37 second performance. Consider both your working time and the time of your quartet carefully. Appoint one member of your group timekeeper.

Use the **duet** material you have just performed (including movement and writing). Combine the two duets into one quartet. Include the writing that has not been used (date time and place and spoken text).

Use the specific **space** that we have assigned to each quartet in the room as one of your materials. Think of how the space will affect your movement and text. Adapt your existing material to the new site. Consider where the audience will be when watching the performance.

Consider your **working process**. Present your material to the group. Rotate the task of directing the performance so the performance reflects 4 different minds or sensibilities.

The 5 points above are practical collaborative performance tools that will help you work together and compose a quartet.

[BS]

4.3 *Quartet writing*

Consider **a fragment** that you or another member of your group brought into your process today. Write what you remember about this fragment.

Consider **a second fragment** (with a different author) that was brought into your process today. Write what you remember about this fragment.

Write a list of words, thoughts, phrases, or ideas that **link** these two fragments: a list of possible links or linkages. These may have been already observed and noted in your process, and now you are simply recording them, or they may occur to you now for the first time.

Write a list of words, thoughts, phrases, or ideas that **counter** both of these two fragments.

Blankness is an important quality that is completely ignored, especially by architects. It creates a kind of horror at its emptiness, but it is a very important thing to allow and to come to terms with. Our profession is indoctrinated to never allow something to remain empty, or undecided, or undetermined. That goes from the large scale to the small scale. Now there is an enormous birth of detailing. On one hand that is fantastic, but on the other it creates an incredible feeling of pressure: every chair has a hundred thousand ideas, an ambition to express something, perhaps the way it is put together, that simply draws attention to itself. Great attention is given to the packaging of space, but no attention to the space itself.

(Rem Koolhaas 1996: 63)

Write about the particular **blankness**, or relationship to blankness, in your group performance. What are its qualities? Does it relate to sound, silence, space, an approach to performing, or some other aspect of the performance? Maybe you discovered it today, or maybe you are thinking about it now for the first time.

Write about the particular quality of the **force** or energy captured by your group and your group's performance. What are the specific, unusual, or valuable qualities of the force that your group captures?

[MG]

4.4 Collaborative methods

4.4.1 Find a structure in which every voice is heard. If you tend to speak a great deal, try to make sure you wait and listen occasionally. If you normally remain silent, try to speak now and then. Remember that having *a voice* need not always connote speaking. Sometimes a quality of attention can become a kind of voice.

4.4.2 Work from people's strengths. Make sure everyone is challenged creatively. Allow the entire group to work from each strength of each individual. For example, pretend everyone in the group is as good as the best dancer.

4.4.3 Work toward complexity rather than simplicity.

4.4.4 Do not expect to understand everything intellectually or rationally while creating or performing. There are many forms of understanding. Also, if you work from a position of *not knowing*, you may find understanding will come later.

4.4.5 Contribute a fragment rather than a complete idea. Through the group process, the ideas complete one another.

4.4.6 Balance talking with doing.

4.4.7 Begin the collaborative process with *showing* the material each member has created rather than *telling* each member about the material or about an idea.

4.4.8 Try different approaches, such as allowing each member to take responsibility for one portion or aspect of the process. Each member may oversee one part of the performance as a director. One member may become the designated timekeeper. One member may oversee choreography, while another oversees spoken text. Or the responsibilities may divide in other ways.

4.4.9 If you encounter problems during the process, try doing another activity together, such as taking a walk or drinking tea.

4.4.10 Try everyone's ideas even if you think you have an instant dislike to those ideas.

4.4.11 If you think you have no connection to someone else's material and are having trouble performing it, try to allow your vision and yourself to expand to include that person's material, and to learn from it.

[KC, MG, LH, MJ, BS, LW]

5 Presentation

Thoughts on commitment

Goat Island summer school, Chicago, July 25, 2006

Sometimes just before a performance, our minds can be occupied with practicalities and stage management responsibilities rather than with the concerns of performing. We might also be subject to exhaustion and anxiety. I have found it helpful to take a moment to consider the following thoughts on commitment and doubt.

Two questions sometimes come up at this point, on the day before a public presentation. Although we haven't heard any of you ask them, we wanted to anticipate them and propose some answers.

The first question is this: "What if we just suck?"

It is important to anticipate this question, because even if it has not occurred to you yet, it might occur to you during the actual performance. To propose an answer, we have to look at the question itself. There we encounter the "we" problem. To explain what I mean by this, I have a quote from David Warrilow. He was a self-trained actor who premiered many of Samuel Beckett's late works for theater. This is what he said.

> There was a time when my perception of the audience was "us" and "them." I was so full of anxiety and insecurity that I was not able to enter into the proper flow of the exchange, as I now perceive it can be and ideally must be . . . I therefore was for a long time in the position of investing a great deal of energy in defending what I was doing against supposed critics—often because of the unusual nature of the material or style that I was involved in.
>
> What I had to understand about the actor's relationship to the audience . . . with a piece of work that one would consider dense and difficult and to some people dark was to what point members of an audience are willing to be challenged, the degree of courage that they bring to the theatre experience.
>
> If I as an actor invest myself to the best of my ability in the work I have chosen to present—if I give it my best energy—then there's a chance that the audience can trust what is going on on stage. If I hold back, if I sit in judgment on myself or the material or the audience, then there is less chance that the audience is going to be justified in trusting and therefore joining the experience. If the actor is willing to go through some kind of transmutation, then the audience can, too.
>
> (Zarilli 1995: 319–321)

The "we" problem lies in the distinction the question makes between performer and audience. This is why the question is a false one. The division between performer and audience arises as the result of fear; fear of the material, the experience, the responsibility of committing oneself to it.

By commitment I mean a quality of focused attention. We cannot make an easy distinction between the material and the manner of its performance. Intensity of concentration transforms the material. This quality of focused attention lends the material its sense of value.

This commitment (as Lin mentioned Monday morning) establishes an anchor, an energy that can bring the audience into the event, rather than allowing the event to react to the energy of the audience.

This commitment is also a commitment to the unlikely—to the impractical, not-normal activity of performance.

This commitment establishes a sympathetic vibration that eradicates the distinction, even if only for a moment, between the performer and the audience, it destabilizes the "us/them" difference, and falsifies the question, "What if we just suck?"

This commitment more than anything else requires courage. Courage is fearlessness. By this I do not mean that you have no fear, or that if you feel fear or anxiety or doubt you are doing something wrong. I only mean that if you experience fear, anxiety, or doubt, you allow those feelings to occupy a place of lesser importance. Those feelings are normal and common, and less important than the uncommonness of the performance.

This may bring up the second question: "What if this is not what I had hoped for? What if this is not the performance I had wanted to make?"

The answer to this also involves courage—the courage to accept difference, and to accept doing less than what you are capable of *as* if it is not less; to accept doing something different than what you had hoped to do *as* if it were not different; to accept the task of doing something you think you are not good at *as* if it were your specialty.

To illustrate this, I have an anecdote.

It is raining. You have just been to the grocery store. At the bus stop, you set your grocery bag down on the bench, and the bottom of it gets wet. It's a paper bag. When you finally get home, just outside your door when you are about to go in, the bottom of the bag tears out and all the groceries fall through and are ruined.

In Zen they call this enlightenment.

The past (all the groceries you bought and carried all the way home) and the future (all the wonderful meals you had planned to cook) have vanished in an instant. All you have left is the startling lightness of the present, a simultaneous great sense of relief that you no longer have to carry that weight, and a feeling of disappointment for what has been lost. Is this all I have? This is all I have. You experience the infinitely less and the infinitely more of this present moment. An accident, an overflow, a collision with the unexpected—has forced you to commit to this present. In that commitment, there is no us and them, but only us. There is no good or bad, better or best, right or wrong, but only the fact of now.

So let the great future that you had planned fall out of the bottom of the bag. Let the past that you brought with you fall out of the bottom of the bag. Let them get out of the way so you can pay proper attention to the fact of now. Commit to what you have, the lightness of the present. You need nothing more than this.

What you have made is full of miracles—incidents of the apparent suspension of the normal laws of nature. They may not be the miracles you thought you would make, or the ones you wanted to make—but they are miracles nonetheless.

Your commitment to your performances is what allows us to recognize the miraculous in them, and what makes the returns they give us infinite and unexpected.

You have no more work to do than that, and we have nothing more to say but thank you.

[MG]

6 Creative response

6.1 Introduction

When we engage the creative mind, the object upon which we focus our energy seems to proliferate. For example, if we attempt to make a collection of green things, and we engage the creative mind for this task, we begin to see green everywhere.

Often we think we can engage the critical mind separately from the creative mind. We think that to be critical means to be negative. In fact, critical simply means discerning, or able to separate the observed object into parts. The critical mind turns out to be another version of the creative mind.

If we think of critical as negative, however, if we think our critical task is to observe and make a collection of problems to be corrected, then problems become the object of our creative mind masquerading as a critical mind. We then start to see problems everywhere. We become proficient at observing problems. We become one who is defined by the ability to observe a proliferation of problems. Because of this approach, the creative mind seems to shut down when the critical mind is engaged. In fact, the creative mind has only been engaged negatively, and because of this habit, when we set out to make our own work, to engage our creative mind deliberately, we experience paralysis because we have trained ourselves to observe only problems.

For now we will try an experiment. We will engage the critical mind to observe the moments in the work we are looking at that seem to us the most exceptional and inspiring—the miraculous moments. Maybe this approach will allow us to keep the creative mind deliberately engaged as we engage the critical mind. Maybe we will start to see miraculous moments everywhere. We will become one who is defined by the ability to observe a proliferation of miracles.

Rather than making a critical response to the work you are observing, make a creative response to it. Think of the creative response as your own work that would not have existed without the work you are responding to. Start with the most obvious miraculous (exceptional, inspiring, unusual, transcendent, or otherwise engaging) moment that you see in the work. What appears obvious to you may not appear obvious to anyone else.

You may have an association with that moment that makes the moment miraculous for you. You may echo the moment in your creative response, multiply it, work out from it in some other way. The moment may have been intentional or accidental. Instead of a moment, maybe you respond to a structural element, a visual element, a spatial element, or some other quality in the work observed.

If we can destabilize the boundaries between the critical and the creative, we may enrich them both, and discover a communal practice—one that relies on one another for inspiration and energy, both critically and creatively.

[MG]

6.2 Version 1: silent response

Each individual in your quartet will devise a silent response to the work of one of the other quartets. You will devise your response as a solo. The four members of your quartet will begin by standing in a line. Then your quartet will present all four responses simultaneously. You do not need to plan as a group how the four solos will work together. Since you are all devising with the same intention, you may allow the responses to align accidentally.

Consider placement in space, timing, rhythm, color, the weight of movement, and that your response will occur simultaneously with three others. As you compose your response, consider what silence offers. Try to present material that actively avoids the use of sound rather than material that has had the sound removed from it.

[KC]

6.3 Version 2: three line response

Write three lines in response to the quartet to which you have been assigned to respond.

Decide on a still position or posture from which to speak your three lines aloud.

Organize your three lines into a sequence, and revise them with this sequence in mind. Make the line to be spoken second exactly three words long.

[MG]

7 Conversation

Write six sentences to share with the group in response to your own performance, with one sentence addressing each of the following six criteria.

1 An insight you gained from yourself.
2 An insight you gained from one or more other members of your quartet.
3 An insight you gained by accident.
4 An insight you gained from a creative response to your quartet.
5 A turning point.
6 Free sentence.

[MG, LH, MJ, BS]

00: To conclude—Writing: community

"A universal community" excluding no-one is a contradiction in terms; communities always have an inside and an outside. That is why Derrida's comments on "community"—which is otherwise a mom-and-apple-pie word, at the very sound of which every politician's knee must bend—are always extremely guarded, on guard against the guard that communities station around themselves to watch out for the other. . . . We might say that a "community" in deconstruction would always have to be what he calls "another community," "an open quasi-community," which is of course always a "community to come," and a "community without community" . . . One might even dream of a community of dreamers who come together to dream of what is to come.

(John D. Caputo 1997: 108, 124)

Prepare your writing materials, but do not begin writing yet.

Consider the **actual community** in which you create work. It might be a community of one, of two, or of many. Begin writing by describing this community, its characteristics and activities. What is in this community that gives you support?

Consider an **imagined community** that supports you and your creative practice. Continue writing by describing this imagined community's characteristics and activities in detail.

Record a **dialogue** between yourself and an individual in the imagined community.

Something unexpected transpires in the imagined community. Continue writing by describing this **unexpected event**.

Describe the **steps** you might take **to actualize the imagined** community from the actual community that you have now.

[LH]

C. LETTER TO A YOUNG PRACTITIONER (2007)

The members of Goat Island wrote "Letter to a Young Practitioner" collaboratively, and delivered it for the first time at The School of the Art Institute of Chicago on March 16, 2000. This 2007 revision reduces the six original contributions to make space for a new contribution by Litó Walkey.

Transitions from one writer to the next are marked by / . The authors progress in the order in which their names appear at the end, which was determined by chance.

Italicized passages have been appropriated and/or adapted from writings by Sappho, Virginia Woolf, Rainer Maria Rilke, and Marcel Proust.

To a Young Practitioner,

"You can render a high service to your own community, and to the whole country, by co-operating with all movements to accelerate building constructions, especially of family dwellings, new roads and public works. These measures will provide employment, enlarge buying power, increase the circulation of money, create markets for farms and factories, and assure prosperity and contented homes."

I found this text during a Goat Island workshop, on a research visit to the Elks Memorial Building in Chicago. It was one of a series of texts, images, and sounds collected on the trip, which later served as a resource for making a collaborative performance. Instructions for the research trip included finding: (1) a gigantic detail; and (2) an echo from two different constructional forms, examples being a wall/painting—or ornament/furniture.

Friends unfamiliar with Goat Island's performances ask me what they do, and I tell them: they use text, but not to tell a standard theatrical narrative; and they use movement, though it's not what you would expect by the term "dance." And combining those texts and movements creates something beyond those individual components of text and movement, and the best word we have for that is "performance."

Bryan has said "we practice creative research and assembly." Lin sees "research as an agent from the outside that transforms the material within; that brings nutrients to the digestion of our personal, individual experiences."

Through collaboration, concepts of individual authorship are blurred; the creative material connects to others, and is completed by them. Creative tools are developed which focus on process, systems, and structures. Use what is around you: the other workshop participants, the room you're in, the building, the city. Use your memory as a resource, not as a route to nostalgia or therapy, not necessarily to tell your story, but to reveal the extent to which your body contains multiple narratives. Critical evaluation is transformed into the need to respond creatively. The work exists in the moment, perhaps not yet even assimilated or understood by the artists who made it. Think formally, then thematically.

Keep a journal observing the incidence of the color yellow.

And in ten years you will find yourself living in San Francisco, writing a letter, which says: "CJ refuses to believe in the existence of the absolute. I have found it." And you will mail this letter to the person who, ten years earlier, wore your left black leather glove at the same time you wore your right black leather glove.

This is not everything I have to say, but this is all the time / for all we've experienced together. I would like to review now. Seven thoughts for youth:

#1 Remember other people.
Focus outside yourself. Concentrate on your co-workers, your audience and those who have nothing to do with you or your art. Remember that there are people who live outside your world. We like to remember these because there is more to life than art. We like to remember these because there is hunger and injustice outside. Remember these others congregate nearby and share your ground.

#2 Beware of Genius.
Look for a sense of humor in those you collaborate with. Work with your friends. Look for conflict resolution skills, forgiveness, the ability to listen, the ability to place faith in your fragmented ideas, a comfortability with failure, a commitment to respect difference, a disciplined nature, and a love of work.

#3 Make small plans.
Temper your big dreams. Dream the smallest thing you can think of and try to perfect that. It's good to have one tiny perfect thing in your history. There are infinite details to perfect in a small venture and the changes force themselves in, expanding the vision.

#4 Value your body.
This physical body is the meeting place of worlds. Spiritual, social, political, emotional and intellectual worlds are interpreted through this physical body. When we work with our hands and body to materialize an idea from within, we imprint the work with a sweat signature; the glisten and odor which only the physical body can produce. These are the byproducts of the convocation of worlds through the physical body. It is visible evidence of the practice and effort to progress from conception to production.

#5 Work slowly.
We appreciate the works of old world artists because of the time they invested in their art. Their bodies were not more capable than ours to join wood or paint masterpieces, but they did have a different concept of time. Perhaps they were more at ease with its passing. Look for long periods of time at your project. Keep a vigil for hours beside it. Practice sustainability. Put it away and forget about it. Bring it back years later to finish it after you have become a different person.

#6 Learn to say no.
If you work slowly you will not have time for everything you desire, so you will pass up creative opportunities. The chance of a lifetime actually comes quite frequently to those who are looking. You will regret having said no to great prospects and you will learn to live with that regret. In return, you will have time.

#7 Be thankful for your fears.

Curiosity leads you to this edge.

Add this to the others as / the day is still beginning.
Never take the same route, always vary your path.
Don't write with a slow pen get one that flows well.

See as a new eye, as a novice, as someone who isn't jaded by fixed notions.
Invent 7 ways to exit your chair.
Stand with the smile of a sad person. Mark the place where your soul lives.
Breathe out through the nose like my grandmother's labored breathing. Life was heavy and hard and she lived long and did not believe she would die, no not that way.
Breathe in with light and lift.

She said: *With my arms I don't think I could touch the sky.*
But you can.

Dive a hundred times into a harbor.
Fall into the grip of another.
Perform a whirling dance to purge the toxic spider venom.
Move in place as seven body parts step in the same spot at least twice before you can make a new footprint. Breathe only once every fourteen moves.
All that my heart longs for, may you achieve, and be my accomplice.

Get your writing materials ready. Close your eyes.
Adjust your body so that you are sitting comfortably.
Take a deep breath. Let your shoulders relax.
Let your forehead relax.
I forgive you all the endless hours you were away.

Coming apart at the seams, I need to get a hold on things in my brain. A building is coming down across the street. Men are turning the bricks and mortar to fine silt with a huge machine and the dust shoots out into a pile.

The dust is everywhere and settling in my room.

But when, from a long distant past nothing subsists, after the people are dead, after the things are broken and scattered, taste and smell alone more fragile, more faithful, remain poised a long time, like souls, remembering, waiting, hoping, amid the ruins of all the rest; hear unflinchingly in the tiny and almost imperceptible drop of their essence the vast structure of recollection.

Memorize to perform. Perform to remember.

You are probably wondering / if you can do this.
Maybe you can, maybe you can't. Just try it.

Where will you find what you want to do? Will you find it in what you separate for contemplation? Or is it somewhere else, in the attitude you adopt, the way you receive things in order to sustain a special quality of experience?

What you do, that thing you choose to try, isn't something separate from life. It is a natural activity. Rather than something to learn to do, it is something you can participate in with a certain adjustment of attention.

You need less to be someone who has something to say, and more to be someone who finds a process. Finding a process will bring up things that you would not have thought of if you had not started to do them.

Don't be too full with intention. Being in a hurry and competition can be harmful to creativity. Being too effective doesn't help you in being a good guide in the tentative activity of creating.

Remember, it has never been done before. You are not going to be communicating any already discovered "truths." You are engaging in a job of experiment. It's like any discovery job; you don't know what's going to happen until you try it. All life is like that. You don't make life be what you've decided it should be. You find out what life is trying to be.

"Now, look carefully, in those trees, you may be able to see the owl better than I can."

Find time and stay receptive. Being receptive is accepting what occurs and being willing to fail.

Don't bother with high standards. Get into action and don't let anything stop you.

You are following a process.
You are making something new.
Something that has not been done before.

No one else can guide you, so become coherent.
Lead yourself to connections.

"Take a deep breath, dive in, and sometimes you can swim." (My mother told me that.)

It's not always easy to know when, but at some point you have to abandon. It is not up to you to determine or value what you've done. Others will decide the significance. They will do this through a sequence of reboundings.

Encourage people to trust that there is reason for what occurs to them. If they behave as alertly and readily as you have, they will not dismiss their own idea, their own pictures and their own puzzlement.

And then, when you can, answer me this. It is my last question: / How do you continue to sustain a practice? I am now trying to decide this as I write to you. I still consider myself a young practitioner.

I am at a point of preparing now; paying close attention to all the details, small and large that present themselves in ideas, research and actions.

In an exercise on departure during a Goat Island Summer School, I was given a white sheet of paper from a participant with a single word written on it. The word was openness. We asked each participant to take the single words given to them as a gesture of a gift to take with them, and possibly guide and incorporate into their lives throughout the year.

Openness is now Blu-tacked onto the wall next to my work desk at home. This single word I have taken into my daily life.

The act of receiving, and the acceptance of this gift is an important philosophy I adhere to, especially in the practice of one's artwork. Through receiving one can see many different levels of how to be influenced, to take on others' thoughts as presents and reinterrupt them into your own mind and body. Once the digestion of the gift has been articulated in oneself then you can begin to understand the nature and the power of sharing. This idea of ownership becomes a wider participation, and one of interaction, circulation and creativity.

Roger Bourke, conceptual installation artist and teacher, once advised me to stop first, and then look, and most importantly listen and be patient with your work. Do not rush; allow us the viewer to see what you are making. Be confident and allow the material to come to you, begin to see with different eyes and learn the value of listening, the silence of yourself and others.

In hearing these words of guidance it allowed for confidence to build. The act of mentoring and listening is a large part of my teaching and arts practice. To create a space where seeing and hearing is an integral and pivotal role in how to be understood and acknowledged. As a young practitioner it is your decision whom you wish to take from and be influenced by. Choose wisely. Identify possible situations you wouldn't normally come into contact with. Allow for a great deal of care.

Be open to new discoveries. Be excited by the many languages you are able to learn and allow the act of creation to / understand who you are.
Understand who you could be.
Understand the gap between the two.
Sometimes, close the gap.
Become who you might be for a moment.
What if we call that moment: "the classroom"?
I have had enough of the rules.
How straight the path, and how strict.
This you must do; this you must not.
That explains why we repeat the same thing over and over again.
Ask yourself in the stillest hour of your night, will that ever be your homework?

Or might this be your homework?

1 What is shaped like a hand?
2 What can you lift?
3 What is the opposite of music?
4 What unbalances?

Take as much time as you need.
Strain the machine.
Never think yourself singular.
Don't labor under the burden of importance.
Don't use up all your energy chasing the dollar.
There are children in America who haven't learned how to play.
They sit immobilized, strapped into cars, into videogames, approaching their imprisonable years.
The municipality has removed their sidewalks.
Concentrate.
Do one thing at a time.
Because what if we call that moment: "the performance"?
I saw a dance, people I did not know, doing things I did not understand.
Yet I felt I knew them, and I understood.

And as I left the theater, I saw everything reel, as one does when one falls from a horse or bicycle, and I asked myself whether there was not an existence altogether different from the one I knew, in direct contradiction to it, but itself the real one, which, being suddenly revealed to me, filled me with that hesitation which sculptors, in representing the Last Judgment, have given to the awakened dead who find themselves at the gates of the next world.
I knew then that I had a place, and that I had found it.
I will love the experience longer than the rest because I have taken longer to get to love it.
Forgive me . . . I have been unwell all this time.
Writing comes hard to me, and so you must take these few lines for more.
I think of you often, and with such concentrated wishes that that in itself really ought to help you somehow.
Whether this letter can really be a help, I often doubt.

But what if we prepare ourselves not for the world as it is, but for the world as it might become?

In this preparation, we experience this world as it becomes that one, for a moment.

For now / I cannot speak without hearing your voice. It sits inside my voice and then outside my voice. I exist does not come before we exist. You start twelve mechanical birds chirping, read me directions to a ghost town. A woman walks by in a grass dress. You kick my imagination into the air. Like a dust particle it floats with your imagination. The two settle together on the floor. I cannot teach without you teaching me.

One does not always want to be thinking in the future, if as sometimes happens, one is living in the present.

At twenty, I expected in the coming years to live the life of an artist. Having had artist friends in high school who jumped chain-linked fences to swim in pools late at night when the gates were locked while I was trying unsuccessfully to fake an injury to remove myself from cheerleading; and having painted in a college studio with skylights, where Professor Thompson sat in the corner with a free-standing ashtray at his elbow flicking a long-ashed cigarette as he told me to observe the beauty when I turned my paintings upside down; having had these experiences I had an idea of the life of an artist. I was not prepared for researching pooper-scoopers, toys, and ear plugs for a patent office and delivering french toast to craving customers, leaving only fractions of night-time to make art. I pooled my energy with others, and together we had enough usable heat to make a performance. But then I saw the work of Pina Bausch, Tadeuz Kantor, and Tadashi Suzuki. I needed to work harder, much harder. These artists did not stop where I stopped. They ran so far that the distance covered caught me up and overtook me. I could make work of this distance only by taking time. I found collaborators who were not in a hurry. I rested in each moment and the moments accumulated. It was mundane, a plodding ordinariness, a daily step taking of two years to make a work, mundane in the sense of seventeenth-century astrology when the word pertained to the horizon—that visible line between time to come and time elapsed. The final performances had a rigor I liked. No one told me about this methodical, caught-in-the-moment beauty.

All you need now is to stand at the window and let your rhythmical sense open and shut, open and shut, boldly and freely, until one-thing melts in another, until taxis are dancing with the daffodils.

Yours,
CJ
Bryan
Karen
Litó
Mark
Matthew
and Lin

EPILOGUE

An Announcement Chicago, June 4, 2006

This afternoon we will present for you the first work-in-progress of a new performance. We started work on this piece in June, 2005. We hope to premier it in the fall of 2007. We anticipate that the finished piece will have three parts. Today we will present about 40 minutes of material of excerpts from part 1 and part 2. We hope you can stay for a 20-minute discussion after a short break.

We began this piece with an imagined research trip to the Hagia Sophia in Istanbul. We were fascinated by the lifespan of a building that had begun as a Byzantine church, was converted to a mosque, and then converted again to a museum. We wondered what alterations might have been made to the space to accommodate these conflicting uses, and we wondered what kind of a performance we might make in response. However, we lacked the funds to travel to Turkey, and instead found ourselves researching a similar building in Zagreb, Croatia, where our tour of our last performance took us. This round building in Zagreb was a museum, then a mosque, then a museum again. It is still referred to as the *dzamija*, the Croatian word for mosque.

In the space of our performance, we wanted to consider these changes not as conflicting theologies, but as movements encountered on different planes. We have given our performance a temporal structure reflecting the historical trajectory of Hagia Sophia, the triple life of church/mosque/museum.

Part 1 of our performance is a **Dance** in 13 rounds. Each round adds a triad of detailed movement. Through the course of the 39 movements, the performers diverge and reconverge, to a regular beat with irregular measures. We built this structure off the dome of Zagreb's dzamija, and we will present a portion of this dance today. In this part, we considered the interiority, the polyphonic proliferation of images, and the endurance aspects of Byzantine architecture and ritual.

Part 2 of our performance relies on **Instructions** for performance sent to us from invited writers and contributors. We present micro-performance fragments on a bare stage in response to each recited instruction. This is a sort of journey with no destination, but only a quality of attention. For this part, we considered the exteriority, the absence of representation, the emphasis on language, the call and response of Islamic architecture and ritual.

Part 3 of the performance will be a sort of **Concert**, and archive. For that part, we consider the overlapping histories, energies, and ghosts of the museum.

This structure, and each of its parts, especially part 3, have been informed by a second directive, which we introduced to the process after we began studying buildings with multiple religious uses. This second directive, we have come to call *lastness*.

This directive, first and foremost a creative one, derives from the decision that we have made as a company. This piece, our ninth performance, will be the last Goat Island piece. After we have completed creating and performing it, the company will end.

This decision comes from the challenge that all artists face: how to continue to grow, to venture into the unknown. We intend this end to present itself as a beginning. We have considered what comes after Goat Island—the multiple futures of company members, associate members, friends, audiences, students—those encountered and those yet to be encountered. We will do what we can to help sustain and multiply the practices of collaboration that the 20+ years of Goat Island have brought us. Each of us will continue to work in, and to advocate for, the field of performance. Our attitude as we arrive at this decision is one of gratefulness. It is time to find the change that growth necessitates. We end Goat Island in order to make a space for the unknown that will follow.

We have initiated this change ourselves, not in response to internal or external adversity, but creatively. We approach it, as we have tried to approach all changes —through a collaborative creative process. We want to provide an example of ending, of lastness, but it is an example we have not yet defined. We hope to discover that example through the two-year process of making this performance. We will show you this evening 40 minutes of what our research has presented to us thus far. Our lastness is no more and no less significant than our study of buildings.

Thank you.

❖❖❖

from: *A directive for our ninth performance in the form of last*

Last is a verb in the sense of continuing in time; surviving; remaining in good condition.

Lasting is the adjective that comes from this verb like lasting in the following seven book titles:

A Lasting Peace
A Lasting Spring
The Thyroid Diet: Manage Your Diet for Lasting Weight Loss
Thucydides' Theory of International Relations: A Lasting Possession
Lasting Visions of X—The Haunted Artist
The Headache RX: A Doctor's Proven Guide to Lasting Headache Relief
Landscaping with Roses: Planting Rose Gardens of Lasting Beauty

Last is a block or form shaped like a human foot and used in the making of shoes.

And *last* (chiefly British) is a unit of volume or weight varying for different commodities and in different districts, equal to about 80 bushels, 640 gallons, or two tons.

A directive:
Construct a last performance in the form of a human foot that weighs two tons and remains in good condition.

GOAT ISLAND TIMELINE

Fall, 1986	Work on a collaborative performance begins with Lin Hixson as director, and Matthew Goulish, Greg McCain, and Timothy McCain as performers.
Spring, 1987	*Soldier, Child, Tortured Man* premieres, Wellington Avenue Church gymnasium, Chicago.
Spring, 1988	Company selects name *Goat Island. Soldier, Child, Tortured Man* tours the US until spring, 1989.
Fall, 1988	Joan Dickinson joins company as performer/collaborator.
Fall, 1989	*We Got A Date* premieres at Wellington Avenue Church gymnasium, Chicago, subsequently tours US, UK and Europe until fall, 1992.
Winter, 1989	Karen Christopher joins company as performer/collaborator. Joan Dickinson departs company.
Spring, 1990	*Can't Take Johnny to the Funeral* premieres, Vooruit Centre d'Arts Teaterzaal, Ghent, Belgium, subsequently tours UK and US until summer, 1995.
Summer, 1993	*It's Shifting, Hank* premieres, Ferens Live Art Space, Hull, UK, and subsequently is performed in Chicago and tours UK and Europe until summer 1994.
Spring, 1994	*We Got A Date; Can't Take Johnny to the Funeral; It's Shifting, Hank* tour UK as *Goat Island Retrospective.*
Summer, 1995	Greg McCain and Timothy McCain depart company. Antonio Poppe and Bryan Saner join company as performer/collaborators.

Spring, 1996	*How Dear to Me the Hour When Daylight Dies* premieres, Centre for Contemporary Arts, Glasgow, subsequently tours US, UK, Europe, and Canada until end of 1997.
Summer, 1996	After teaching shorter workshops since 1989, the company teaches its first multi-week Summer School at the invitation of Glasgow's CCA. The company continues to teach Summer Schools every year in various international locations, including at The School of the Art Institute of Chicago from 1999 to 2008.
Fall, 1996	Antonio Poppe departs company. Mark Jeffery joins company as performer/collaborator.
Fall, 1998	*The Sea & Poison* premieres, Centre for Contemporary Arts, Glasgow, subsequently tours US, UK, and Europe until spring, 2002.
Summer, 2001	*It's an Earthquake in My Heart* premieres, Wiener Festwochen, Vienna, Austria, subsequently is performed in Chicago and tours UK and Europe until spring, 2003.
Winter, 2001	Litó Walkey joins company as performer/collaborator.
Fall, 2004	*When will the September roses bloom? Last night was only a comedy (a double performance)* premieres, Battersea Arts Centre, London, is performed in Chicago, and subsequently tours UK and Europe until winter, 2007.
Summer, 2005	In recognition of their ongoing close collaboration with the company, Goat Island adds associate members Cynthia J. Ashby (clothing design), Lucy Cash (film and video), CJ Mitchell (development), Judd Morrissey (hypertext projects), Margaret L. Nelson (technical direction), and Chantal Zakari (graphic design).
Summer, 2006	Company announces the ninth performance work, scheduled to premiere in fall, 2007, will be its last.
Fall, 2007	*The Lastmaker* scheduled to premiere at Teatar &TD in Zagreb, Croatia, followed by UK, US, and European tours.

BIBLIOGRAPHY

Agamben, Giorgio 2004. *The Open: Man and Animal*, trans. Kevin Attell. Stanford, CA: Stanford University Press.

Apple, Jacki 1991. "The Life and Times of Lin Hixson: The L.A. Years." *The Drama Review* 35.4 (Winter), pp. 27–45.

Bailes, Sara Jane 2001. "Goat Island." *New Art Examiner* 28.10 (July–August), pp. 44–49, 101.

—— 2004. "Report on a Process: Being in Waiting." In "*When will the September roses bloom? Last night was only a comedy*: Reflections on the Process," special edn of *Frakcija* Performing Arts Magazine, no. 32 (Summer), Goat Island, section 05, np.

Baker, Steve 2000. *The Postmodern Animal*. London: Reaktion Books.

Banes, Sally 1987. *Terpsichore in Sneakers: Post-Modern Dance*, 2nd edn. Hanover, NH: Wesleyan University Press.

—— 1993. *Democracy's Body: Judson Dance Theater, 1962–1964*. Durham, NC and London: Duke University Press.

Barthes, Roland 2000. *Camera Lucida: Reflections on Photography*, trans. Richard Howard. London: Vintage.

Bateson, Gregory 1980. *Metaphor and the World of Mental Process*. West Stockbridge, MA: Lindisfarne Association.

—— 2000 [1972]. *Steps to an Ecology of Mind*. Chicago, IL and London: University of Chicago Press.

—— 2002 [1980]. *Mind and Nature: A Necessary Unity*. Cresskill, NJ: Hampton Press.

Baudrillard, Jean 1996. *The Perfect Crime*, trans. Chris Turner. London: Verso.

Becker, Carol 1994. "The Physicality of Ideas." In *Hankbook: Process and Performance of* It's Shifting, Hank (Chicago, IL: Goat Island), pp. 57–64.

—— 1996. *Zones of Contention: Essays on Art, Institutions, Gender and Anxiety*. New York: SUNY Press.

Bergson, Henri 1911a. *Creative Evolution*. London: Macmillan.

—— 1911b. *Matter and Memory*. London: Macmillan.

Blocker, Jane 2004. *What the Body Cost: Desire, History and Performance*. Minneapolis, MN: University of Minnesota Press.

Bohm, David 1980. *Wholeness and the Implicate Order*. London and New York: Routledge.

Bottoms, Stephen J. 1996. "Re-staging Roy: Citizen Cohn and the Search for Xanadu." *Theatre Journal* 48.2 (May), pp. 157–184.

—— 1998. "The Tangled Flora of Goat Island: Rhizome, Repetition, Reality." *Theatre Journal* 50.4 (December), pp. 421–446.

—— 2000. "Biochemically Stressed: Goat Island, the Body, Technology and Poison." Paper presented at "Performative Sites: Intersecting the Body, Art and Technology." Symposium at Penn State University, October 26.

—— 2004. "*Poor Theater: A Series of Simulacra.*" Performance review. *Theatre Journal* 56.4 (2004), pp. 693–695.

Cage, John 1961. *Silence.* Hanover, NH: Wesleyan University Press.

—— 1992. *Roaratorio.* New York: mode records 28/29.

—— 1993. *Freeman Etudes, Books 1 and 2.* New York: mode records 32.

Calasso, Roberto 2001. *The Forty-Nine Steps*, trans. John Shepley. Minneapolis, MN: University of Minnesota Press.

Calvino, Italo 1993. *Six Memos for the Next Millennium*, trans. Patrick Creagh. New York: Vintage.

Capra, Fritjof 1996. *The Web of Life.* New York: Random House.

Caputo, John D. 1997. *Deconstruction in a Nutshell: A Conversation with Jacques Derrida.* New York: Fordham University Press.

Celan, Paul 2001. *Selected Poems and Prose of Paul Celan*, trans. John Felstiner. New York and London: W.W. Norton.

Charney, Leo 1998. *Empty Moments: Cinema, Modernity, and Drift.* Durham, NC and London: Duke University Press.

Chaudhuri, Una 1994. "'There Must Be a Lot of Fish in That Lake': Toward an Ecological Theater." *Theater* 25.1, pp. 23–31.

—— 1995. *Staging Place: The Geography of Modern Drama.* Ann Arbor, MI: Michigan University Press.

Christopher, Karen 1996. "Body Intelligence." Talk presented at the Goat Island Summer School, Glasgow. July. Printed in Goat Island 1997, pp. 75–79.

—— 1998. "Beginnings." Talk presented at the Goat Island Summer School, Glasgow. July.

—— 1999a. "Lighthouse." Talk presented at the Goat Island Summer School, Chicago, IL. July 22.

—— 1999b. "Faith and Pressure." Talk presented at the ArtNow conference, State University of New York, New Paltz. October 1.

—— 2001. "Goat Island makes *Earthquake.*" Text written for 6-minute video of same name, aired on *Art Beat Chicago* (WTTW public television), June.

—— 2002. "Stopping Time." Talk presented at Goat Island workshop, Kampnagel, Hamburg, Germany. April.

—— 2005. "Waiting, Wondering, Wavering and Wanting: The Performance of Silence." In "*When will the September roses bloom? Last night was only a comedy*: Reflections on the Performance," special edn of *Frakcija* Performing Arts Magazine, no. 35 (Spring), Goat Island, section 3, np.

—— and Bryan Saner 2003. Unpublished interview with Stephen Bottoms. Glasgow, March 7.

Cixous, Hélène 1993. *Three Steps on the Ladder of Writing*, trans. S. Cornell and S. Sellers. New York: Columbia University Press.

—— 1998. *Stigmata: Escaping Texts* (various translators). London and New York: Routledge.

Coetzee, J. M. 2004. *2003 Nobel Lecture: He and His Man*. London: Penguin.

Crain, Patricia 2000. *The Story of A: The Alphabetization of America from The New England Primer to The Scarlet Letter*. Stanford, CA: Stanford University Press.

Critical Art Ensemble 1998. *Flesh Machine: Cyborgs, Designer Babies and New Eugenic Consciousness*. New York: Autonomedia.

Crouch, David 2003. "Performances and Constitutions of Natures: a Consideration of the Performance of Lay Geographies." In *Nature Performed: Environment, Culture and Performance*, eds Bronislaw Szersynski, Wallace Heim and Claire Waterton (Oxford: Blackwell), pp. 17–30.

Debord, Guy 1983. *The Society of the Spectacle*, rev. edn, anon. trans. Detroit, MI: Black and Red.

Defoe, Daniel 2003. *Robinson Crusoe*. London: Penguin.

Deleuze, Gilles 1991. *Bergsonism*, trans. Hugh Tomlinson and Barbara Habberjam. New York: Zone Books.

—— 2003. *Francis Bacon: The Logic of Sensation*, trans. Daniel W. Smith. London and New York: Continuum.

—— 2004. *Desert Islands and Other Texts*, trans. Michael Taormina. Los Angeles, CA and New York: Semiotext(e).

—— and Claire Parnet 1986. *Dialogues*, trans. Hugh Tomlinson and Barbara Habberjam. New York: Columbia University Press.

—— and Félix Guattari 1987. *A Thousand Plateaus: Capitalism and Schizophrenia*, trans. Brian Massumi. Minneapolis, MN: Minnesota University Press.

Derrida, Jaques 1992. *The Other Heading: Reflections on Today's Europe*, trans. Pascale-Anne Brault and Michael Nas. Bloomington, IN: Indiana University Press.

Edson, Russell 1994. *The Tunnel: Selected Poems*. Oberlin: Oberlin College Press.

Faulconer, James E. 2002. "Levinas: The Unconscious and the Reason of Obligation." In *Psychology for the Other: Levinas, Ethics and the Practice of Psychology*, eds Edwin E. Gantt and Richard N. Williams (Pittsburgh, PA: Duquesne University Press) pp. 102–117.

Foster, Hal 1996. *The Return of the Real: The Avant-Garde at the End of the Century*. Cambridge, MA: MIT Press.

Foucault, Michel 1979. *Discipline and Punish*. New York: Vintage.

Freire, Paolo 1985. *The Politics of Education*, trans. D. Macedo. Granby, MA: Bergin & Garvey.

Fuchs, Elinor and Una Chaudhuri (eds) 2002. *Land/Scape/Theater*. Ann Arbor, MI: University of Michigan Press.

Garoian, Charles 1999. *Performing Pedagogy: Toward an Art of Politics*. New York: SUNY Press.

Giannichi, Gabriella and Nigel Stewart (eds) 2005. *Performing Nature: Explorations of Ecology and the Arts*. Berlin: Peter Lang.

Gibson, William 1999. *All Tomorrow's Parties.* London and New York: Viking.

Goat Island 1991a. "Talking with Goat Island: An Interview with Joan Dickinson, Karen Christopher, Matthew Goulish, Greg McCain." Conducted by Irene Tsatsos. *The Drama Review* 35.4 (Winter), pp. 66–74.

—— 1991b. "*We Got a Date.*" Photographic documentation of performance. *Whitewalls* 27 (Winter), pp. 39–57.

—— 1994. *Hankbook: Process and Performance of* It's Shifting, Hank. Chicago, IL: Goat Island.

—— 1996a. *How Dear to Me the Hour When Daylight Dies:* Programme notes for premiere performances. CCA Glasgow, May.

—— 1996b. "Illusiontext." *Performance Research* 1.3 (Winter), pp. 6–10.

—— 1997. *Schoolbook: Textbook of the 1996 Goat Island Summer School in Glasgow.* Chicago, IL: Goat Island.

—— 1998a. "The Impossible and Poison." *Whitewalls* 39 (Fall/Winter), pp. 16–28.

—— 1998b. *A Reading Companion to The Sea & Poison.* Chicago, IL: Goat Island.

—— 1999a. "The Incredible Shrinking Man Essay and Board Game." Collaborative publication project with students of the Sunflower Community School, Chicago. *The Drama Review* 43.1 (Spring), pp. 13–45.

—— 1999b. "*The Sea & Poison*: Post-show Talk." *Frakcija* 15 (October), pp. 76–83.

—— 2000. *Schoolbook* 2. Chicago, IL: Goat Island.

—— 2001a. *It's an Earthquake in My Heart: A Reading Companion.* Chicago, IL: Goat Island.

—— 2001b. "Goat Island Collaborative Journal Project: 465 Sentences for June 2001." *Frakcija* 20/21 (Autumn), pp. 155–180.

—— 2002. "Letter to a Young Practitioner." Group talk first presented at The School of the Art Institute of Chicago, March 16 2000. In *Theatre in Crisis?: Performance Manifestos for the New Century*, eds Maria M. Delgado and Caridad Svich (Manchester: Manchester University Press), pp. 240–249.

—— 2004a. "*When will the September roses bloom? Last night was only a comedy:* Reflections on the Process." Special edn of *Frakcija* Performing Arts Magazine, No. 32 (Summer).

—— 2004b. *North True South Free.* Collaborative publication project with students of Northside College Preparatory High School. Chicago, IL: Goat Island.

—— 2005a. "*When will the September roses bloom? Last night was only a comedy:* Reflections on the Performance." Special edn of *Frakcija* Performing Arts Magazine, No. 35 (Spring).

—— 2005b. "Propositions." A collaborative lecture by Goat Island delivered at the School of the Art Institute of Chicago, October 20.

Goulish, Matthew 1996. "*How Dear to Me the Hour When Daylight Dies:* in process." Talk presented at CCA Glasgow, March 23.

—— 1997. Unpublished interview with Stephen Bottoms: Chicago, IL, February 7.

—— 2000a. *39 Microlectures: In Proximity of Performance.* London and New York: Routledge.

—— 2000b. "Memory is This." *Performance Research*, 5.3 (Winter), pp. 6–17.

—— 2003. Unpublished interview with Stephen Bottoms: Glasgow, March 8.

—— 2004a. "Eight Memos on the Creation Process of Goat Island's *When will the September roses bloom? Last night was only a comedy*." In "*When will the September roses bloom? Last night was only a comedy*: Reflections on the process," special edn of *Frakcija* Performing Arts Magazine, no. 32 (Summer), Goat Island, section 08, np.

—— 2004b. "A Transparent Lecture." In *After Criticism: New Responses to Art and Performance*, ed. Gavin Butt (Oxford: Blackwell), pp. 176–206.

—— and Lin Hixson 1990. "Locating Goat Island." Interview conducted by David Hughes. *Performance* 61 (September), pp. 11–17.

Graver, David 1995. *The Aesthetics of Disturbance: Anti-Art in Avant-Garde Drama*. Ann Arbor, MI: University of Michigan Press.

Grotowski, Jerzy 1969. *Towards a Poor Theatre*, ed. Eugenio Barba. London: Methuen.

Guattari, Félix 2000. *The Three Ecologies*, trans. Ian Pindar and Paul Sutton. London and New York: Continuum.

Gwilt, Joseph 1982. *The Encyclopedia of Architecture: Historical, Theoretical, and Practical*. New York: Crown Publishers.

Hamilton, Ann (nd). *Ghost: A Border Act*. Quicktime video interview at www.pbs.org/art21/artists/Hamilton/index.html.

Haraway, Donna 1991. *Simians, Cyborgs, and Women: the Reinvention of Nature*. London: Free Association.

—— 2003. *The Companion Species Manifesto: Dogs, People and Significant Otherness*. Chicago, IL: Prickly Paradigm P.

Hayles, N. Katherine 1999. *How We Became Posthuman: Virtual Bodies in Cybernetics, Literature and Informatics*. Chicago, IL and London: University of Chicago Press.

Heathfield, Adrian 2001. "Coming Undone." In *It's an Earthquake in My Heart: A Reading Companion* (Chicago, IL: Goat Island) Goat Island 2001a, pp. 16–20.

—— ed. 2004. *Live: Art and Performance*. New York: Routledge.

Heinrich, Bernd 1987. *One Man's Owl*. Princeton, NJ: Princeton University Press.

Hejinian, Lyn 2000. *The Language of Inquiry*. Berkeley and Los Angeles, CA: University of California Press.

Hijikata Tatsumi 1985. "Kazedaruma." Speech on the eve of the Tokyo Butoh Festival, February 9; trans. Nippon Services Corp. In *Butoh: Dance of the Dark Soul*, eds Mark Holborn and Ethan Hoffman (New York: Aperture 1987), pp. 124–127.

Hillman, James 1996. *The Soul's Code*. New York: Random House.

Hillman, Mayer 2004. *How We Can Save the Planet*. London: Penguin.

Hixson, Lin 1990. "*Soldier, Child, Tortured Man:* The Making of a Performance." *Contact Quarterly* 15.1 (Winter), pp. 12–19.

—— 1991. "Lin Hixson: An Interview" (with Tom Jaremba). *The Drama Review* 35.4 (Winter), pp. 46–49.

—— 1992. "Artifacts." Interview with John Killacky on radio show of that name, KFAI Minneapolis, February 27.

—— 1995. "Feminisms: Responses." *P-Form* 35 (Spring), pp. 22–23.

—— 1996. "Trust, Construction, Digestion." Talk presented at Goat Island Summer School, Glasgow. July. Printed in Goat Island 1997, pp. 90–96.

—— 1997. Unpublished interview with Stephen Bottoms: Chicago, IL, February 7.

—— 1999. "Many-Headed." Talk presented at conference of Performance Studies International, Aberystwyth. April 11.

—— 2000. "Watch." Talk presented at Goat Island Summer School, School of the Art Institute of Chicago, July.

—— 2002a. "Rain Fall." *Women and Performance* 12.2, pp. 99–103.

—— 2002b. "Small Acts of Repair." Talk presented at XIV World Congress of the International Federation for Theatre Research, Amsterdam. July 2. Printed in Goat Island 2004a, Section 02, np.

—— 2003. Unpublished interview with Stephen Bottoms. Nottingham, June 6.

—— 2004. "More Permanent Than Snow." In *Live: Art and Performance*, ed. Adrian Heathfield (New York: Routledge), pp.128–131.

—— 2006. "Starry Night Sky." In *Performance and Place*, eds. Leslie Hill and Helen Paris (Basingstoke: Palgrave Macmillan 2006), pp. 213–223.

Howe, Fanny 2003. *The Wedding Dress: Meditations on Word and Life*. Berkeley and Los Angeles, CA: University of California Press.

Howe, Susan 1985. *My Emily Dickinson*. Berkeley, CA: North Atlantic.

Hughes, David 1996. "Dying Memories." *Dance Theatre Journal* 13.1 (Summer), pp. 32–33.

Jabès, Edmond 1993. *The Book of Margins*, trans. Rosmarie Waldrop. Chicago, IL: University of Chicago Press.

James, William 1981. *Principles of Psychology* Vol. I. Cambridge, MA: Harvard University Press.

Jeffery, Mark 1999a. "Artificial Ice." Unpublished talk for the Goat Island Summer School; School of the Art Institute of Chicago. July 25.

—— 1999b. Untitled talk given at work-in-progress performance of *It's an Earthquake in My Heart*. Wellington Avenue Church, Chicago. November 13.

—— 2000. "Heart Murmur." Talk presented at Goat Island Summer School Symposium, University of Bristol. August 19.

—— 2004a. "The Materiality of Lightness." Talk presented at Ann Hamilton Studio, Columbus, OH, January 13. In "*When will the September roses bloom? Last night was only a comedy*: Reflections on the Process," special edn of *Frakcija* Performing Arts Magazine, no. 32 (Summer), Goat Island, section 06, np.

—— 2004b. "Materiality and Goat Island." Talk presented at Goat Island Summer School, Chicago. School of the Art Institute of Chicago, July 23.

—— 2005. "Notes towards performing." Talk presented at Goat Island Summer School, Chicago. School of the Art Institute of Chicago, July 25.

Kershaw, Baz 1999. *The Radical in Performance: Between Brecht and Baudrillard*. London and New York: Routledge.

—— 2000. "The Theatrical Biosphere and Ecologies of Performance." *New Theatre Quarterly* 16.2 (May), pp. 122–130.

—— 2001. "Oh for Unruly Audiences! Or, Patterns of Participation in Twentieth-Century Theatre." *Modern Drama* 42.2, pp. 133–154.

—— 2002. "Ecoactivist Performance: The Environment as Partner in Protest?" *The Drama Review* 46.1 (Spring), pp. 118–130.

Koolhaas, Rem 1996. *Conversations with Students*, ed. Sanford Kwinter. New York: Princeton Architectural Press.

Krauss, Ruth 1989 [1952]. *A Hole is to Dig: A First Book of First Definitions*. New York: Harper Collins.

Kruger, Loren 1999. "Goat Island: *The Sea and Poison*." *Frakcija* 15 (October), pp. 71–75.

Lauterbach, Ann 2005. *The Night Sky: Writings on the Poetics of Experience*. New York: Viking.

Lepecki, André 2000. "Still: On the Vibratile Microscopy of Dance." In *ReMembering the Body*, eds Gabriele Brandstetter and Hortensia Völckers (Ostfilden-Ruit: Hatje Cantz), pp. 334–366.

Levinas, Emmanuel 1969. *Totality and Infinity: An Essay on Exteriority*, trans. A. Lingis. Pittsburgh, PA: Duquesne University Press.

—— 1996. *Emmanuel Levinas: Basic Philosophical Writings*, ed. Peperzak, Critchley, and Bernasconi. Bloomington, IN: Indiana University Press.

Likens, G. E. and F. H. Bormann 1995. *Biogeochemistry of a Forested Ecosystem*, 2nd edn, New York: Springer Verlag.

McDonough, William and Michael Braungart 2002. *Cradle to Cradle: Remaking the Way We Make Things*. New York: North Point Press.

Marranca, Bonnie 1996. *Ecologies of Theater: Essays at the Century Turning*. Baltimore, MD: Johns Hopkins University Press.

Meredith Publishing Company 1957. *Better Homes and Gardens Handyman's Book*.

Mills, Chris 2000. "Walking into the Future, Thinking about the Past: Yvonne Rainer, Goat Island and a little bit of Hope." Paper presented at the conference of Performance Studies International, Mainz.

Mitchell, CJ 1999. "Untitled Talk." Presented at the ArtNow conference, State University of New York, New Paltz. October 1.

Murchie, Peter 1999. "A Personal Response to *The Sea & Poison*." After-show talk at Wellington Avenue Church, Chicago. May 1.

Nowotny, Helga 1996. *Time: The Modern and Postmodern Experience*. Cambridge: Polity Press.

Pesic, Peter 2002. *Seeing Double: Sharing Identities in Physics, Philosophy and Literature*. Cambridge, MA: MIT Press.

Phelan, Peggy 2002. "Tenderness, for Lynda Hart." *Women and Performance: A Journal of Feminist Theory* 13.1, pp. 19–26.

—— 2004. "Marina Abramovic: Witnessing Shadows." *Theatre Journal* 56.4 (December), pp. 569–577.

Plato 1987. *The Republic*, trans. Desmond Lee. London: Penguin.

Rainer, Yvonne 1965. "Some retrospective notes on a dance for 10 people and 12 mattresses called *Parts of Some Sextets*." Reprinted in *Happenings and Other Acts*, ed. Mariellen R. Sandford (London and New York: Routledge, 1995), pp. 160–167.

Read, Alan 1993. *Theatre and Everyday Life: An Ethics of Performance.* London and New York: Routledge.

Reznikoff, Charles 2005. *The Poems of Charles Reznikoff 1918–1975*, ed. S. Cooney. Boston, MA: Black Sparrow.

Ross, Andrew 1994. "The Ecology of Images." In *Visual Culture: Images and Interpretation*, eds Norma Bryson, Michael Ann Holly and Keith Moxey (Hanover, NH: Wesleyan University Press), pp. 325–346.

Saner, Bryan 1996. "Stealing." Talk presented at CCA Glasgow, March 23. Printed in Goat Island, 1997, pp. 71–74.

—— 1997. Unpublished interview with Stephen Bottoms. Chicago, IL. February 8.

—— 1998. "Work." Talk presented at Goat Island 3-Day Spring Intensive Workshop. Chicago. May 1.

—— 1999a. Untitled talk presented at the Goat Island Summer School, School of the Art Institute of Chicago. July 25.

—— 1999b. Untitled talk presented at work-in-progress performance of *It's an Earthquake in My Heart*. Wellington Avenue Church, Chicago. November 13.

—— 2001. "Alternative Spaces and Vision." Talk presented at the Goat Island Summer School; School of the Art Institute of Chicago. July 11.

—— 2005. "Interior Eye." In "*When will the September roses bloom: Last night was only a comedy*: Reflections on the Performance," special edn of *Frakcija* Performing Arts Magazine, no. 35 (Spring), Goat Island, section 3, np.

Sarraute, Nathalie 1984. *Childhood*, trans. Barbara Wright. New York: George Braziller.

Savran 1988. *Breaking the Rules: The Wooster Group.* New York: Theatre Communications Group.

—— 2005. "The Death of the Avantgarde." *The Drama Review* 49.3 (Fall), pp.10–42.

Sayre, Henry 1989. *The Object of Performance: The American Avant-Garde since 1970*. Chicago, IL: University of Chicago Press.

—— 1996. "Performance and the Question of Authenticity." Unpublished paper presented at the Performance Art, Culture, Pedagogy Symposium, Penn State University. November.

—— 2004. "In the Space of Duration." In *Live: Art and Performance*, ed. Adrian Heathfield (New York: Routledge), pp. 38–45.

Schneider, Rebecca 2000. "On Critical Art Ensemble." *The Drama Review* 44.4 (Winter), pp.120–131.

Schwartz, K. Robert 1996. *Minimalists*. London: Phaidon.

Sebald, W. G. 2001. *Austerlitz*, trans. Anthea Bell. New York: Random House.

Seremetakis, C. Nadia (ed.) 1994. *The Senses Still.* Chicago, IL: University of Chicago Press.

Shepard, Sam 1984. *Fool for Love and Other Plays*. New York: Bantam.

Simmel, Georg 1997. *Simmel on Culture: Selected Writings*. London: Sage.

Stanier, Philip 2005. "Process, Repair and the Obligations of Performance: Goat Island's *When will the September roses bloom? Last night was only a comedy*." *Dance Theatre Journal* 20.4 (March), pp. 37–40.

Stein, Gertrude 1985. *Lectures in America*. Boston, MA: Beacon Press.

—— 1994. *Stanzas in Meditation*. Los Angeles, CA: Sun and Moon Press.

Stelarc, nd. "Obsolete Body." www.stelarc.va.com.au/obsolete/obsolete.html.

Stewart, Susan 1993. *On Longing: Narratives of the Miniature, the Gigantic, the Souvenir, the Collection*. Durham, NC: Duke University Press.

—— 2002. *Poetry and the Fate of the Senses*. Chicago, IL and London: The University of Chicago Press, p. 330.

Szersynski, Bronislaw, Wallace Heim and Claire Waterton (eds) 2003. *Nature Performed: Environment, Culture and Performance*. Oxford: Blackwell.

Tarkovsky, Andrei 1996. *Sculpting in Time: Reflections on the Cinema*, trans. Kitty Hunter-Blair. Austin, TX: University of Texas Press.

Townsend, Colin R., Michael Begon and John L. Harper 2003. *Essentials of Ecology*, 2nd edn, Oxford: Blackwell.

Virgil 2004. *The Georgics of Virgil*, trans. Peter Fallon. Loughcrew, Co. Meath: Gallery Books.

Virilio, Paul 1986. *Speed and Politics*, trans. Mark Polizzotti. New York: Semiotext(e).

—— 1991. *The Aesthetics of Disappearance*, trans. Philip Beitchman. New York: Semiotext(e).

—— 1997. *Open Sky*, trans. Julie Rose. London: Verso.

Wackernagel, Mathis and William Rees 1996. *Our Ecological Footprint: Reducing Human Impact on the Earth*. Gabriola Island, BC: New Society Publishers.

Waddington, C. H. 1969. *Behind Appearance: A Study of the Relationship Between Painting and the Natural Sciences in this Century*. Edinburgh: Edinburgh University Press.

Waldrop, Rosmarie 2002. *Lavish Absence: Recalling and Rereading Edmond Jabès*. Middletown, CT: Wesleyan University Press.

Walkey, Litó 2003. Unpublished interview with Stephen Bottoms. Nottingham. June 6.

Wallace, Irving and Amy Wallace 1978. *The Two: The Story of the Original Siamese Twins*. New York: Simon & Schuster.

Watts, Alan 1957. *The Way of Zen*. New York: Pantheon.

Weil, Simone 1970. *First and Last Notebooks*, trans. Richard Rees. New York and Toronto: Oxford University Press.

—— 1992. *Gravity and Grace*, trans. Emma Craufurd. London and New York: Routledge.

Wheeler, Wendy 1999. *A New Modernity?: Change in Science, Literature and Politics*. London: Lawrence and Wishart.

Williams, Raymond 1983. *Keywords: A Vocabulary of Culture and Society*, rev. edn, New York: Oxford University Press.

Woolf, Virginia 1984. *The Virginia Woolf Reader*, ed. Mitchell A. Leaska. New York and London: Harcourt Brace & Company.

Wright, C. D. 2005. *Cooling Time: An American Poetry Vigil*. Port Townsend, WA: Copper Canyon Press.

Zarilli, Phillp B., ed. 1995. *Acting (Re)Considered*. London and New York: Routledge.

Zupancic, Alenka 2001. "On Evil: An Interview with Alenka Zupancic," conducted by Christopher Cox. *Cabinet* No. 5 (Winter).

INDEX

Acker, Kathy 136
acting 83–84, 208
activism 25, 117
Agamben, Giorgio 163
Akhmatova, Anna 150
alphabet 53–55, 131–132
amateurism 11, 13
animals 6, 7, 8, 12, 49, 54–55, 86–89, 98, 162–165, 169–170
see also dogs
Antin, David 63
appropriation xi, 17, 60–65, 74, 135–138, 156–161
architecture 2, 30–32, 38, 40, 47, 62, 84–85, 141–142, 206, 214, 222–223
Aristosthenes 41
artifice 45–48, 86, 121
Ashby, Cynthia 226
Asturias, Miguel 150
audience response 13, 15, 17–18, 35–36, 40, 50–67, 72–73, 83–84, 85, 94–96, 106, 148, 208, 210–211
authenticity 2–5, 43, 46, 66
authorship 66–67

Bachelard, Gaston 109
Bacon, Francis 163
Bailes, Sara Jane ix, 97, 108–109
Barthes, Roland 58
Bartok, Bela xiv
Bateson, Gregory 8–12, 15, 17, 18–22, 24, 35, 80, 140–141
Bateson, Mary Catherine 18
Baudrillard, Jean 172–173
Bausch, Pina 63, 74, 91, 136, 156, 157–161, 221
Becker, Carol vi, ix, 50, 71–72, 87
Beckett, Samuel 63, 189–190, 208
becoming(s) 12, 55–56, 86–89, 149, 160, 163–165, 220
beginnings xiii–xiv, 51–53, 128–130, 133–135
Bel, Jerome 156–157
Bergson, Henri 56, 86, 128
Bernhard, Thomas 84
Blake, William 12, 25
Blocker, Jane 77
Bohm, David 123
Book of Life 103
Bottoms, Stephen ix
writing by xi–xii, 3–25 (alternate pages), 33–37, 42–44, 55–58, 62–66, 73–78, 80–83, 86–88, 91–93, 101–105, 135–138, 149, 176
Bourke, Roger 219
Boy with Green Hair, The 46
Bresson, Robert 162
Burbank, Carol 83

Cage, John xvi, 53–54, 105, 107, 128, 131, 135
Calvino, Italo 12, 16
Can't Take Johnny to the Funeral 29, 30, 51–52, 60, 71–72, 87, 91, 127, 150, 225
Caputo, John D. 212
Cash, Lucy 182, 226

Celan, Paul xv, xvi, 84, 90, 95–96, 104, 105, 139, 165, 169–170, 175, 191
Chang and Eng 123–126
Chaudhuri, Una 19, 34, 43
Christopher, Karen ix, xiii, 11, 13, 15, 45, 48, 67, 71, 80, 81–82, 85, 87–89, 90, 99–101, 102, 103, 104, 121, 122, 124, 131–132, 138, 139, 154, 155, 156, 159, 162, 164, 173, 180, 225
  writing by 51–53, 60, 67, 83–85, 89, 94, 106–108, 119–120, 135, 145–147, 201–202, 211, 216–217
Chuma, Yochiko 183
Churchill, Caryl 189
Cixous, Hélène 16, 192
climate change *see* global warming
Cockburn, Bruce 105
Coe, Sue 60
Coetzee, J.M. 12, 14
collaboration 40, 83, 115–118, 121–126, 193, 204–207, 215, 221, 223
collage 61–62, 150–151
commitment 71–73, 207–210
community 193, 211, 212–213
compactness 179–180
Cooper, Tommy 63, 64
Critical Art Ensemble 11, 25
criticism 210–211
crops 7, 42–43, 91, 119
Crouch, David 42–43
cyborgs 7, 15, 75, 80

dance (and non-dance) 13, 54, 61, 63, 69, 70, 71, 74, 152, 156–162, 183
  see also movement
Dando, Jill 47
Darwin, Charles 10, 19, 21, 56, 177
Day, Doris 53
Debord, Guy 48
Defoe, Daniel 12
Deleuze, Gilles 36, 56, 128, 160, 163–164, 192
  and Félix Guattari 64–65, 78, 86–88, 135, 138
Derrida, Jacques 25, 212
Dickinson, Joan 74, 225
documentation xiv–xv, 3
dogs 55, 63, 71, 87–88, 131–132, 162–165, 204
dreams 97, 212
Dryden, John 123
duration 56–58, 106, 152–154, 167–168
  see also time, slowness

Earhart, Amelia 60, 61, 85, 138
ecology vi, 4, 7–10, 12, 15, 19–23, 25, 32, 34–36, 41, 43, 56, 75, 77, 91–93, 114, 119–120, 133, 177–178
economics 4, 9, 10, 23, 35, 75, 114, 116–120, 144–145
Edson, Richard 87, 124
Eno, Brian 81
entropy 8, 15, 19
environment 8, 10, 21, 23, 44, 47, 84, 119, 144
environmental theatre 34–35
ethics 18, 69–70, 124, 191
evolution 10, 19

failure 42, 77, 142, 156, 157, 179
Farocki, Harun 9, 104
fascism 8, 131, 142
Faulconer, James 124
feminism 69–70, 75, 77, 115–116
Feminist Art Workers 116
film 51, 60, 90–91, 107, 167, 173
Fitzsimmons, Bob 60, 138
Forsythe, William 63
Foster, Hal 58
Foucault, Michel 76
found objects *see* materials
found texts *see* appropriation
Freire, Paolo 192

ghosts 82, 170–172, 175
Gibson, William 75
Gish, Lillian 84, 95, 131, 139, 181
global warming 9, 19
Goat Island
  founding of xiii–xiv, 116–117, 128

funding of xiii–xvii, 116–118
group writing by xiii–xvii, 206–07, 214–221, 222–223
performances by *see* individual titles
working process xiv, 13, 19, 30–31, 41–42, 45–46, 119–125, 128–143, 147, 149–155, 158–182, 214–215
Goulish, Matthew ix, xiii, 3, 17, 30, 31, 32–33, 44, 46, 48, 63, 67, 71–72, 74, 75, 80, 81, 85, 87–89, 96, 101–103, 104, 122, 124, 128, 131–132, 136–138, 139, 155, 156, 187–190, 225
writing by 2–18 (alternate pages), 53–55, 58–59, 66, 97, 105, 126–127, 128–129, 140, 149–150, 152–155, 156–160, 162–165, 175, 177–180, 192–193, 194–197, 205–212, 219–220
grass 20, 22, 64, 65
Graver, David 62–63
Gray, Spalding 62
Grotowski, Jerzi 32, 63, 73
Guattari, Félix vi, 23, 32, 55, 92
see also Deleuze and Guattari
Gulf War (1991) 48, 91, 183

Hadid, Zaha 84–85
Hamilton, Ann 172
Hamlet 122
Haraway, Donna 75
Harp of Burma, The 60, 65–66
Harris, Ed 136
Hartley, Hal 103
Hayles, Katherine 17, 75–76
Heathfield, Adrian x, 35, 50, 74, 79–80, 101
Hejinian, Lyn 14
Hijikata, Tatsumi xiv, 96, 98–101, 102
Hillman, James 142
Hillman, Mayer 9
Hitchcock, Alfred 60, 136
Hixson, Lin x, xiii–xiv, 13, 23, 25, 35, 69, 83, 90–91, 135–136, 142–143, 149, 153, 154, 157, 159, 162, 164, 168, 179, 180, 215, 225
writing by 29–32, 48–49, 58, 70–71, 85–86, 98–101, 113–114, 115–117, 121–126, 129–132, 138–139, 147–149, 150–152, 156, 169–170, 173–174, 175, 181–183, 193, 202–204, 212–213, 221
Hoffmann, Hans 62
How Dear to Me the Hour When Daylight Dies 30, 52–53, 56–58, 60, 63–66, 81–83, 85, 93–94, 109, 113, 133–138, 140, 150, 152, 226
Howe, Susan 114
How to Live in the German Federal Republic 9, 104, 173
Hughes, David 65, 93–94
humanism 74–76, 86

Ichikawa, Kon 60, 65
impossibility xiii, xvi–xvii, 3, 25, 131, 141, 152–155, 157, 190, 194, 199, 202
Incredible Shrinking Man, The 49, 89
individual(ism) 115, 123
Institute Benjamenta 105
interpretation *see* audience response
intuition 56, 145–146, 149
Islam 222–223
islands 12, 36, 177
It's an Earthquake in My Heart 9, 13, 15, 30, 35, 38–39, 44–45, 55, 63, 74, 78–81, 98–104, 113, 138, 156–162, 173, 226
It's Shifting, Hank 30, 53, 55, 72–73, 83, 89, 142–143, 150, 225

Jabès, Edmond 32, 95, 192
James, William 100
Jeffery, Mark x, xiii, 48, 63, 67, 78, 80, 85, 86, 87–89, 98, 101, 102, 103, 121, 131–132, 155, 156, 159, 169, 173, 180, 226
writing by 41–42, 45–48, 114–115, 161, 166, 170–172, 174–175, 197–198, 204, 218–219
Judson Dance Theatre 63, 69, 74

Kantor, Tadeusz 91, 221
Kershaw, Baz 34, 36, 43
Killacky, John 29, 69
Koolhaas, Rem 2–4, 9, 206
Kruger, Loren 37
Kurosawa, Akira 60, 109

Labowitz, Leslie 116
Lacy, Suzanne 116
landscape 19, 34, 36, 44, 114
language 13, 14, 16, 51, 54, 95, 104, 149, 172–173, 192
Lartigue, Jacques-Henri 162, 164–165, 172
last(ing)ness 113, 223–224
Lastmaker, The 222–224, 226
Lauterbach, Ann 191, 192
Lepecki, André 184
Levinas, Emmanuel 124, 191
Liebeskind, Daniel 38
lighting 33, 37
Linke, Susanne 156–157
logic 11, 20, 22, 23, 58, 123, 178

McCain, Greg xiii–xiv, 51–52, 71–73, 74, 128, 129, 138, 142–143, 147, 225
McCain, Timothy xiii–xiv, 51–52, 71–72, 128, 142–143, 147–148, 225
McDonough, William and Michael Braungart 120
machines 75–82, 173
Marranca, Bonnie 34
materials, materiality 41–43, 46, 121–122, 174–175
Matheson, Richard 49
media culture 23, 44, 46–47, 90–93, 101–102
Melville, Herman 60
memory 61, 93–95, 98–101, 109, 145, 169–175, 215, 217
Mercy, Dominique 136, 157–160, 162
metaphor 18, 19, 20, 22, 152
Miller, Arthur 62
Mills, Chris 69–70, 187
miniaturization 44, 47–49, 199–200
Mitchell, CJ x, xiii, 67, 128, 159, 214–215, 226
Molière 9,11
Mondrian, Piet 32
montage 63
Morrissey, Judd 226
movement 13, 23, 33, 51–53, 56–57, 60, 61, 69–78, 85–88, 136, 146–166, 171, 173, 182–183, 197–205
see also dance
Murchie, Peter 21
music 53, 81, 192

Nelson, Margaret xiii, 226
Newman, Paul 142–143
Newton, Isaac 58
Night of the Hunter 181

Ondaatje, Michael 150

Palm Beach Story 165
Parks, Suzan-Lori 189
Paxton, Steve 74
pedagogy 187–189
see also teaching
Phelan, Peggy x, 187–190, 191
photographs 58, 60, 71, 149–150, 172
Piano, Renzo 38
Plato 43, 188
pollution 9, 21, 23, 48, 144–145
poor theatre 32–33, 35, 62–63, 73
Poppe, Antonio 225, 226
posthumanism 74–76, 80
postmodernism 64
Pound, Ezra 55, 143
props *see* materials
proscenium staging 29, 34, 37–38, 40
prostheses 80, 93
Proust, Marcel 214, 217, 220
puppets 48–49, 56–57, 74, 89, 138

Quay Brothers 105

Rainer, Yvonne xiv, 69–70
Ratzel, Friedrich 8

Rauschenberg, Robert 62
Reagan, Ronald xiv
recycling 17, 30, 41, 75, 91
Renoir, Jean 60
repair xv, xvii, 23, 25, 31, 41, 95, 104, 106, 109, 119, 129–130, 175, 201
repetition 17, 40, 53–54, 56–58, 74, 106, 109, 139, 152–155, 182, 188–190
Reznikoff, Charles 192
rhizome 64–65, 135
Rilke, Rainer Maria 214, 220
Rogers, Kenny 65
Rosenthal, Rachel 116
Ross, Andrew 91
Rotman, Brian 179

Saner, Bryan x, xiii, 25, 44, 48, 65, 81, 85, 87–89, 90, 94, 97–98, 102, 105, 106, 121–122, 137, 155, 156, 159, 162, 169, 175, 176, 179, 187–189, 215, 225
  writing by 37–41, 60–62, 78, 117–118, 144–145, 167–169, 199–200, 215–216
Sappho 214, 217
Sarraute, Nathalie 99, 100
Savage, Robert 188
Sayre, Henry 63–64, 66
Sea & Poison, The xvi, 21, 30, 43, 45–49, 67–68, 76–78, 81, 86–87, 97, 121–125, 127, 152–155, 187–190, 226
Sebald, W.G. 63, 95, 164
September 11th, 2001 25, 101–104
Seremetakis, Nadia 184
Sert, Jacques 60
Shakespeare, William 122, 189–190
Shepard, Sam 87, 136
silence 67, 105–107, 211
Simmel, Georg 126
Sitte, Camillo 32
slowness xiv, 2–5, 58, 115, 118, 170, 204, 216
smallness xv, 25, 130
  see also miniaturization
Smith, Patti 150
Socrates 4, 6, 10, 16, 18, 20, 22, 188
Soldier, Child, Tortured Man 30, 76, 116, 128–129, 147–149, 168, 225
Sometimes a Great Notion 142–143
sports 71, 147, 149–150
Stanier, Philip x, 94–96
stage space 29–31, 34–41
stealing *see* appropriation
Stein, Gertrude 19, 34, 103, 130
Stelarc 75, 77, 80
Stewart, Susan 47, 170
stillness 105–107, 182–183, 201, 203, 204
structure xi, 66, 139–142, 178–180, 205, 206, 214–215
Sturges, Preston 165
Suzuki, Tadashi 221

Tarkovsky, Andrei 174
task 13, 70, 71, 77, 149, 150–152, 199, 202
Taylor, James 31, 64, 95, 131, 169, 184
teaching (and learning) xiv, 54–55, 115, 128, 141, 187–189, 192–213, 226
Thirty Nine Steps, The 60, 136–137
Thornton, Leslie 60, 137–138
time 2–5, 13, 47–48, 51–53, 56–58, 60, 65, 67, 90–109, 115, 167–171, 182–183, 203, 205, 216, 221
  see also memory, duration, slowness
traffic 5, 32, 78, 80, 84, 144–145, 161
trauma 58, 82, 101, 102, 104, 109, 170–172
trees 44, 89, 189–190, 218
Trump, Donald 32
Tsatsos, Irene 74
Turim, Maureen 65

Uexküll, Jacob von 6, 8, 10

Van Eyck, Aldo 30–32
Van Gogh, Vincent 127
Vawter, Ron 136–138
video 60, 137–138, 181–182
Virgil 192
Virilio, Paul 44, 92–93, 181–182

Waiting for Godot 189–190
Walker, Mike 59, 60, 81–83, 85, 138, 140
Walkey, Litó x, xiii, 43, 88, 90, 105, 131, 132, 162, 164, 176, 180, 182–184, 226
writing by 164–165, 200–201, 217–218
Warhol, Andy 58
Warrilow, David 208
Watts, Alan 42
We Got A Date 30, 33, 76, 225
Weil, Simone xiv, xvi, 64, 84, 88, 95, 109, 139, 162–163, 175
Wellington Avenue Church 36–37, 117, 126–127, 147
When will the September roses bloom? Last night was only a comedy xi, 23, 25, 31, 41–42, 43, 55, 63, 80, 84, 88, 94–96, 104–109, 130–132, 162–166, 169–170, 175, 178–183 , 226
Whitehead, Alfred North 56, 59
Wilder, Thornton 62
Wilson, Robert 34
Wind, The xv, 95, 131,139
Woolf, Virginia xvii, 214, 219–220
Wooster Group, The 62–63, 136
Wright, C.D. 191
writing exercises 194–197, 205–206, 211–212, 217, 220

Young, LaMonte 132

Zakari, Chantal 226
Zupancic, Alenka xvi, 131

RELATED TITLES FROM ROUTLEDGE

39 Microlectures
In Proximity of Performance
Matthew Goulish

'A series of accidents has brought you this book.

You may think of it not as a book, but as a library, an elevator, an amateur performance in a nearby theatre.

Open it to the table of contents.

Turn to the page that sounds the most interesting to you.

Read a sentence or two.

Repeat the process.

Read this book as a creative act, and feel encouraged.'

39 Microlectures: In Proximity of Performance is a collection of miniature stories, parables, musings and thinkpieces on the nature of reading, writing, art, collaboration, performance, life, death, the universe and everything. It is a unique and moving document for our times, full of curiosity and wonder, thoughtfulness and pain. Matthew Goulish, founder member of performance group Goat Island, meditates on these and other diverse themes, proving, along the way, that the boundaries between poetry and criticism, and between creativity and theory, are a lot less fixed than they may seem. The book is revelatory, solemn yet at times hilarious, and genuinely written to inspire – or perhaps provoke – creativity and thought.

ISBN13: 978–0–415–21392–9 (hbk)
ISBN13: 978–0–415–21393–6 (pbk)